IMAGES
of America

WESLEY CHAPEL

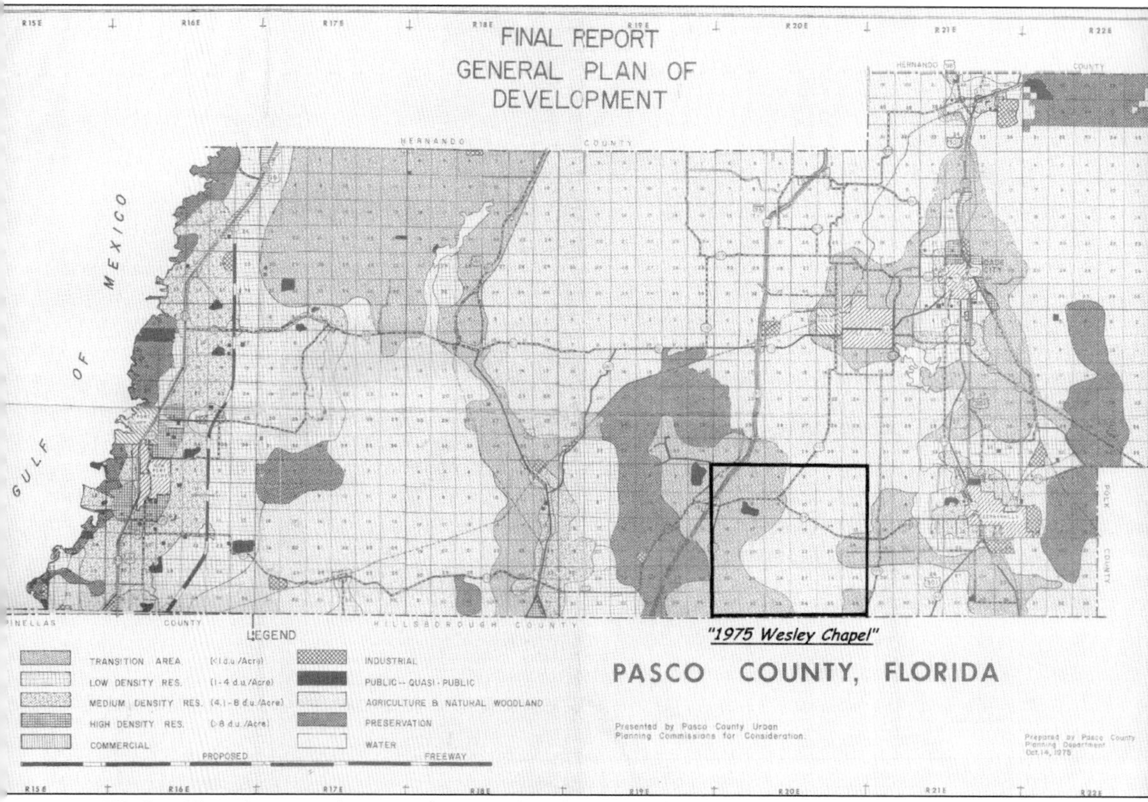

Wesley Chapel was predominantly agricultural and rural throughout its history. The Pasco County development map from October 14, 1975, does not notate the name of Wesley Chapel because of the scarcity of population. In 1975, the community was comprised of "agricultural and natural woodland" and "transitional land" only, according to the county planning department. (Courtesy of Pasco County Planning Department.)

On the Cover: Gator hunting was done at night in the swamps of Wesley Chapel. Lonnie Tucker, at far left with a light on his forehead, guides two visitors through the swamp. His daughter, Anna Jo Bracknell, said it was typical for Lonnie to harvest three to four gators per evening. She considers gator tail a culinary delicacy. In preparation, the gator tail is split at a row of muscle and sliced into steaks. The hides are skinned, salted, and then rolled up in pillow cases and put in the freezer until sold. Leon Moody similarly remembered hunting rattlesnakes with Lonnie and gathering 11 in one trip to King Lake. (Courtesy of Anna Jo Bracknell.)

IMAGES
of America

WESLEY CHAPEL

Madonna Jervis Wise

ARCADIA
PUBLISHING

ISBN 978-1-4671-1615-2

Published by Arcadia Publishing
Charleston, South Carolina

Printed in the United States of America

Library of Congress Control Number: 2015952091

For all general information, please contact Arcadia Publishing:
Telephone 843-853-2070
Fax 843-853-0044
E-mail sales@arcadiapublishing.com
For customer service and orders:
Toll-Free 1-888-313-2665

Visit us on the Internet at www.arcadiapublishing.com

This book is dedicated to Ernest Edward Wise. Although a scientist by professional training, Ernest and I share a love of family genealogy and history. We value the friends, family, and communities that have shaped our lives.

Contents

Acknowledgments

I enjoyed serving as an educator in Pasco County. Ernest E. Wise and I worked with a team to bring this book to realization. I appreciated the ongoing collaboration of Jeff Miller of the West Pasco Historical Association. Special thanks go to Ruth Smith Adams, Stephanie Brown Benson, Cullen Ricardo Boyette, Deborah Boyette, Michael C. Boyette, Sue Boyette, Anna Jo Bracknell, David L. Brown, Sarah Robinson Downs Bruce, Clereen Morrill Brunty, Jim Dennison, Charlie Estepp, Mark Gallo, Melton Godwin III, Clarence Cooter Hale, Beth Kersey Hayes, Eddie Herrmann, Eddie Lee Hill, Marlo Hilton Johnson, Delores Lanigan, Keith Lane, Etta Lindsey, Nick Linville, B.C. Manion, Eunice Ryals McElveen, Quinn Porter Miller, Vickie Strickland Pavone, Cletia Pierce, James Don "J.D." Porter Jr., William Porter, Scott Searles, Shirley Hill Sheppard, William Raleigh "Bill" Smith, Shawn Sombutmai, Lillie Eva Sapp Stanley, Marco Edward Stanley, Roscoe "Rocky" Stanley, Theresa "Lou" Stanley, Kenneth Stewart, Elisabeth Strickland, Anne Elkins Sweat, Wayne Sweat, Eugene Wells, and Kenneth T. "Ted" Williams for their consultation.

Thanks go to everyone who contributed to the book via kind smiles, answered questions, or insightful stories. The book is intended as an invitation to learn more about Wesley Chapel and an enticement to drive along Bruce B. Downs Boulevard, visit the Shops of Wiregrass or the Grove at Wesley Chapel, dine in a café, or attend a community event. History must be shared to be passed to the next generation!

Introduction

Frontier independence was prevalent amongst strong, hardworking pioneer settlers. Settlers maintained a fierce network of community for safety and political, social, and economic realities. They arrived in the 1840s to an area that was variously known as Godwin, Double Branch, Westley, Lemon, Gatorville, and eventually Wesley Chapel. Wesley Chapel was a true community, where everyone helped each other and pitched in to mentor children. David L. Brown, a descendant of pioneer Francis "Ruben" Barnes, explained, "Everyone cared for one another but did not bother each other."

Early human inhabitants date to 10,000 BC. It has been recorded that the location was occupied by Native Americans of the Muscogee Creek nation when Spanish explorers arrived in the 16th century, however research does not substantiate this. Dr. Jerald Milanich, author of *Florida Indians and the Invasion from Europe*, attempted to retrace the expedition of Hernando de Soto through Florida. The Spanish saw the first native cornfields, known as the Plain of Guacozo, yet there is no conclusive evidence of which tribe the Spanish encountered. However, many native groups across Florida were decimated by European-introduced diseases, leading to a population "vacuum" by the early 18th century. In the mid-18th century, various southeastern Indians, the majority of whom were Creek, began settling the area. They became known as the Seminoles. From 1835 until 1858, the United States and the Seminoles were at war. Three Seminole Wars occurred: the First Seminole War (1817–1818), the Second Seminole War (1835–1842), and the Third Seminole War (1855–1858), which drove the Seminoles from the region, encouraging further white settlement.

Asbel, Barnes, Boyette, Bradley, Cooper, Ellerbee, Geiger, Gillette, Godwin, Hill, Kersey, O'Berry, Overstreet, Ryals, Smith, Stanley, Strickland, Thomas, and Tucker are a few settler names as identified by primary sources as well as census records, range maps, and historical writings. Settlement occurred in the 1840s and after the Civil War. The Homestead Act was a motivator for families, offering 160 acres with provisions such as residing for five years and improving the land. Pasco County formed in September 1887 and included Precinct 4, which was Wesley Chapel.

According to genealogical research done by Michael C. Boyette, land was granted to his ancestor Edward Boyette Sr. in the Florida Armed Occupation Act of 1842. Thomas Ashley Boyette founded the church that stood across from the present-day location of the Double Branch Church on Highway 54. Boyette's grandson and namesake, Edward, called the area "Double Branch" for the twin creeks that flowed through his property. Since its founding in 1878, the Double Branch Church (now the First Baptist Church) was the community center. As more pioneers settled, a Methodist chapel was built at the northwest corner of Highway 54 and Boyette Road.

William Sebron Standley and his wife, Frances "Fannie" Bradley, settled near Gatorville after the Civil War. Spellings differ on the various pioneer names, as indicated by Standley/Stanley;

the *d* was dropped by family members. Fannie was the daughter of Capt. Robert Duke Bradley from the Bradley Massacre, which occurred in May 1856. Stanley's son Lewis Napoleon set up his homestead on Tupper Road across from present-day Saddlebrook Resort.

There was no recognizable town nucleus, yet the community possessed two sawmills, a general store, and a post office. Two post offices actually claimed the early settlement. The village of Godwin, named for Jacob Godwin, operated from 1888 to 1915 with four postmasters—Jacob Godwin, Matilda Godwin, Abraham L. Godwin, and William P. Smith. It was located across from present-day Quail Hollow Golf Course. The Wesley Chapel Post Office functioned from 1897 to 1902, also with four postmasters—Elizabeth F. Smith, Lawrence M. Strickland, Abraham L. Godwin, and Ephraim B. Cooper.

Laurin McQueen Strickland homesteaded in April 1890. He and his wife, Emaline, migrated from Georgia. William Riley Smith settled in Wesley Chapel after the Civil War, around the time he married Anne E. Sims in 1867. Lewis Wesley "Dee" Wells was the county's impounding officer during Florida Free Range. Dee was a descendant of Jacob Wells, who was the first armed occupation homesteader in 1842 in what is now Pasco County.

Pioneer women of Wesley Chapel were revered for their tireless days of toil, with a nurturing spirit and the skill to raise large families. The Barnes family is a prime example. Francis Asbury Barnes owned huge acreage—sections 10, 11, 12, 13, and part of 15—in Wesley Chapel. Barnes's granddaughters Martha and Vida were industrious managers of land and cattle. Longtime foreman of the K-Bar Ranch Clarence Hale, who often assisted at other nearby ranches such as Wiregrass and Barnes, remarked on Martha's agility in penning cattle and physical labor on the farm. "The Barnes family is related to the fellow pioneer families of Strickland, Redbrook, Godwin, Leggett, Smith and Hill," reads a description on the engraved entrance marker of the Brown Family Cemetery, where Martha was buried in 1986. Thelma Hale prepared the food for the cowhands and delivered it to the area across from present-day Bruce B. Downs Boulevard on horseback. Other women, such as Sallie Godwin, Emaline V. Strickland, Lillie Sapp Stanley, Ella Mae McKendree Wells, Esther McKendree Boyette, Ruth Smith Adams, Isabel Helveston Barnes, and Martha McDonald Porter, are mentioned in interviews and documented in research as resilient pioneers.

Wesley Chapel was known for singing. Whenever the fifth Sunday of a month occurred (about five times per year), the church hosted a singing convention. "I'll Fly Away" and "Leaning on the Everlasting Arms" were among the gospel hymns that incorporated audience participation. Music was printed in paperback convention books using a musical system known as seven-shape notation to make it easier for folks to read without formal training. The seven-shape notational system includes an equilateral triangle (do), semicircle (re), diamond (mi), right triangle (fa), oval (sol), rectangle (la), and quarter circle (ti). Singing conventions originated in Georgia and caught on throughout rural Florida. The tradition of dinner on the grounds capped off the celebration.

Wesley Chapel School was a two-room schoolhouse with a room for lower grades and a room for upper grades through grade eight. It sat beside the Double Branch Church and replaced an earlier nearby log cabin schoolhouse. It operated until the 1950s. A big educational change began with the opening of Quail Hollow Elementary in 1974. The area now has two high schools and associated elementary and middle schools as well as Pasco-Hernando State College.

Historical cemeteries included Holton Cemetery on McKendree Road, Double Branch Cemetery adjacent to First Baptist Church of Wesley Chapel, and County Line Cemetery. Land was donated by Julia Elizabeth Holton for Holton Cemetery, and descendants host an annual gathering there each October.

Informal Wesley Chapel socializing occurred at the general store. Cullen Boyette said, "Jesse Stanley's Store was a place for just a few items . . . not major groceries or supplies . . . things like canned goods, cheese, and a pop. Remember, we didn't have electricity, so the gasoline pump would move in graduation, and you had to pump it before inserting the nozzle to get gasoline for your vehicle." Stanley's store was located at Tupper Road near Highway 54. It closed in the

1940s. Later, there was a garage at Pasco Cooper's place at the intersection of Curley Road and County Road 54. Subsequently, the Wells General Store was operated by Delbert and Ella Mae Wells and the Hill Grocery by James Henry Hill and Ida Geiger Hill and later their son, James Monroe Hill.

As for transportation, Highway 54 runs east-west and I-75 and Bruce B. Downs Boulevard are the north-south thoroughfares. Highway 54 was originally named Denham–Dade City Road and was used for carts carrying lumber and turpentine. It was colloquially known as a "2-2-20" Road, because as gravel replaced dirt in the 1920s, it was said to take two years to build, two years to wear out, and 20 years to pay for. Bill Smith remembered that his father, Luther, dug some of the original one-lane road by mule after returning from World War I. Others recalled the paving of Highway 54 in 1942 and Highway 43 by prison inmates who dug the roadbed by hand. Unlike contemporary Wesley Chapel, the road was quiet and rarely traversed. "Kids could play in the middle of Highway 54 with no worry, because you wouldn't see a car for two hours," said David L. Brown. The construction of I-75 in 1963 transformed Wesley Chapel. In more recent years, "broosbeedowns" is uttered when giving directions to Bruce B. Downs Boulevard, named in 2000 by Gov. Jeb Bush for a public administrator who worked at the Florida Transportation Department and Hillsborough County. Bruce B. Downs Boulevard (originally Thirtieth Street in Tampa) had been a desolate two-lane road that locals referred to as the "Road to Nowhere" for abruptly ending at the county line. Political squabbling left the road—intended as a hurricane evacuation route from Tampa Bay—unfinished. A series of clandestine crimes occurred in the 1970s and 1980s along the span of road.

Agriculture was the livelihood. Subsistence farming prompted by land grants gave way to larger-scale ranching and logging. Crops that provided food for the settlers and commodities for bartering included sweet potatoes, sugarcane, peas, velvet beans, okra, corn, guavas, citrus from seedling groves, and bananas.

When times were hard, gator hunting, charcoal production, rattlesnake harvesting, and frog gigging were fallback skills. Native Lonnie Tucker said, "I'd stand in the water, about waist deep and grunt like a gator to make it come out. When it did, I'd hit him right in the head with an axe." Lonnie would take the hide off the gator, which sold for $25, and then take the tail meat home to eat. As for rattlesnake hunting, Lonnie said he killed as many as 23 snakes in one day. His daughter, Anna Jo Bracknell, said her father would typically bring home three gators in a nighttime hunting excursion. In untamed Florida, before prevalent paved roads and state regulations, lush vegetation concealed many activities.

Timber and turpentine pervaded the area. Logging companies surrounded the Big Cypress Swamp, and large cypress trees were cut down for many years. A series of tram roads were built to connect the area to Tampa and also to Abbott, where Greer's Mill harvested the timber. The tram roads were laid to accommodate log carts; as trees were felled, hooks were used to load them into the wagons. Remnants of the tram roads, which were also used to transport turpentine, can be seen throughout. A turpentine community existed near Stanley Station (on what was later the Barnes Ranch) about 150 years ago, with a commissary, workers' homes, a cemetery, a well, and a turpentine still. One of the turpentine houses still stands on the Ruben Barnes Ranch. It is suspected that this turpentine still was in operation during the late 1800s or early 1900s. The size of the operation is not known, but due to the extensiveness of the tram road network, it appears to have been large.

According to avid historian and collector Wayne Sweat, moonshining was prevalent throughout Wesley Chapel. Sweat has gathered arrowheads for years and frequently finds remnants of demijohns (classic moonshining jugs) along the woods and streams. If only those demijohns could talk! By 1927, Sheriff Hudson declared "war" on moonshiners, claiming that 90 percent of the stills and liquor supplying Tampa were in Wesley Chapel. Not surprisingly, there was a prevailing opposition to Prohibition in Wesley Chapel. A poll in October 1888 to decide whether liquor could be sold in Pasco County had shown a majority against it, except in the villages of Wesley Chapel and St. Thomas, where sales were favored.

Lumber trusts in the early 1900s exemplified an era of growth, and the timber industry was part of trustification. Much of the future ranch land of Wesley Chapel was owned by John D. Rockefeller, Otto Hermann Kahn, and Edwin Wiley Grove. Timberlands were controlled by the Rockefeller-Weyerhaeuser group. Louis F. Post, assistant secretary of labor, said in 1919, "In the southern pine region, the prices have risen from $1 or $2 an acre to $60 . . . and in Florida, three holders had 4,200,000 acres, and the largest timber holder in Florida appeared to hold over 16,990,000 acres—about one-eighth of the land area of the state." Rockefeller was known for eliminating waste, so to optimize costs for his oil industry, he began making his own oil barrels by buying tracts of timber for the vessels. Not surprisingly, the Rockefeller Land Trust as well as the Otto Hermann Kahn Trust owned thousands of acres of the timberland that now makes up the Wesley Chapel community.

The present-day Wiregrass Ranch property has a complex history. Around 1937, James Barney Porter purchased land that now houses the nearby Zephyrhills Municipal Airport. In the early days of World War II, the Army Air Corps wanted that land for an air training station. Porter's great-grandson J.D. Porter said, "When the land was condemned by the Army Air Corps, the proceeds were parlayed into a purchase of 15,000 acres from the Rockefeller Land Trust." James Barney Porter, who lived with his wife, Kathryn Virginia Hatcher, and children Martha, Margaret, James Hatcher, and Robert Paul, in Plant City, bequeathed land parcels to his sons and their wives. James H. Porter moved to the ranch in 1946 with his wife, Martha McDonald, and their three sons—James "Don," Tom, and William "Bill." They worked the ranch, raising cattle, citrus, and crops.

James H. Porter was referred to as "Wiregrass." It was his late friend Dade City Buick dealer Ed Madill who was most responsible for the iconic nickname. Each Christmas, Madill sent Porter a box of matches with instructions to burn wiregrass on the ranch. The ashes fertilized grass for the cattle, and the name stuck. Once, when Madill was in Mexico, he wrote a postcard to his friend and addressed the envelope simply to "Wiregrass Porter, Gatorville, Florida, USA." In 1972, Wiregrass Porter made a land sale for portions of Saddlebrook Resort. The next year, the land that was to become Meadow Pointe was sold. The Porters donated land for a Pasco-Hernando State College campus and several other civic sites.

Ranch names permeate the area. For example, K-Bar (Krusen Grove & Cattle) borders a large portion of Cross Creek Boulevard. In the 1930s, I.A. Krusen purchased 13,000 acres for just over $2 an acre. Krusen constructed a sawmill and paid off the land by selling lumber. His son-in-law Henry Douglas said that the Atlantic Tank Company of New York was an important buyer of tank cypress. It came from the heart of the trees, coined "wood eternal," and was used to build water tanks on the top of buildings, placed in case of fire. The wood was also used for brewer's tanks, oil tanks, and cannery tanks. From one of these trees, Krusen was able to saw out 9,000 board feet of lumber. Pebble Creek Subdivision is on land that used to be part of the original 13,000 acres. In 1994, Christine Douglas described the pasture that extended just north of Tampa Palms, saying, "That area was what we called Red Brook Hammock, and when we sold it, we rounded up the cattle right where the clubhouse now stands."

Present-day Wesley Chapel has many late-20th-century and early-21st-century landmarks.

One

Pioneers of Wesley Chapel, Goodwin, and Gatorville

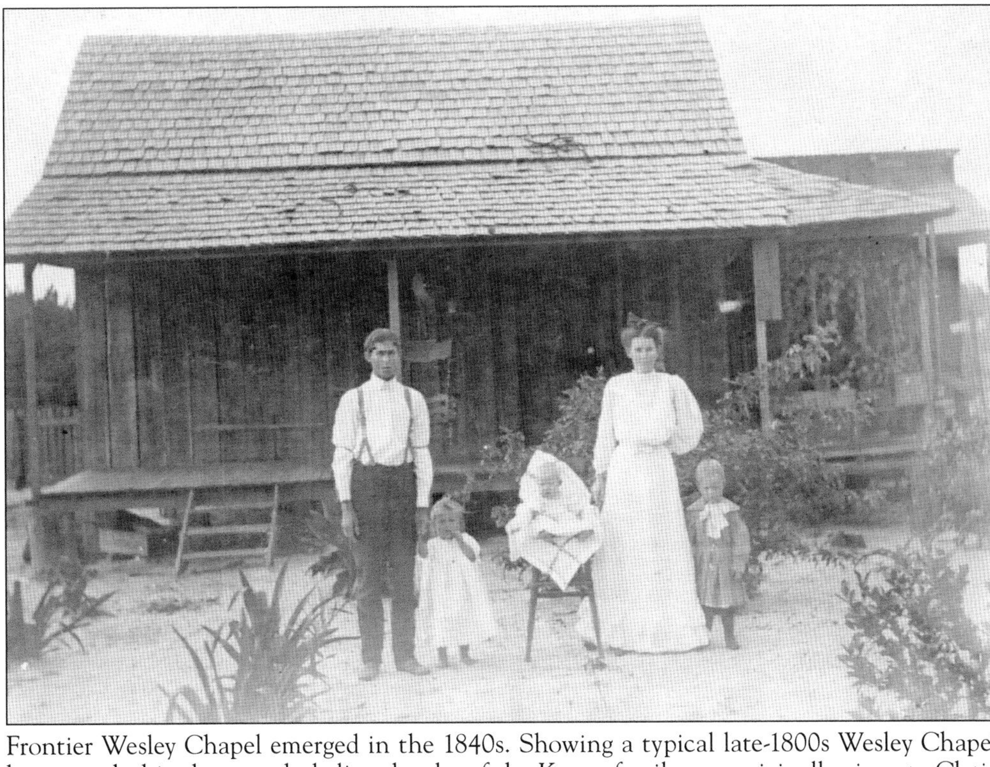

Frontier Wesley Chapel emerged in the 1840s. Showing a typical late-1800s Wesley Chapel homestead, this photograph, believed to be of the Kersey family, was originally given to Cletia Pierce by Wesley Chapel residents James Fernie Cooper and Marjorie Mae Orine Williams Cooper. Sharon Boyette Macklin, descendant of the Boyette homesteading family, explained that the early houses were built with a passageway separating the kitchen from the living quarters. With the precautionary split configuration, if one experienced a kitchen fire, the living quarters were left standing. (Courtesy of Cletia Pierce.)

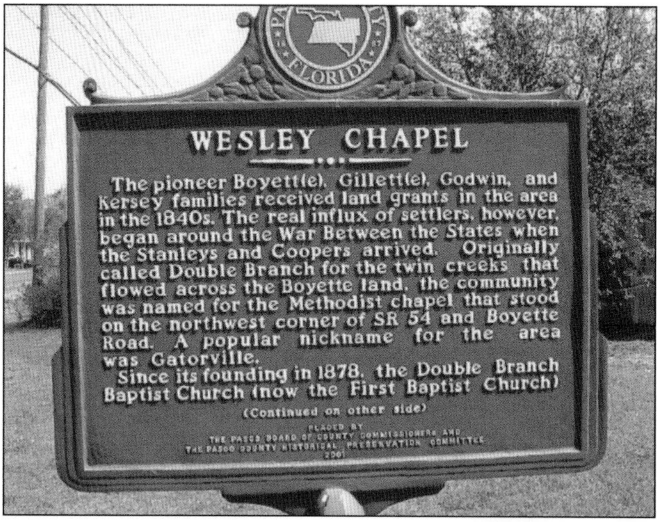

Settlers arrived in the 1840s, and the area remained chiefly agricultural and rural until around 1990. In the 1935 Florida census, Wesley Chapel was unincorporated. Residents had several post office addresses. The 193 Wesley Chapel residents documented in the census were broken down as follows: 127 with a Zephyrhills RFD, 36 with a Lutz RFD, 10 with a Dade City RFD, and 20 with a San Antonio RFD. (Courtesy of Ernest Wise.)

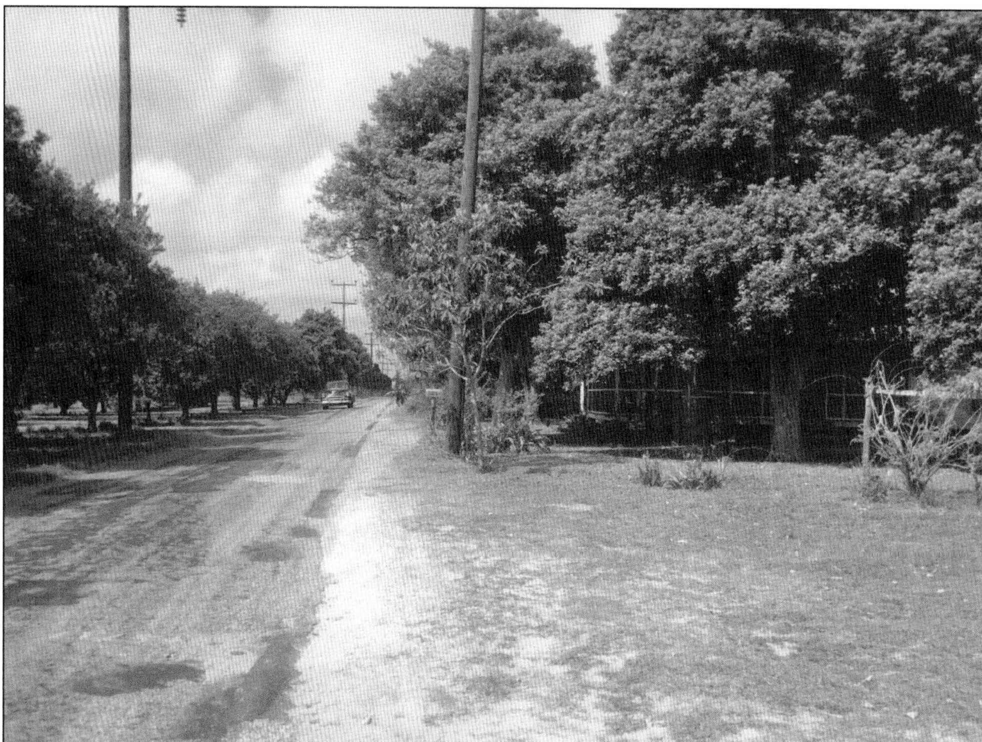

In 1921, county commissioner W.H. Mayo wrote, "Answering the inquiry as to what Wesley Chapel had to offer as an inducement to the homeseeker, I might first geographically outline our position relative to our sister localities. Wesley Chapel district is located in the interior of the much favored county of Pasco, twelve miles southwest of Dade City, our county seat, and six miles south of San Antonio, twenty-three miles north of the city of Tampa, and on the shortest and most direct public highway connecting the above towns and cities. It is eight miles from Zephyrhills, from which we have daily free delivery mail service, the same being situated on the main line of the Seaboard railway, from Tampa to Jacksonville." (Courtesy of Florida State Road Department, Florida Library & Archives, Florida Department of State.)

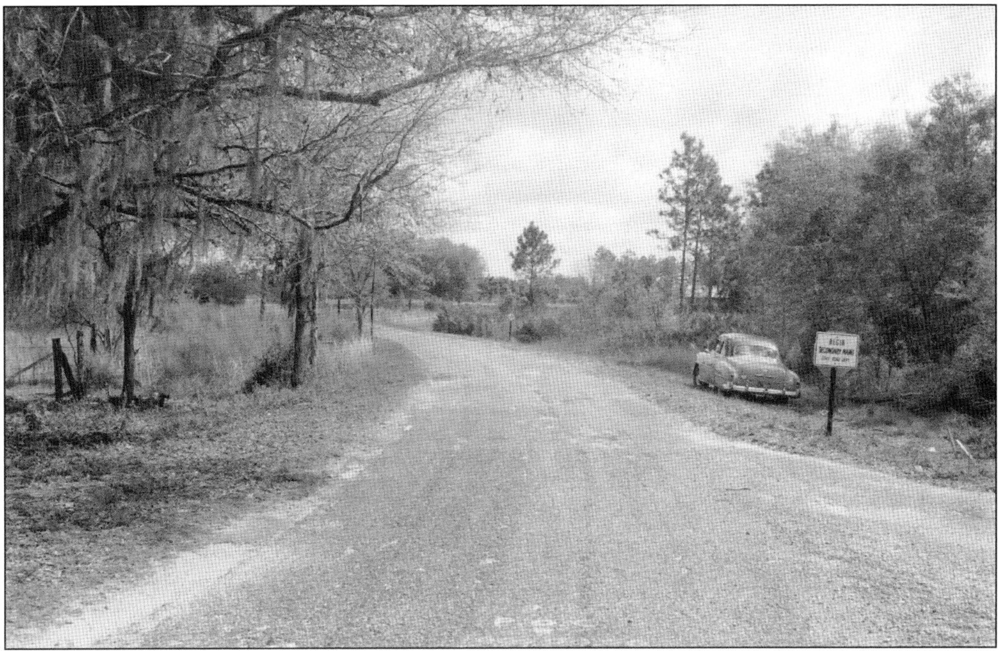

In 1922, C.B. Taylor wrote that Wesley Chapel was located on some of the finest farming land, most of which was low and flat, held moisture well, and adapted to almost any kind of growing. Because of remoteness and bum roads, very little trucking was done. (Courtesy of Florida State Road Department, Florida Library & Archives, Florida Department of State.)

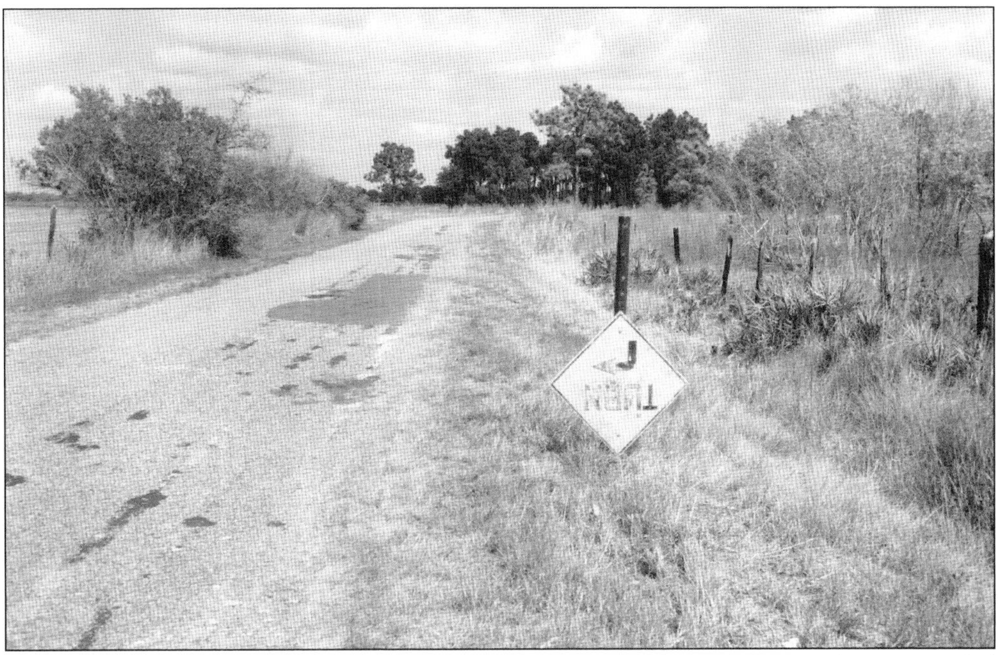

Farming and two sawmills were the principal industries in early 1920s. A general store attended to the physical needs of the community. "When I was a kid, I could walk down to Highway 54, sometimes for an hour, and wouldn't see one car!" said Cullen Boyette. (Courtesy of Florida State Road Department, Florida Library & Archives, Florida Department of State.)

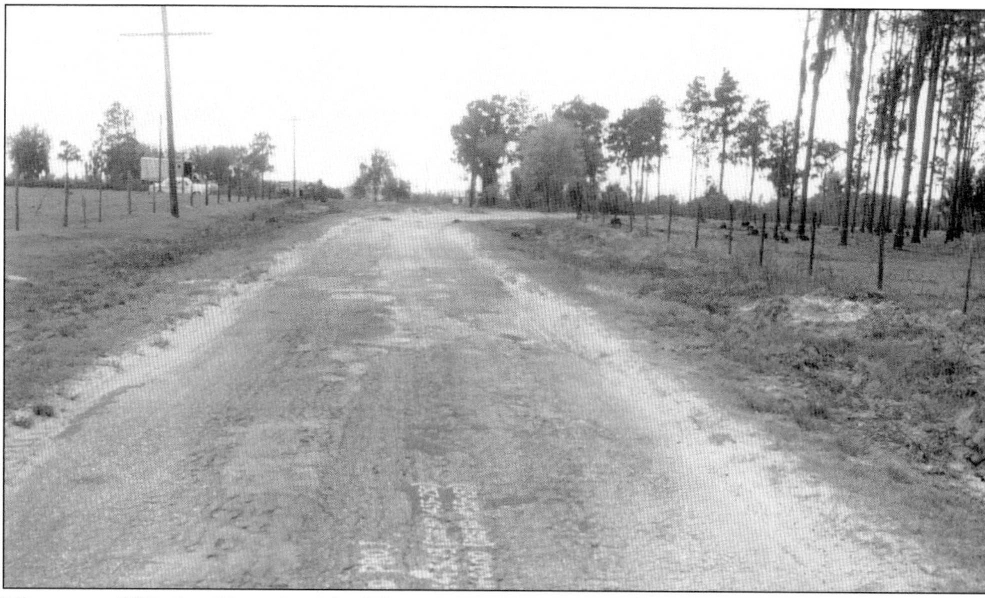

The area of Wesley Chapel applied for a post office, originally under the name "Lemon." The name was denied, but a post office was established on September 15, 1897; however, it closed on September 30, 1902, and service was transferred to nearby Abbott, Florida. A post office was again opened in Wesley Chapel in recent years, located just north of the northeast corner of Boyette Road and Highway 54. (Courtesy of Florida State Road Department, Florida Library & Archives, Florida Department of State.)

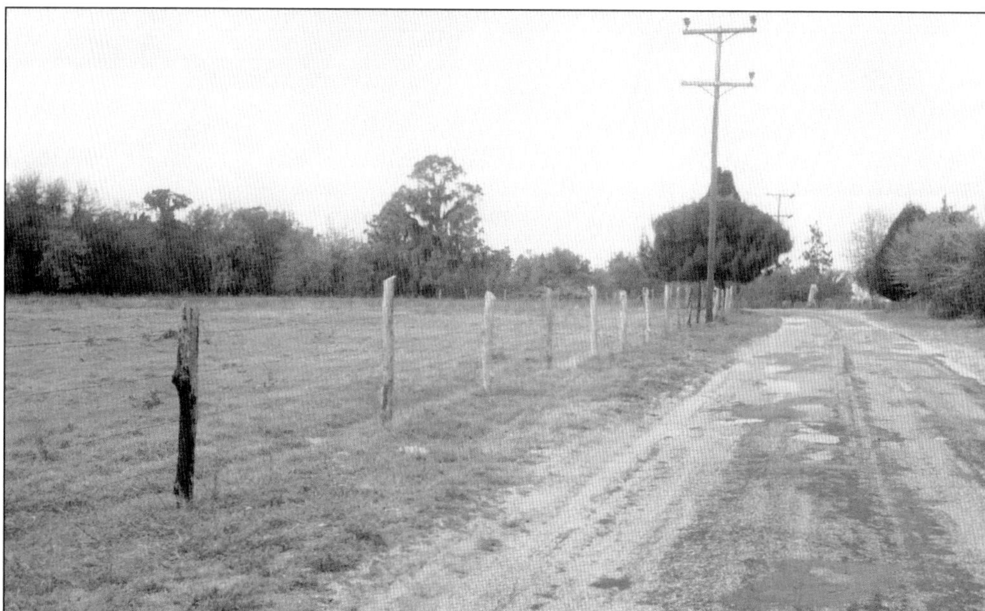

The stretch from Zephyrhills to Wesley Chapel shows the rural countryside of Highway 54. "Wesley Chapel was a stand-alone community. Kids could play in the middle of Highway 54 with no worry, because you simply wouldn't see a car for two hours. People looked after each other's children, so you were always cared for," said David L. Brown of his home community. (Courtesy of Florida State Road Department, Florida Library & Archives, Florida Department of State.)

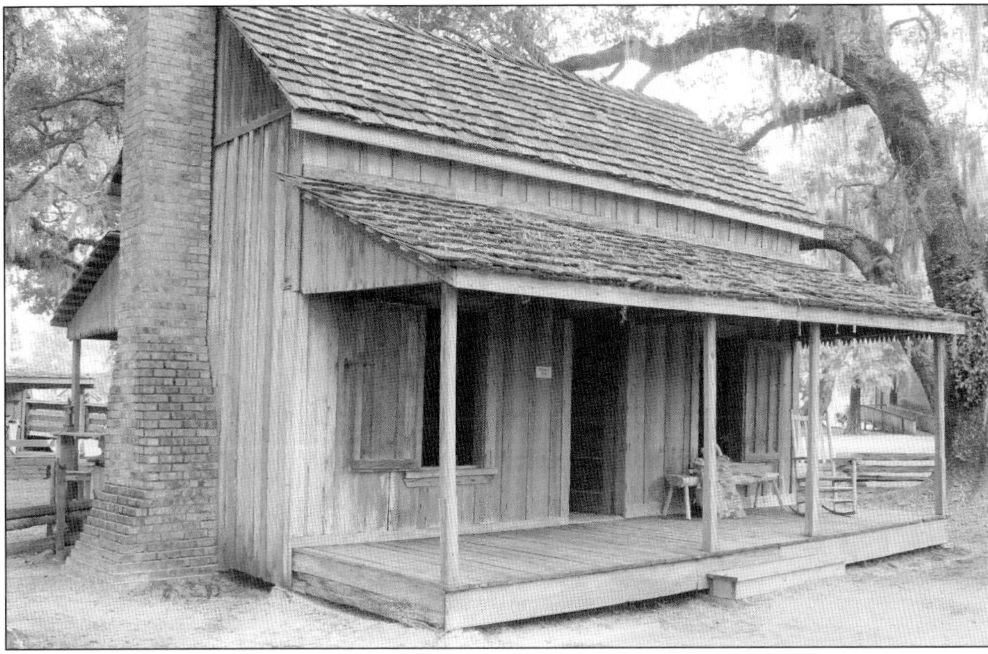

Friends and neighbors of Daniel H. Smith and Elizabeth Geiger gathered for a barn raising–style celebration in 1894 to build a frontier home for the engaged couple. The house was donated in 1979 by the Smiths' grandson, Willie Smith, to the hands-on exhibit at the Florida State Fairgrounds in Tampa known as "Cracker Country." (Courtesy of Ernest Wise.)

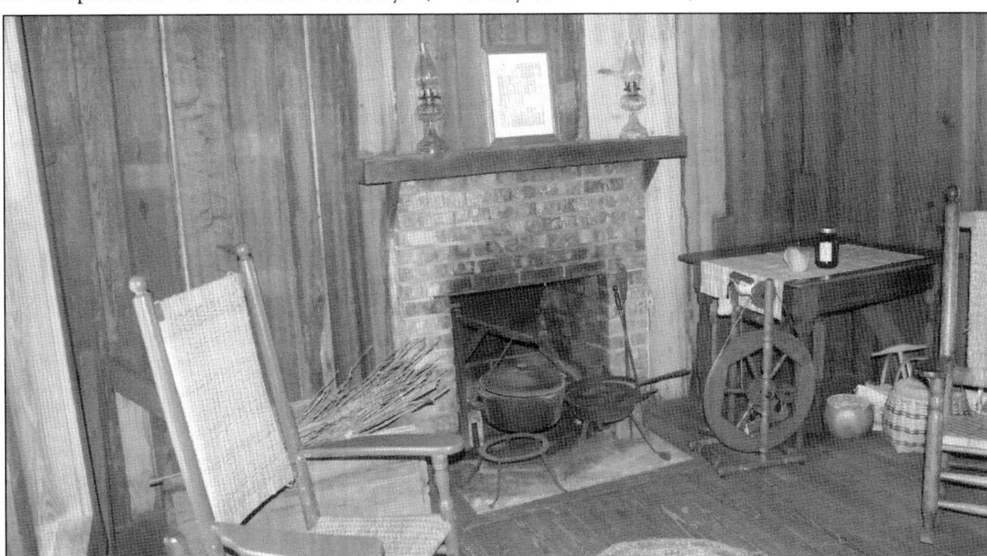

The interior of the 1894 Smith home reveals lumber harvested from the land. The shell was completed in three days and topped with cedar shingles. In the customary style of the day, the kitchen was a separate structure to prevent fire from invading the sleeping area. Daniel and Elizabeth had four sons who were ranchers and farmers in the area. For many years after the house was donated to "Cracker Country" as a museum exhibit, Smith descendants attended the Florida State Fair to give lectures and give demonstrations of Florida pioneer customs. (Courtesy of Ernest Wise.)

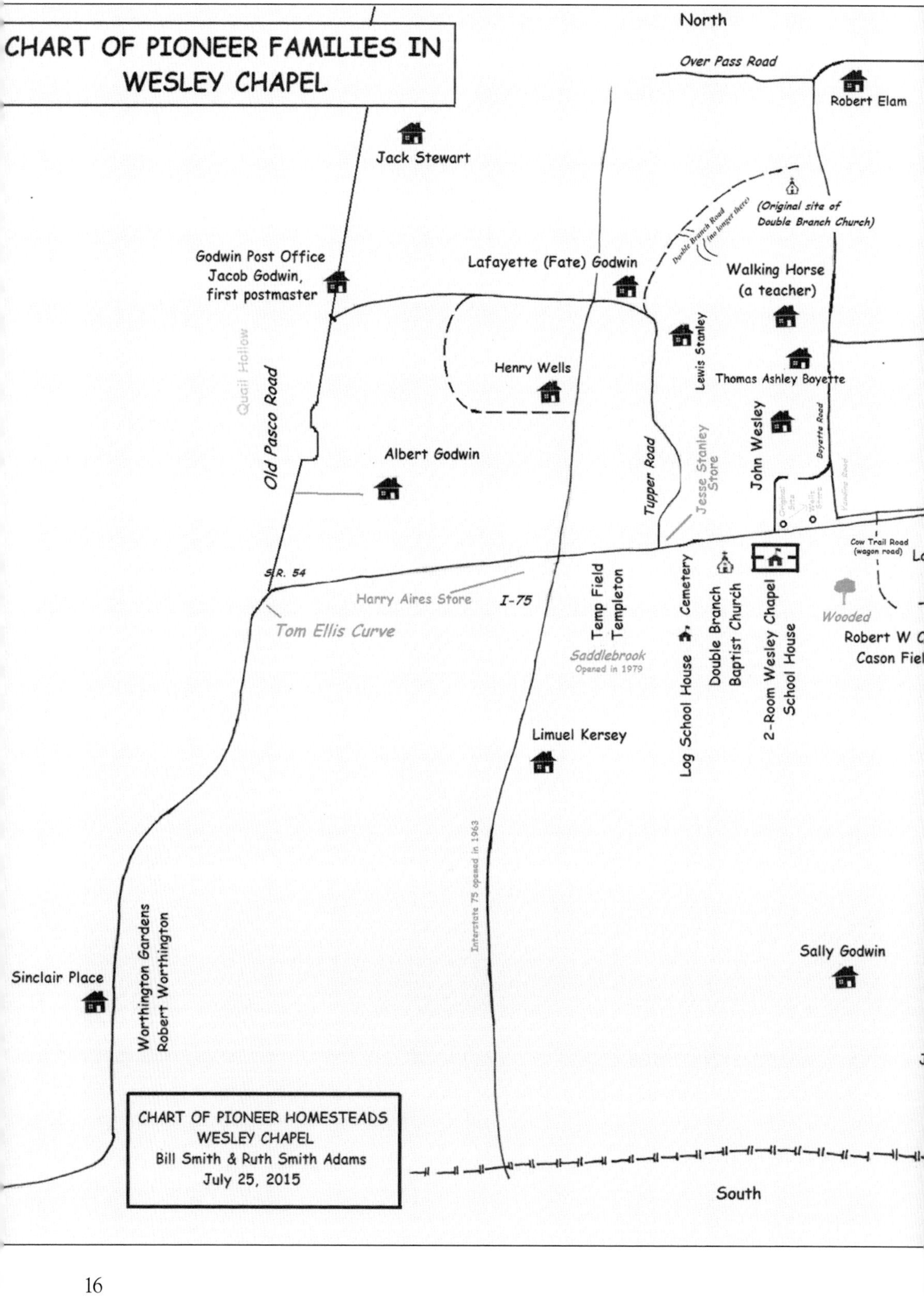
CHART OF PIONEER FAMILIES IN WESLEY CHAPEL
North
Over Pass Road
Robert Elam
Jack Stewart
(Original site of Double Branch Church)
Double Branch Road (no longer there)
Godwin Post Office
Jacob Godwin, first postmaster
Lafayette (Fate) Godwin
Walking Horse (a teacher)
Lewis Stanley
Quail Hollow
Old Pasco Road
Henry Wells
Thomas Ashley Boyette
John Wesley
Boyette Road
Tupper Road
Jesse Stanley Store
Albert Godwin
Cow Trail Road (wagon road)
S.R. 54
Harry Aires Store
I-75
Temp Field
Templeton
Log School House
Cemetery
Double Branch Baptist Church
2-Room Wesley Chapel School House
Wooded
Tom Ellis Curve
Saddlebrook
Opened in 1979
Limuel Kersey
Interstate 75 opened in 1963
Sally Godwin
Sinclair Place
Worthington Gardens
Robert Worthington
CHART OF PIONEER HOMESTEADS
WESLEY CHAPEL
Bill Smith & Ruth Smith Adams
July 25, 2015
South

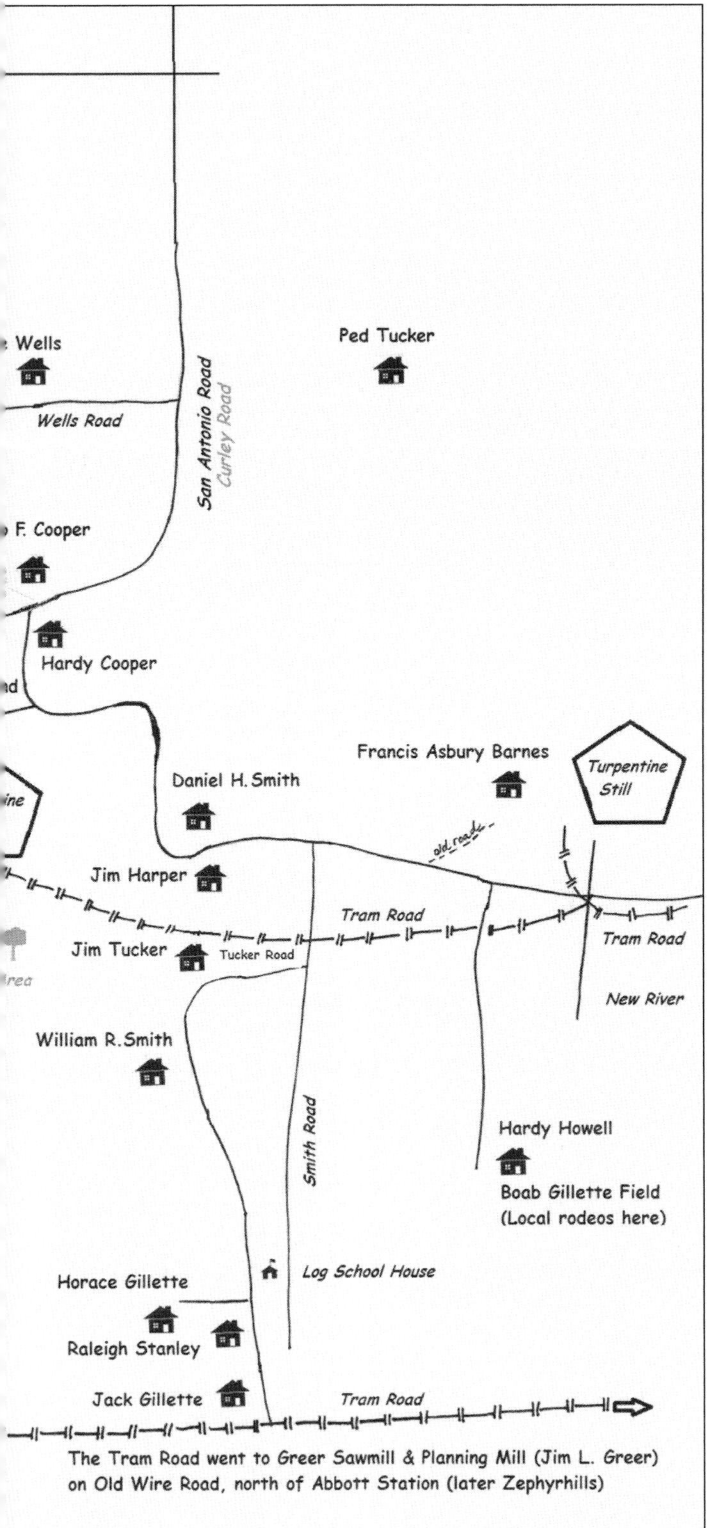

A chart of pioneer families in Wesley Chapel was developed by descendants of settlers. Pioneers mentioned on the map around 1910 include Francis Asbury Barnes, Thomas Ashley Boyette, Robert W. Cason, Hardy Cooper, Pasco F. Cooper, Robert Elam, Boab Gillette, Horace Gillette, Jack Gillette, Albert Godwin, Jacob Godwin, Lafayette "Fate" Godwin, Sally Godwin, Raleigh Stanley, Jim Harper, Hardy Howell, Limuel Kersey, Jay Ryals, Daniel H. Smith, William R. Smith, Raleigh Stanley, Jack Stewart, Lauren Strickland, John Thomas, Jim Tucker, Ped Tucker, Dee Wells, and Henry Wells. (Courtesy of Bill Smith and Ruth Smith Adams.)

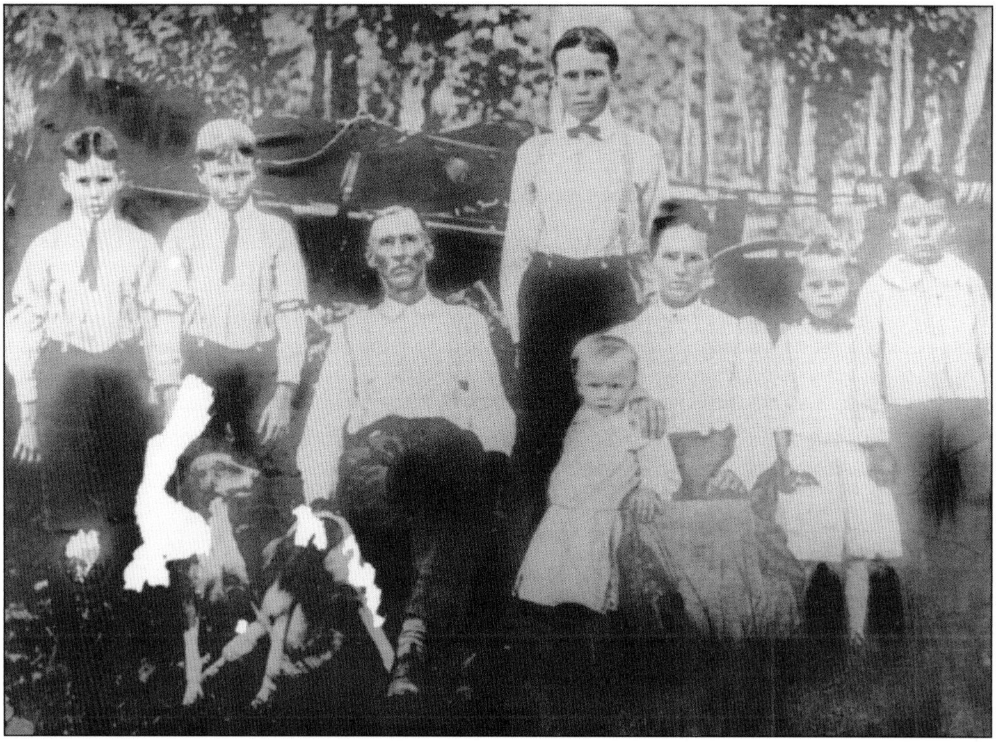

The Laurin McQueen Strickland family poses along with their horse and buggy and prized hounds in the summer of 1906. From left to right are Victor, Robert Drawd "Drawdy," Laurin McQueen (1860–1915), Joseph Lamar, Laurin Morris (child in front), Emaline Virginia Tootle (1867–1937), Selma, and Harry Strickland. Laurin McQueen Strickland was an inspector and clerk for the primary election on May 26, 1898, in Wesley Chapel, along with D.H. Smith and J.J. Gillet, as reported by the *San Antonio Herald*. He was also the District 3 county commissioner for Godwin in 1904. (Courtesy of Elisabeth Strickland.)

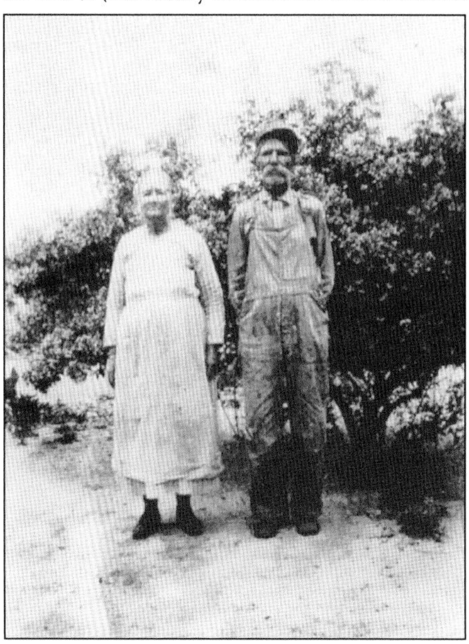

Robert Cooper and his wife, Mary Etta Gillette Cooper, pose in front of a grove on their farm in Wesley Chapel. Chickens appear in the background. Robert was born in 1853 and married Mary Etta in 1875. Mary Etta was born in 1857 in Levy County, Florida, to Joshua Jackson Gillette and Malinda Morgan Gillette. Indicative of the crop farming and subsistence lifestyle of rural Florida, the Coopers were early pioneers in Wesley Chapel who settled after the Civil War. (Courtesy of Marco E. Stanley.)

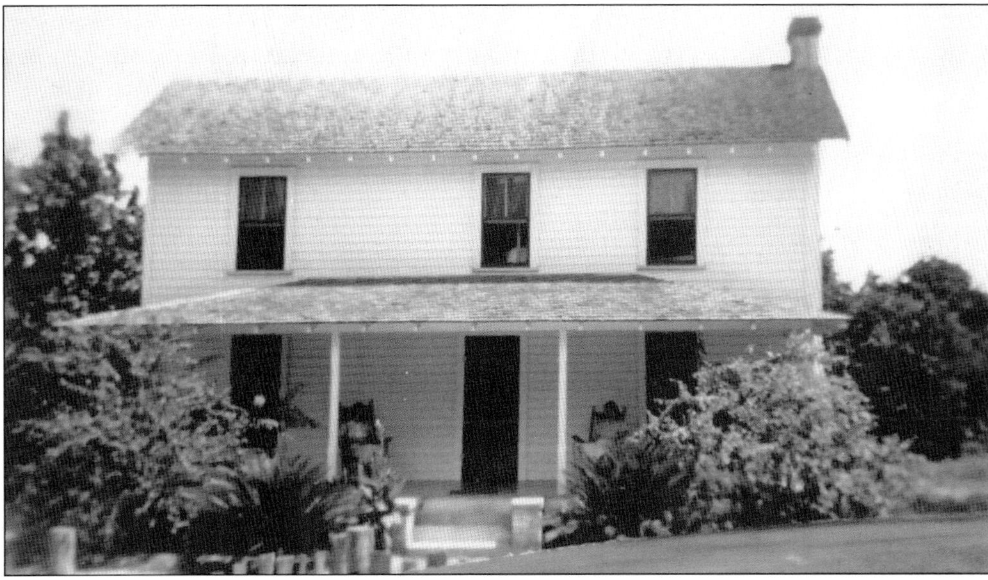

The Ruben Barnes original homestead off Highway 54 was built for his father, Francis "Asbury" Barnes, around 1920. The house is encircled by a barn, corncrib, and hog-boiling kettle constructed by Reese Knapp in 1939. An earlier house sat at the Mulberry Hammock on the homestead, which became the home space for Asbury's granddaughter Vida DePue in later years. (Courtesy of David L. Brown.)

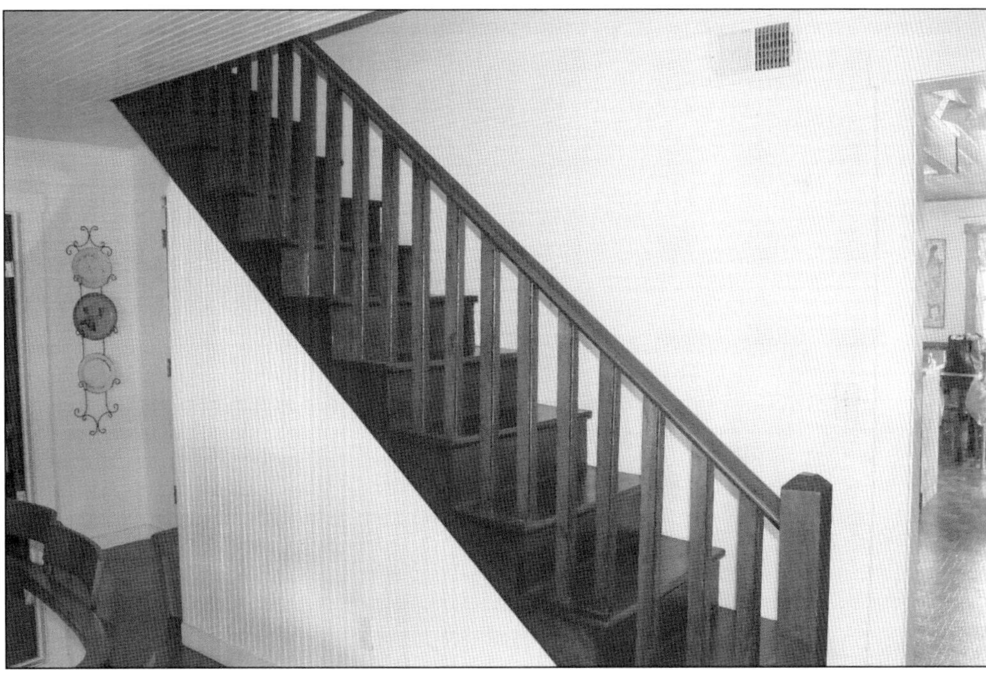

The original wooden staircase of the Ruben Barnes home is surrounded by beadboard walls with floors and a ceiling of solid wood. Beadboard was used in early 1900s. The June 30, 1922, *Dade City Banner* reports that "Barnes has a nice home. A very pretty orange grove was well-loaded but dropped a good deal of the fruit. Barnes is an extensive stock owner." (Courtesy of Ernest Wise.)

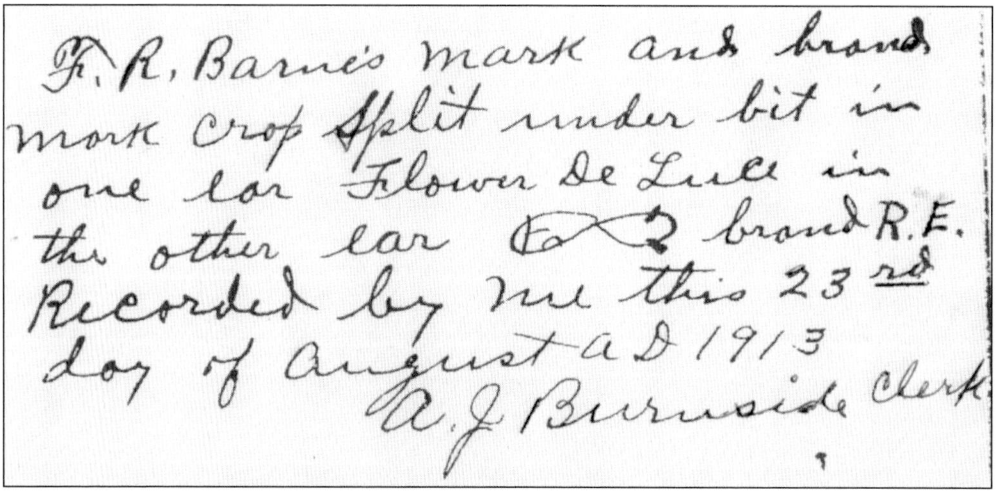
F. R. Barne's mark and brand
mark Crop Split under bit in
one ear Flower De Luce in
the other ear [brand] brand R.F.
Recorded by me this 23rd
day of August A D 1913
A. J. Burnside Clerk

The Ruben Barnes stock brand, dated August 23, 1913, appears on file in the Pasco County Clerk's Office. The complex brand is described and illustrated. Prior to the no-fence law, all cattle and livestock—except the family's milk cow and hogs, which were cooped in a pen for personal use—roamed free. Each family had their particular mark. The branding iron is proudly displayed in the Barnes homestead. (Courtesy of Pasco County Clerk's Office.)

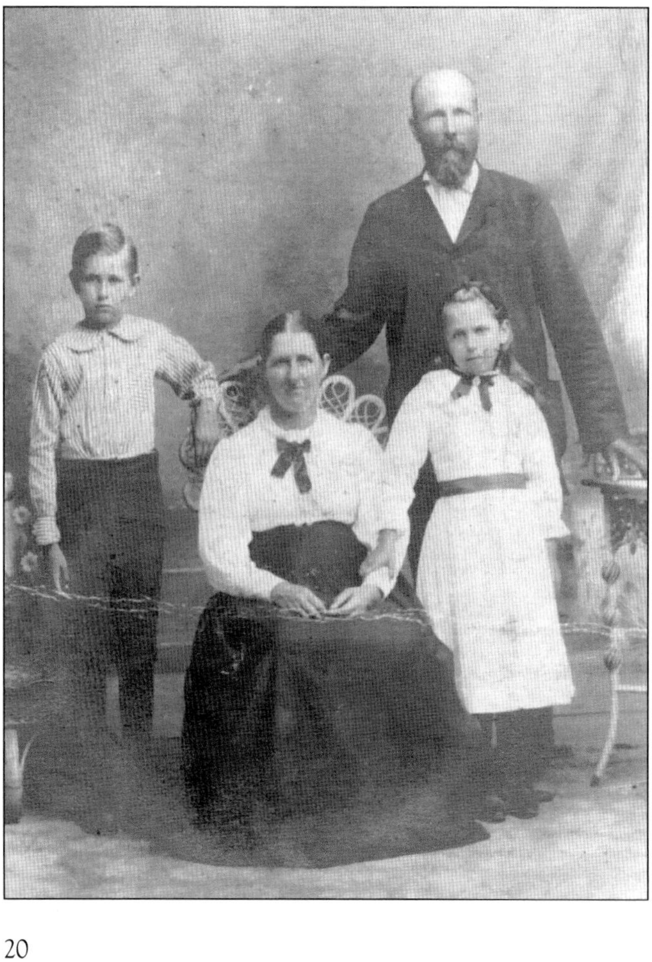

The family of Ruben Barnes is pictured. From left to right are Ruben, Margie Anna Geiger Barnes, Lula Redbrook Barnes Strickland, and Asbury Barnes around 1895 in Wesley Chapel. Margie Anna was the daughter of John Adam Geiger and Mary Jane Dormany Geiger. David L. Brown said, "Ruben Barnes was the quintessential southern gentleman . . . very proper in his demeanor. He called his grandchildren babies. He had two distinctive hats . . . a straw hat, which was his 'going-to-town' hat, and a felt Stetson hat which was his 'work hat.' He was a late bloomer . . . [and] married at age 35." (Courtesy of David L. Brown and Stephanie Brown Benson.)

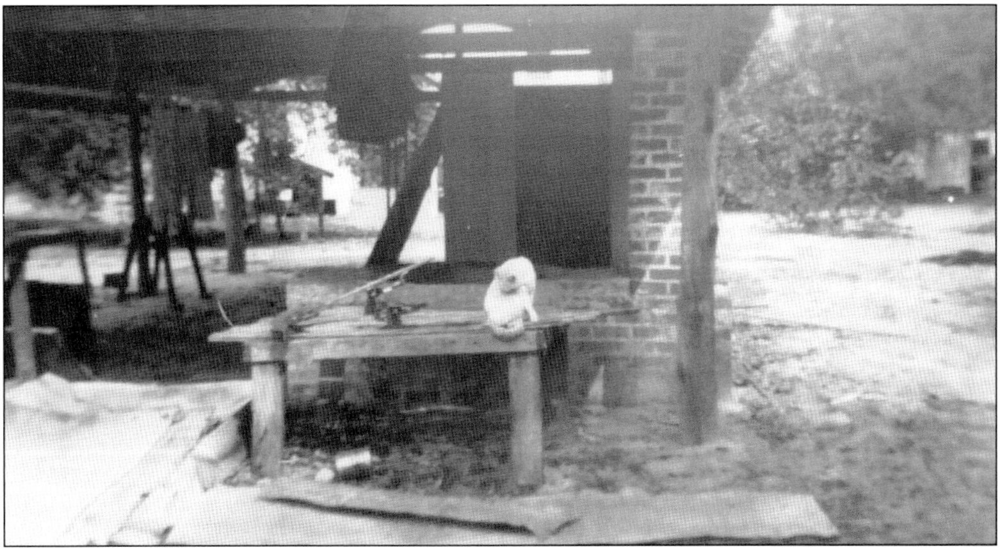

The remnants of a kettle vat for boiling down cane to make syrup and also for scalding hogs in the butchering process is pictured at the Ruben Barnes homestead. Reese Knapp, Faye Gaskin Smith's grandfather, laid the bricks and built the multifunctional structure in 1939. Faye carved the date in the concrete. (Courtesy of David L. Brown.)

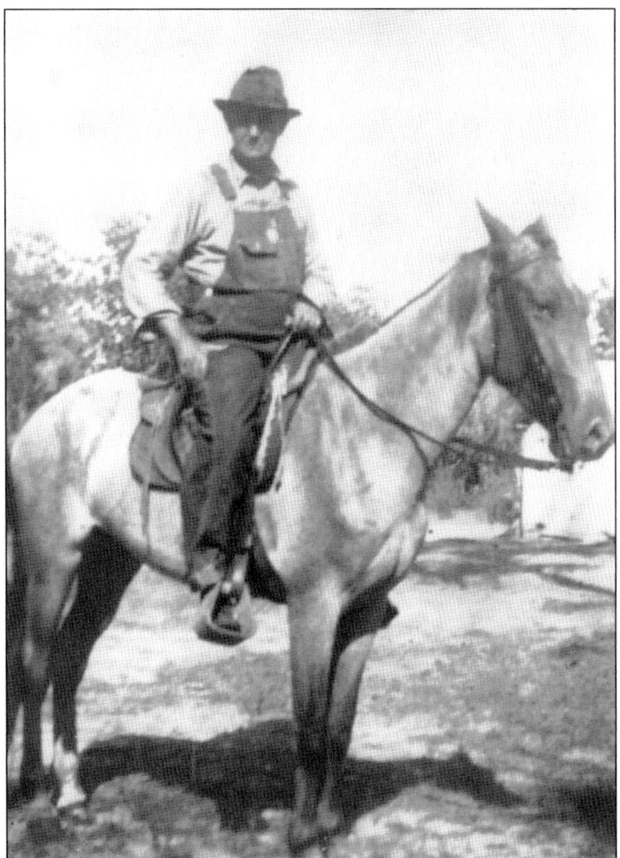

Ruben Barnes looks out over his ranch. Survey notes from 1879 indicate that "the timber and the general surface is almost exclusively pine and is small and scattered—a few scrub oaks are here and there on the more elevated spots: cypress, bay, sweetgum, and ash. In the ponds and swamps, undergrowth of saw palmetto and gall berry shrubs are extensive. Many of the roads through the township are mere paths—often so overgrown with grass as to escape the observation of persons crossing these; hence . . . the line of survey is not measured in the field notes." (Courtesy of David L. Brown.)

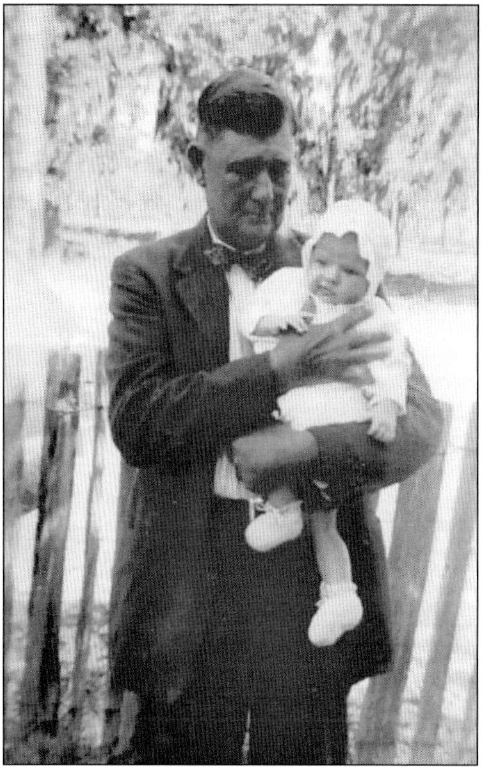

Ruben Barnes affectionately holds his first grandchild, Mary Frances DePue, around 1942. Described as a stoic individual by nature, he displays his soft side in this image. Families were revered and nurtured in frontier Wesley Chapel, and the stories live on of their devotion, hard work, and daily life. (Courtesy of David L. Brown.)

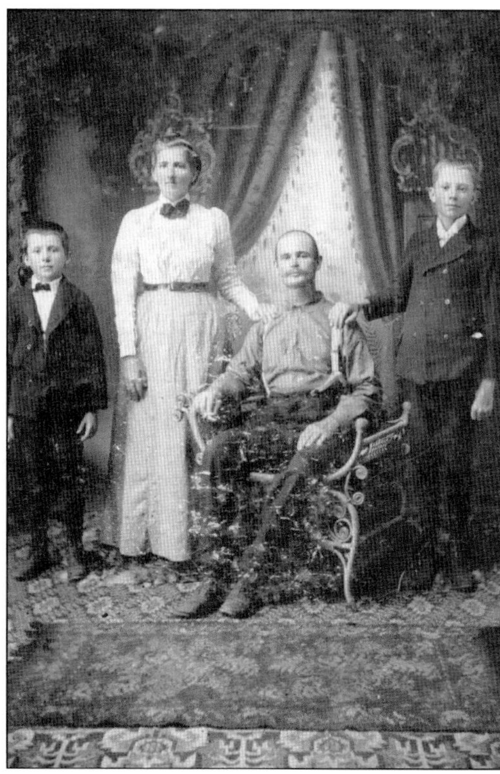

The intertwining of families is evidenced in early history. The Redbrook family is pictured. From left to right are John Asbury Redbrook, Susan Matilda Barnes Redbrook, John Irvin Redbrook, and Arthur Sylvester Redbrook. Susan Matilda Barnes, born in 1869 to Francis Asbury Barnes and Margie Anna Geiger, married John Irvin Redbrook on July 28, 1887. (Photograph by Harry Burgert, courtesy of David L. Brown.)

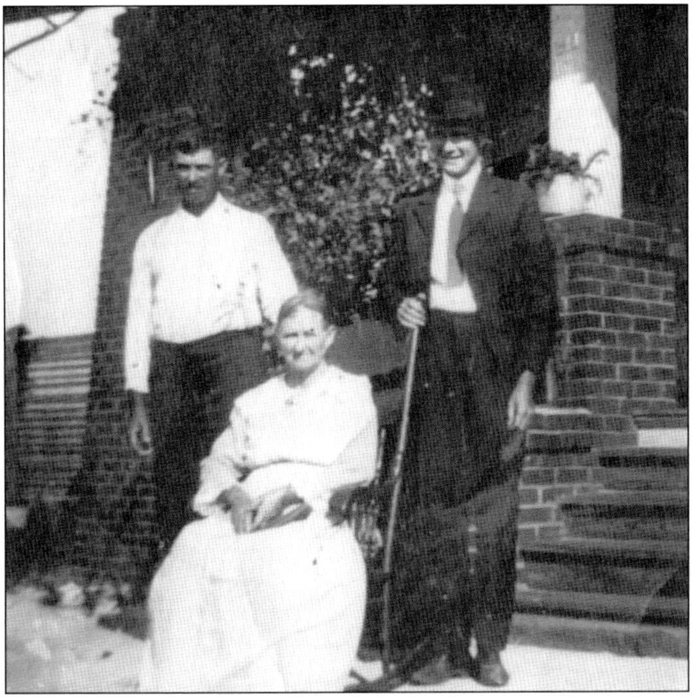

Frank Barnes (left), Margie Anna Geiger, and Ruben Barnes pose in this photograph. Frank was the brother of Ruben. The Barnes family owned the land that was approximately from the intersection of Eiland Boulevard and Highway 54 extending westward to Curley Road and northward to Wells Road. The Barnes Ranch encompassed nearly five sections of land as measured in the public land survey system, each section totaling 640 acres. (Courtesy of David L. Brown.)

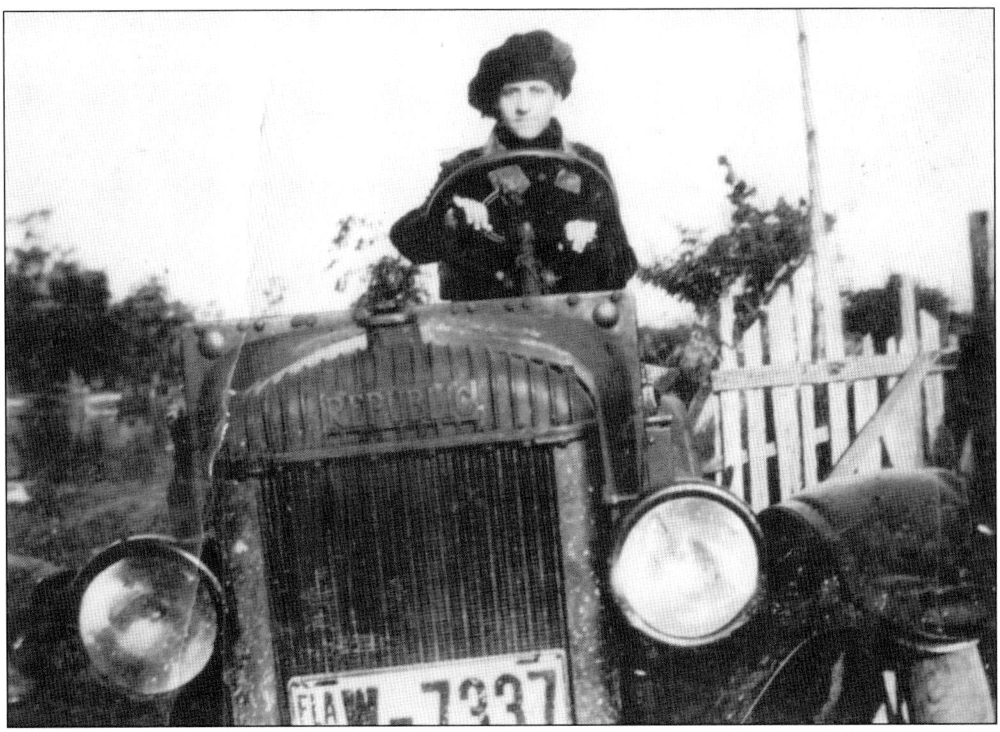

Clara Baines Robinson Barnes drives a Republic Motor truck around 1929 while wearing her motor garb. Wesley Chapel roads were very rugged in this time period. The Republic Motor Truck Company, a major supplier of Liberty trucks during World War I, produced commercial trucks from 1913 to 1929. (Courtesy of David L. Brown.)

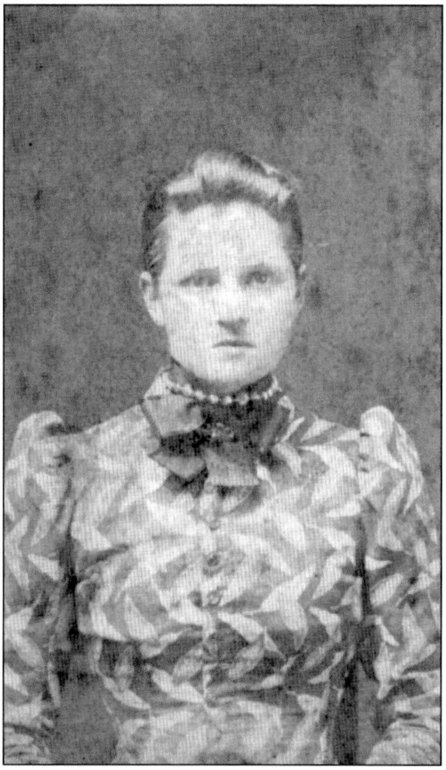

Elizabeth Frances Geiger and Daniel H. Smith were married in December 1894, and their children were Luther, Milton and Dennis. Elizabeth was the daughter of John Adam Geiger and Eliza Jane Carroll. Her simple home is on display at the Florida State Fairgrounds Museum in Tampa and reflects the stark living conditions. In the 19th century, 95 percent of women worked at home. Their work was all consuming. Often working on the land, they were also charged with preparing meals, sewing and mending clothes, planting gardens and preserving foods, as well as rearing children and assuring the family's church attendance and participation. (Courtesy of David L. Brown.)

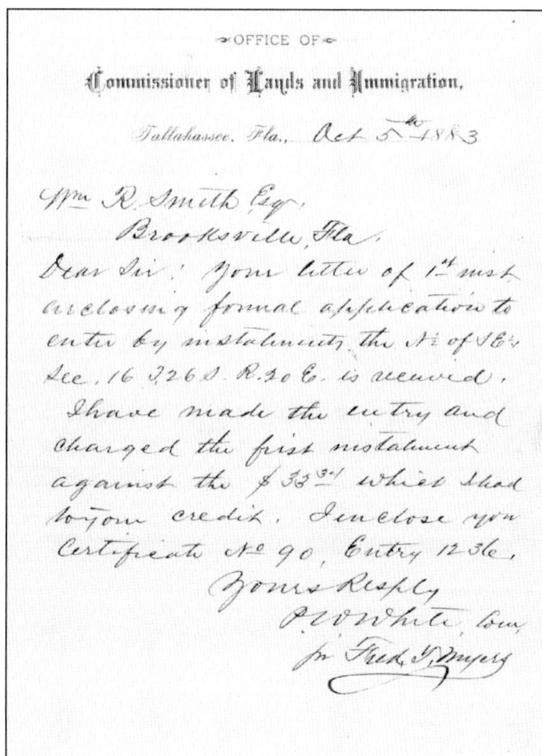

OFFICE OF

Commissioner of Lands and Immigration,

Tallahassee, Fla., Oct 5th 1883

Wm R. Smith Esq.
Brooksville, Fla.

Dear Sir: Your letter of 1st inst enclosing formal application to enter by instalments the N½ of SE¼ Sec. 16 T26 S. R. 20 E. is received.

I have made the entry and charged the first instalment against the $33.34 which I had to your credit. I enclose you Certificate No 90, Entry 1236.

Yours Respy
P. W. White, Clk.
for Fred. T. Myers

A letter dated October 5, 1883, from the Tallahassee commissioner of lands and immigration identifies the section, township, and range of land applied for by William R. Smith from the Homestead Act of 1862. The act provided for the transfer of 160 acres of unoccupied public land to a homesteader for a nominal fee after five years of residency. The pioneers often settled land before it had been surveyed or auctioned by the government. Settlers could expand acreage by paying $50 for 40 acres. They could also file timber claims, which allowed them to obtain an additional 10 acres for planting trees. The philosophy behind homesteading was the belief that the freeholder rather than the tenant would be a supporter of democratic government and community stability. (Courtesy of Ruth Smith Adams.)

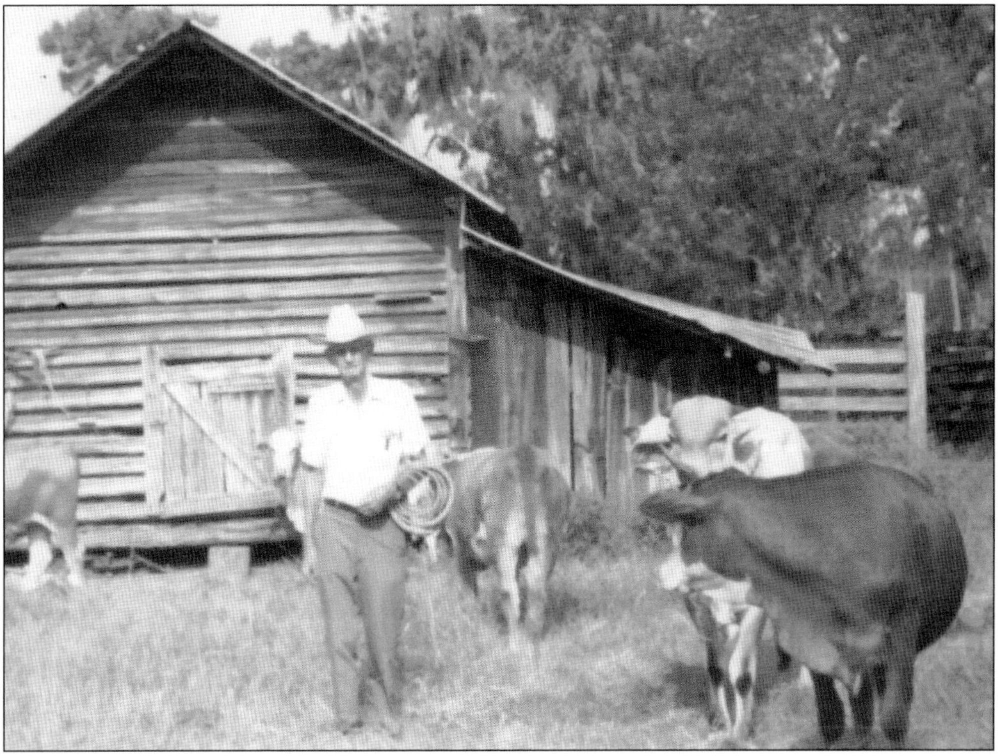

Luther Daniel Smith is shown on his homestead that included 640 acres, in Wesley Chapel. His son explained that the barn was built by neighbors in a barn raising after Luther returned from his military service around 1920. Although the structure has been moved, it remains on the same property and is surrounded by picturesque, pine-laden land that is tucked within the growing contemporary Wesley Chapel on Smith Road. (Courtesy of Bill Smith.)

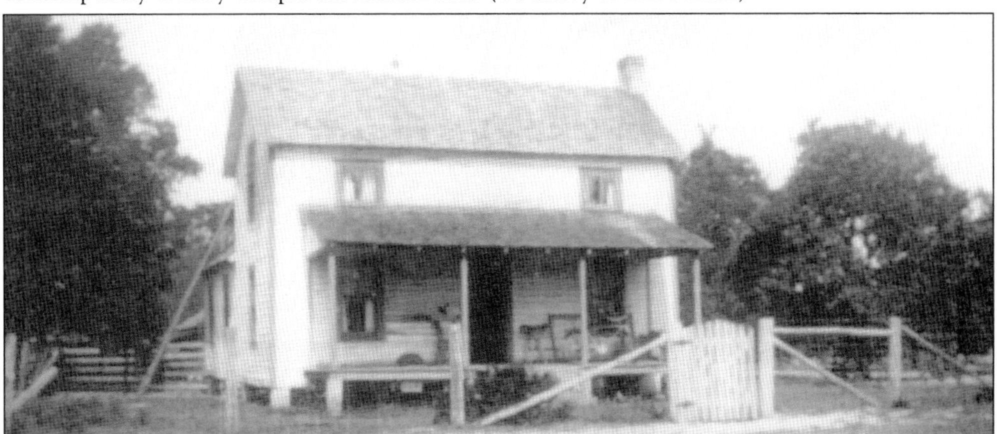

The Luther Daniel Smith homestead was located off Smith Road in Wesley Chapel. Children William Raleigh "Bill" Smith and Ruth Smith were born in the home. They remember walking to Zephyrhills every Saturday for groceries, where their mother would often trade homegrown vegetables, such as sweet potatoes, and eggs for supplies. The town center was a meeting place. "For 25¢, you could see a movie and buy popcorn and candy," said Bill Smith, whose great-grandfather William R. Smith first arrived in Wesley Chapel in 1865. (Courtesy of Bill Smith.)

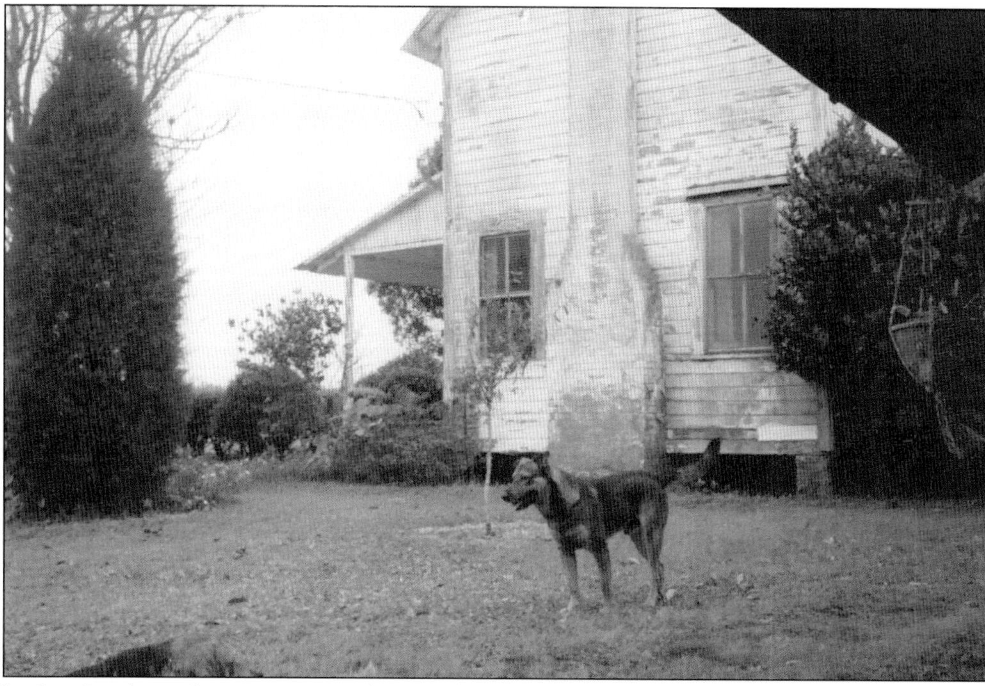

Luther Smith was born in 1886 and married Louneta "Neta" Stanley in Pasco County, Florida. Life in Wesley Chapel was a regiment of hard work, which included farming, ranching, charcoal producing, gator hunting and skinning, turpentining, and moonshining. According to Ruth Smith, electricity came to Wesley Chapel in 1949. (Courtesy of Bill Smith and Ruth Smith Adams.)

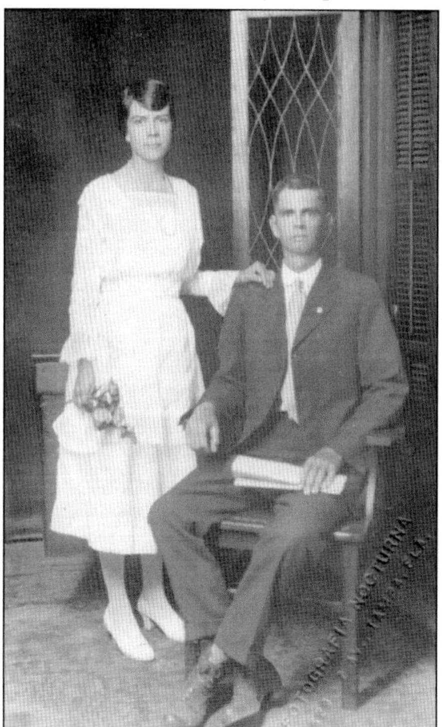

Luther and his wife, Louneta Stanley Smith, lived and worked the land in Wesley Chapel. Generations have lived on this land, beginning with settlers and grandparents William R. Smith and Annie E. Sims Smith. The origin of the name "Wesley Chapel" is uncertain. B.C. Manion reported in 2012: "Debate remains. . . . Many historical accounts theorize it was named after John Wesley, the founder of Methodism. Bill Smith, son of Luther, does not think so. He said the community did not have a large contingent of Methodists. He believes it is more likely that the community was named after a teacher and preacher whose last name was Wesley. While those traveling through the area today will see a community chock full of places to live, work, and play, the people who settled in the community during the early days encountered a much different place." (Courtesy of Marco E. Stanley.)

John Boyette was born in 1875 as the son of John "Berry" Boyette and nephew of Thomas Ashley Boyette. Pictured, from left to right, are Johnnie, John holding William, Ruby, Blanche (John's wife), and Vera. The *Dade City Banner* of December 19, 1919, reports, "Most everybody of Wesley Chapel are grinding cane now. They intend to have something sweet, since we can't get sugar." C.B. Taylor penned that John Boyette had fine-looking sugarcane in 1922. (Courtesy of Cletia Pierce.)

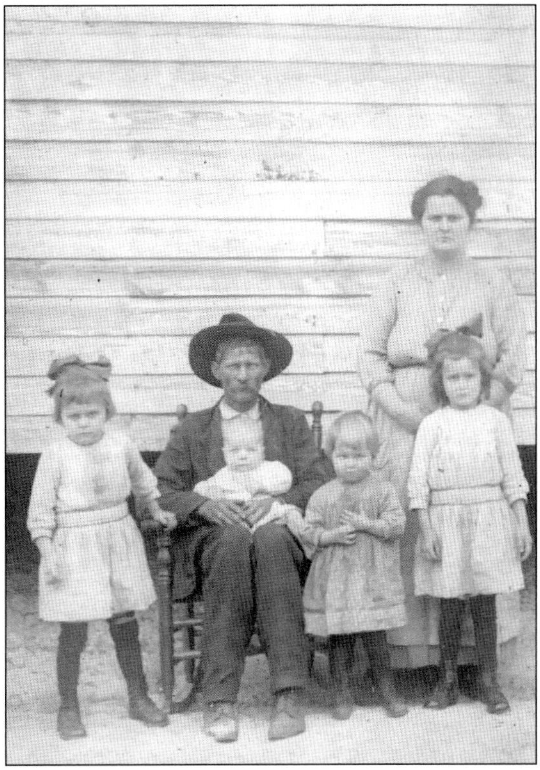

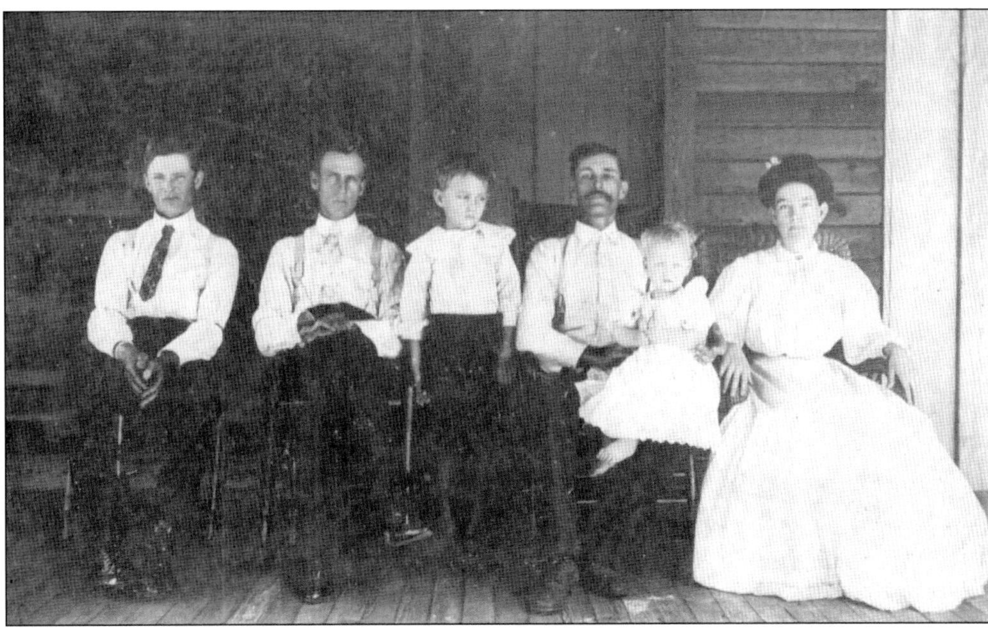

Edwin "Fate" Lafayette Godwin and his wife, Julia Barnes Godwin, sit with their children on the front porch of their home in Wesley Chapel. Their homestead was located up Tupper Road on the west side of Highway 54, directly across from the entrance of the present-day Saddlebrook Resort. Fate was the son of Jacob L. Godwin and Mary Ann Benner Godwin. Pictured are, from left to right, Ivy, Elias, Emanuel, Fate, Ola, and Julia. (Courtesy of David L. Brown.)

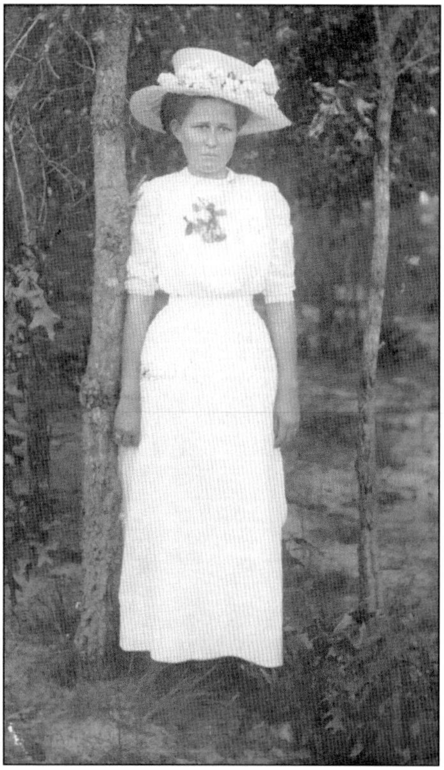

Margery Turner displays her fashionable bonnet on her wedding day, April 18, 1912. She is documented in the Wesley Chapel censuses for 1920 and 1930. In 1930, Margery was 36, and her husband, Sherrod, was 69. Their children were Stanley, 16; Elena, 15; Daniel C., 13; Florence E, 9; and Ruth Ryals 7. Sherrod's first wife, Sophrana Taylor, was born in 1841 and passed away; the couple had no children. Kenneth Cleveland Ryals penned a history of the Daniel C. Ryals family that was published in 1985 and includes accounts of Wesley Chapel residents including Margery Turner Ryals's family. (Courtesy of Marlo Hilton.)

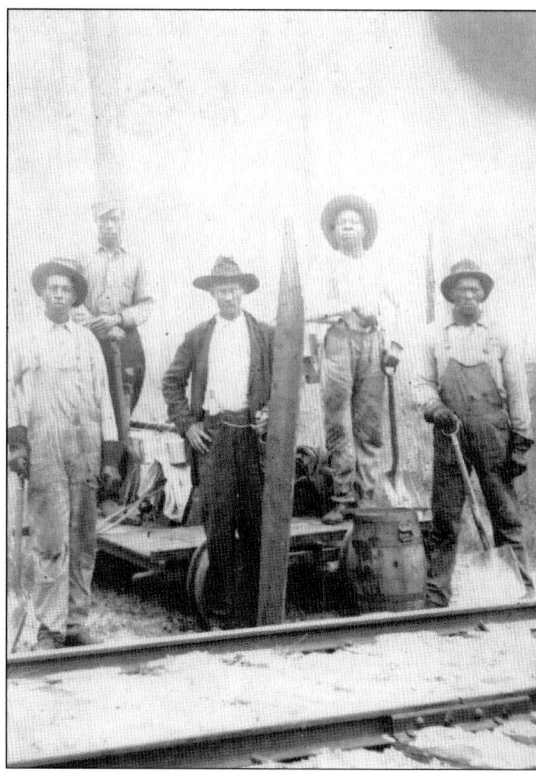

A postcard image depicts John Boyette and his crew of African American workers on the Florida Railroad. The photograph was taken at the railroad, which ran parallel to Pasco Road in Wesley Chapel. Wood racks were positioned along the railway for the trains to stop and fire their boilers. To calculate payment to the woodcutters, there were partitions that showed measurements in cords of wood. The engineer of the train would just leave a check on the rack. (Courtesy of Cletia Pierce.)

Fernie "Pasco" Cooper gives his wife, Mittie Lula Wells—daughter of John Wesley Wells and Mary Elizabeth Gaskins—a hug. "Everybody called Cooper 'bossman'—even his children. He owned a dairy, logging business, and store," Michael C. Boyette shared. "He had a heart of gold, always assisting neighbors in need. When he worried he had lost his homestead in the midst of the Great Depression, his wife revealed that she had painstakingly paid off the mortgage herself with egg money and other household funds." (Courtesy of Michael C. Boyette.)

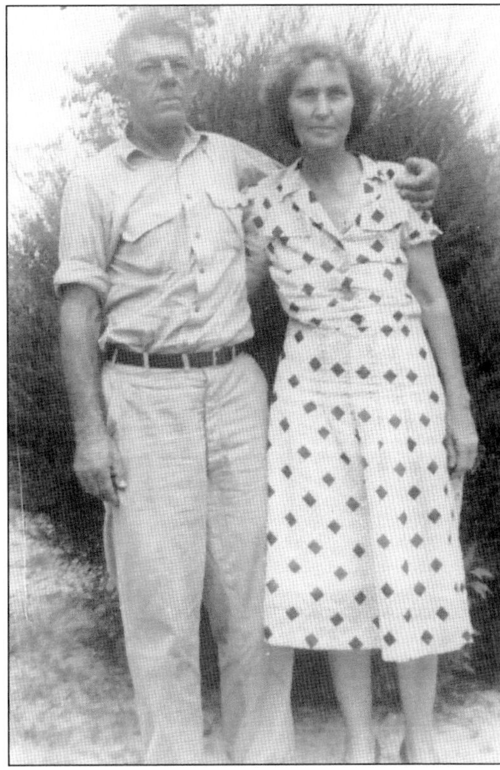

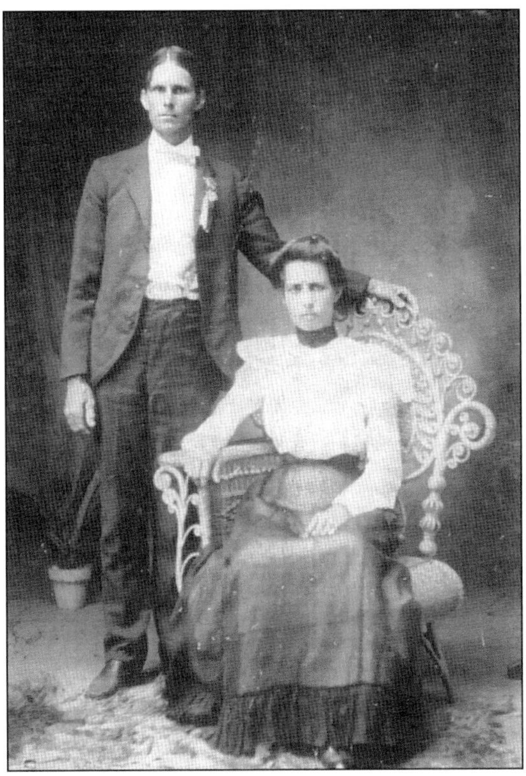

James Monroe and Fannie Lee Stanley Boyette, who married on February 2, 1902, are pictured around that same year. James was the son of Thomas Ashley Boyette and Elizabeth Jane Osburn Boyette. According to Cullen Boyette, the Boyette family migrated from Virginia by way of the Carolinas after the Civil War. The story of Wesley Chapel was the story of a few key families, which included the Boyettes as well as the Coopers, Wells, Stanleys, Gillettes, and others. Cullen's great-uncle was Dee Wells, for whom Wells Road was named. His great-grandfather on the maternal side was Robert Cooper, who also arrived after the Civil War. (Courtesy of Cletia Pierce.)

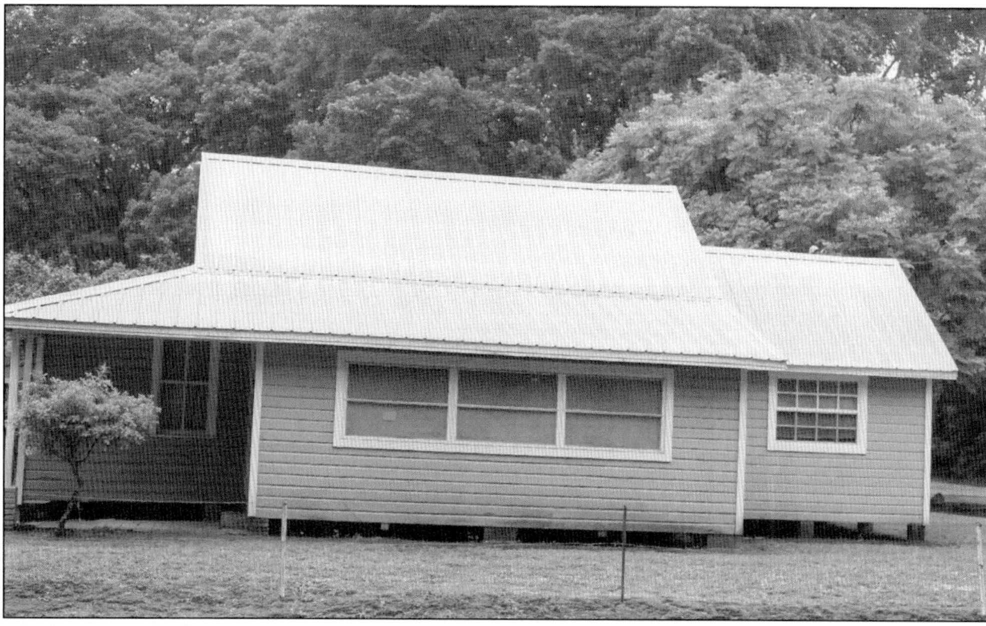

The homestead of James Monroe Boyette on Boyette Road continues to be used as a home. Cullen Boyette said, "When I was a little boy, we had one church, one grocery store, and maybe 35 families . . . everybody was a farmer or a logger. . . . [W]e raised black-eyed peas, corn, peanuts, okra, and watermelons. You'd take produce to the farmers' market in Tampa. The interstate came in the 1960s. To go to Tampa, I would have to drive out to Highway 41." (Courtesy of Ernest Wise.)

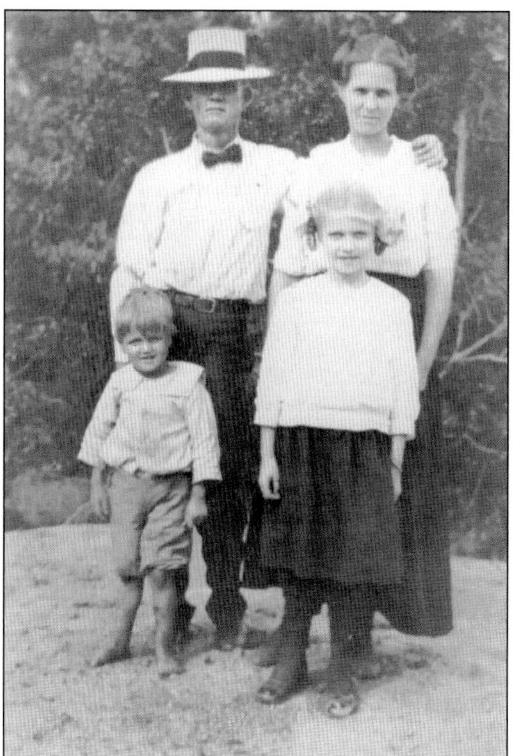

James Hardy Cooper stands proudly with his wife, Sabra Louneda Boyette, son Lonnie C., and daughter Lillian Irene around 1917. Other children were Curtis C., James F., and James Earl. "There was a closeness about the relationships of neighbors of Godwin and others of the central region and along the two rivers. They went in bands from east to west to catch and salt mullet to dry for the year's supply of fish. They traveled together to the county seat, first located at Tampa, then Ocala, and finally at Brooksville," said teacher Rosemary Trottman. (Courtesy of Cletia Pierce.)

Hardy and Sabra Louneda Boyette Cooper pose for a photograph near the Wells Store. Hardy frequented the Wells Grocery Store usually with his grandchildren in tow—often BeBe and Cliffy Cooper. A great place to catch up on the community news, the store was operated by Delbert Wells, who was also known for his extraordinary watermelon patch behind the store. (Courtesy of Cletia Pierce.)

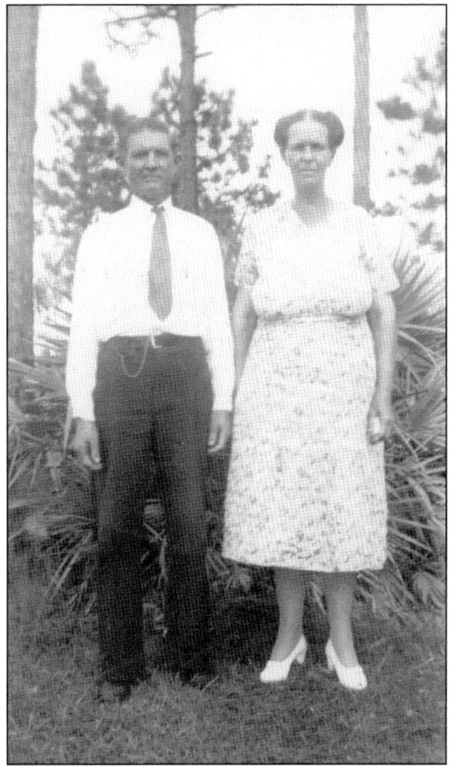

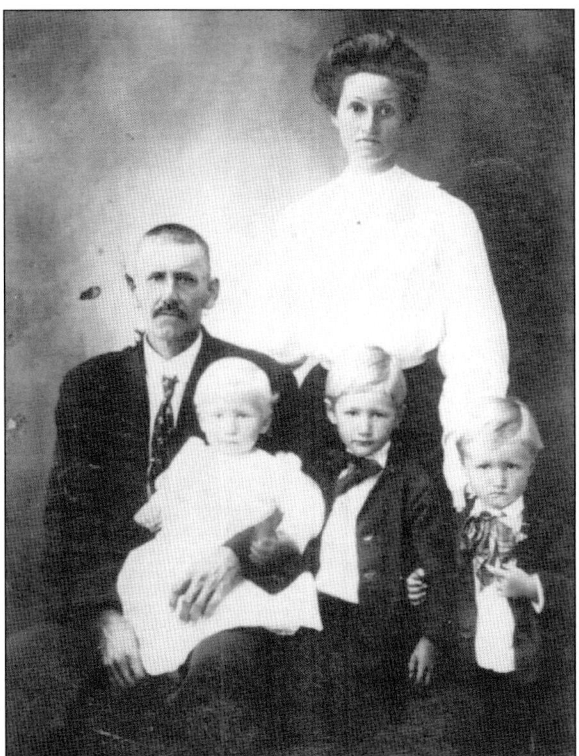

Much of the history of Wesley Chapel is intertwined with the Tucker family. James Tucker and his wife, Sarah Humphries Tucker, sit for this 1917 photograph with children, from left to right, Wilber "Wigg" , Bryant, and Lonnie. Tragedy struck this couple when James became permanently incapacitated by a major illness. Sarah persevered alone to raise their family and manage the homestead, but unfortunately, she succumbed to illness in her mid-30s, leaving the eight Tucker sons to make their own way in the world. As was often the norm, the boys rallied to assist one another. (Courtesy of Anna Jo Bracknell.)

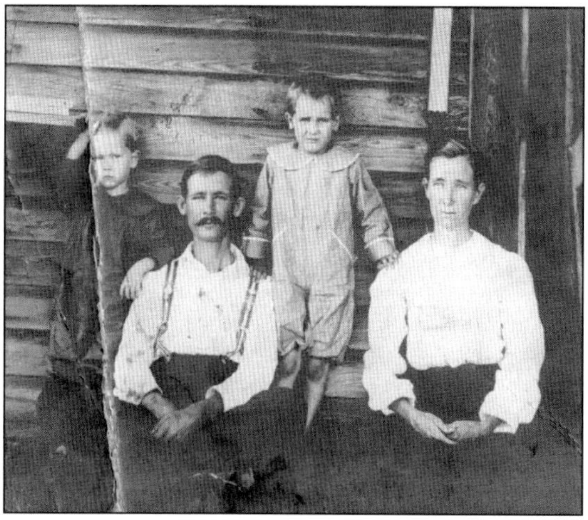

Ephrain Bascom Cooper and Nancy Hill Cooper are pictured at their homestead in Wesley Chapel with their two sons, Wallace and Robert Bascom Cooper. Winifred Madison, their youngest child, was not born at the time of this c. 1909 photograph. Ephrain became the postmaster of Wesley on March 25, 1902. He was the son of John R. Cooper and Mary Etta Gillet. Nancy was the daughter of Robert Madison Hill and Catherine Frances Holder. At the 1998 dedication of the Pasco County Courthouse, the Hills were recognized as a founding family. (Courtesy of Cletia Pierce.)

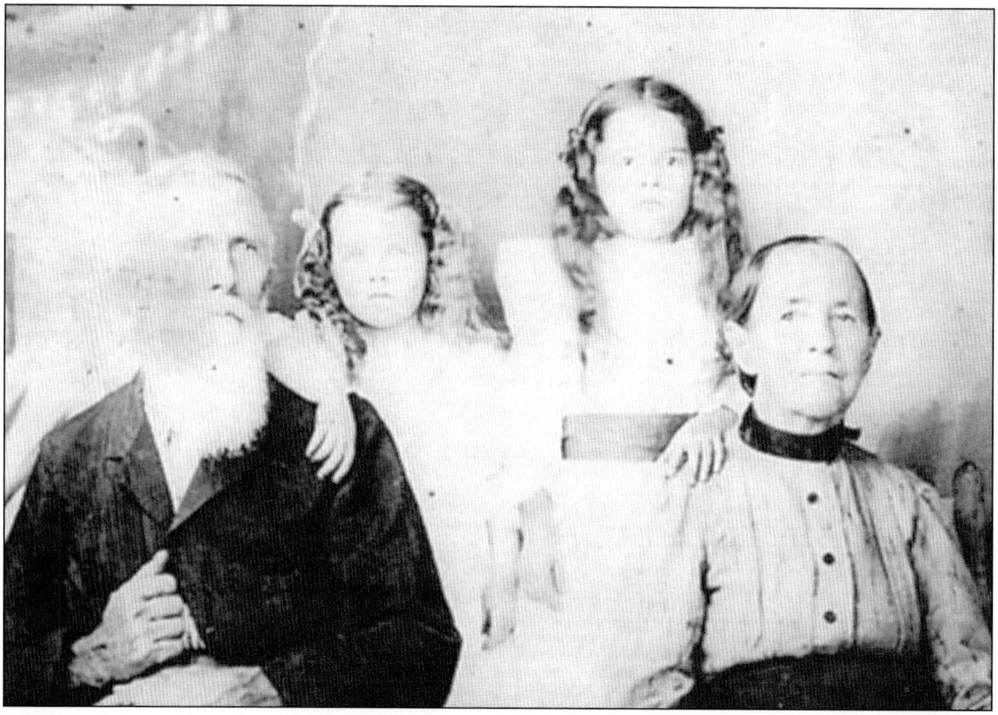

William Sebron Standley and his wife, Fannie Bradley Standley, arrived after the Civil War. Wesley Chapel allegiances were for both the Confederacy and the Union. This photograph includes Annie Stanley and Ruby Stanley, children of Walter Raleigh Stanley. Marco E. Stanley said, "My great-great grandfather is buried in Mount Zion Cemetery in Dade City. He married Capt. Robert Duke Bradley's daughter. Frances "Fannie" Bradley was known for the leadership in the Bradley Massacre (May 5, 1856). The monument in nearby Darby commemorates the battle. The next generation, sons, Lewis Napoleon Stanley and his brother, Walter Raleigh Stanley, dropped the *d* in Standley." (Courtesy of Marco E. Stanley.)

William Sebron Standley was in the Confederate army and took great pride in his military service. He often shared that, even after his capture, he remained loyal to the Confederacy. "I was captured at Murfreesburo, Tennessee by the Federal Army and placed in prison at Camp Chase, Ohio where I was forcibly kept until the surrender of the Confederate Army. I was captured about the 13th day of December, 1860," wrote Standley. His descendants joked that, in reality, he was from the North, so to speak—originally, via his Irish heritage. (Courtesy of Marco E. Stanley.)

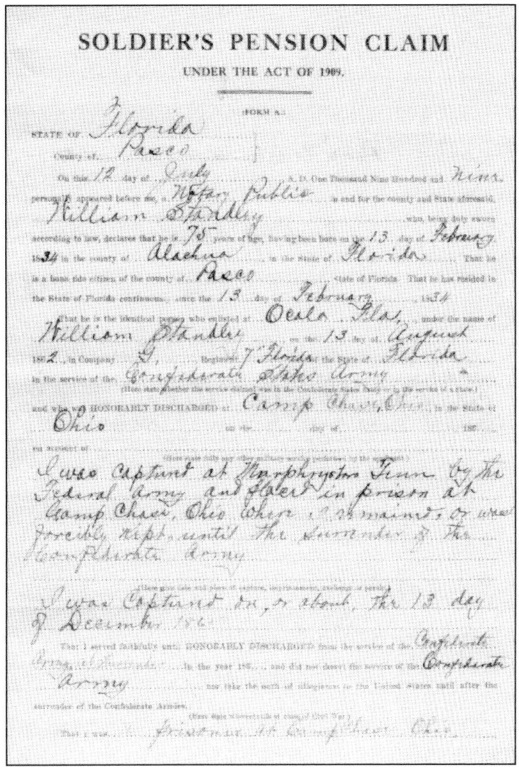
SOLDIER'S PENSION CLAIM

UNDER THE ACT OF 1909.

FORM A.

STATE OF Florida

County of Pasco

On this 12 day of July A. D. One Thousand Nine Hundred and Nine, personally appeared before me, a Notary Public in and for the county and State aforesaid, William Standley who, being duly sworn according to law, declares that he is 75 years of age, having been born on the 13 day of February 1834 in the county of Alachua in the State of Florida. That he is a bona fide citizen of the county of Pasco State of Florida. That he has resided in the State of Florida continuously since the 13 day of February 1834

That he is the identical person who enlisted at Ocala Fla, under the name of William Standley on the 13 day of August 1862, in Company G, Regiment 7 Florida the State of Florida in the service of the Confederate States Army

(Here state whether the service claimed was in the Confederate States Army or in the service of a State.)

and who was HONORABLY DISCHARGED at Camp Chase, Ohio in the State of Ohio on the day of 186

on account of

(Here state fully any other military service performed by the applicant.)

I was captured at Murphreysboro Tenn by the Federal Army and placed in prison at Camp Chase, Ohio where I remained or was forcibly kept until the surrender of the Confederate Army

(Here give date and place of capture, imprisonment, exchange or parole.)

I was captured on, or about, the 13 day of December 186

That I served faithfully until HONORABLY DISCHARGED from the service of the Confederate Army at surrender in the year 186 , and did not desert the service of the Confederate Army nor take the oath of allegiance to the United States until after the surrender of the Confederate Armies.

(Here state whereabouts at close of Civil War.)

That I was prisoner at Camp Chase Ohio

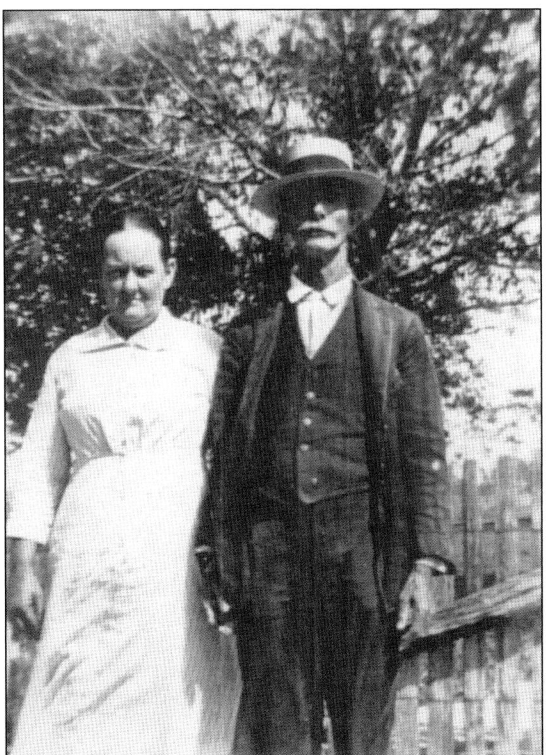

Walter R. Stanley and Mary Abbigail Sellers Stanley are pictured at their homestead. The Stanley name was amongst those of prominent pioneers in the community. Thelma Stanley writes in the February 11, 1938, *Dade City Banner* that "those attending the fair on Tuesday for children's day were Mr. and Mrs. Albert Godwin and family; Mr. and Mrs. J.M. Boyette; Mr. and Mrs. Fritz Boyette and family; Mrs. J.H. Cooper; F.R. Barnes; Lonnie Cooper; Vida and Martha Barnes; and Thelma and Jean Stanley. All reported a good time." (Courtesy of Kimber Ann Ferguson.)

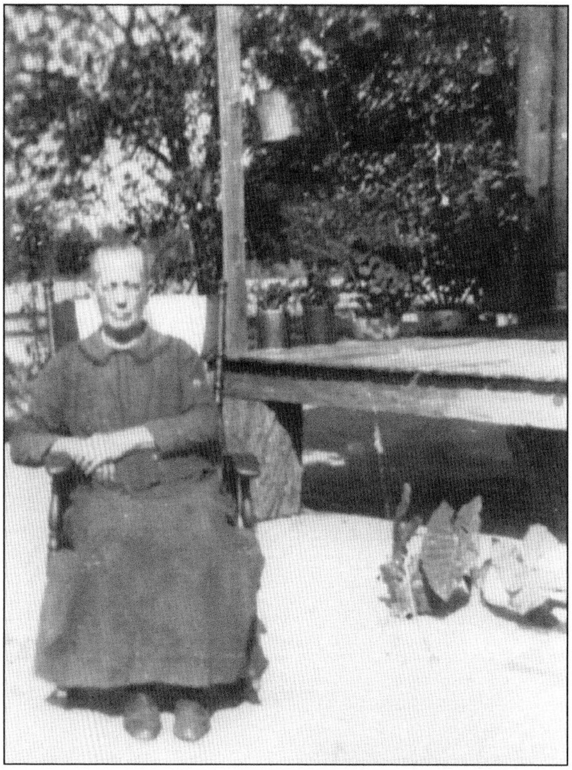

Mary Alice Tomberlin Stanley was born in Gadsden on December 2, 1865, and died in Wesley Chapel on August 31, 1937. In this photograph, she rests in a rocker at the Old Stanley homestead in Wesley Chapel. Her obituary reads: "Mrs. Mary Alice Stanley, aged 71 years, well-known resident of Wesley Chapel, passed away early Tuesday afternoon. Mrs. Stanley was a faithful member of the Baptist Church and Sunday school and a regular attendant, in spite of poor health. She was the widow of L.N. Stanley, who passed away eight years ago." (Courtesy of Kimber Ann Ferguson and Cletia Pierce.)

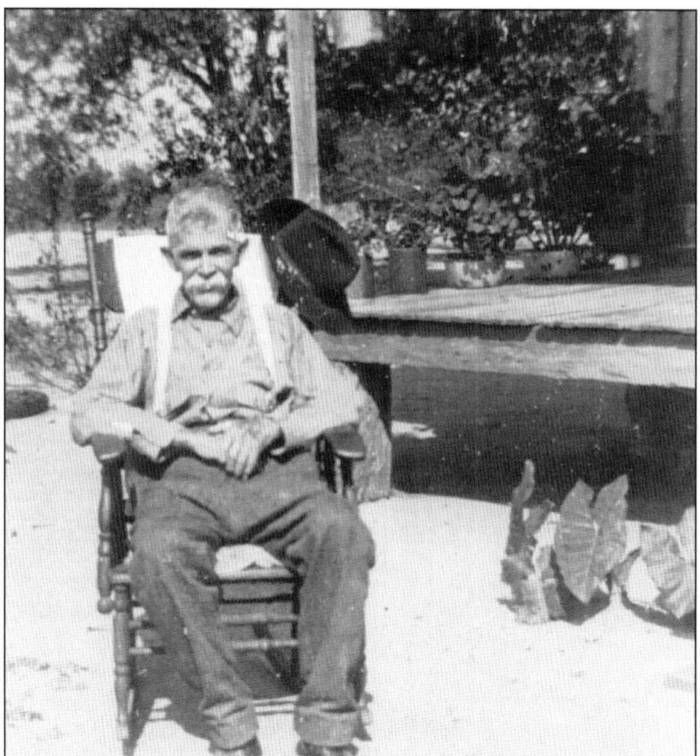

Lewis Napoleon Stanley (pictured) was the father of 15 children. He, like other pioneers, was a subsistence farmer. Food and essentials were produced and timber and sap were harvested at the homestead and in the community. The sap (oleoresins) of pine trees was processed in stills and the liquid was boiled in huge kettles and distilled into turpentine. The residue was sold as rosin. The nearest hub for trade was the port in Tampa at the site of Fort Brooke. (Courtesy of Marco E. Stanley.)

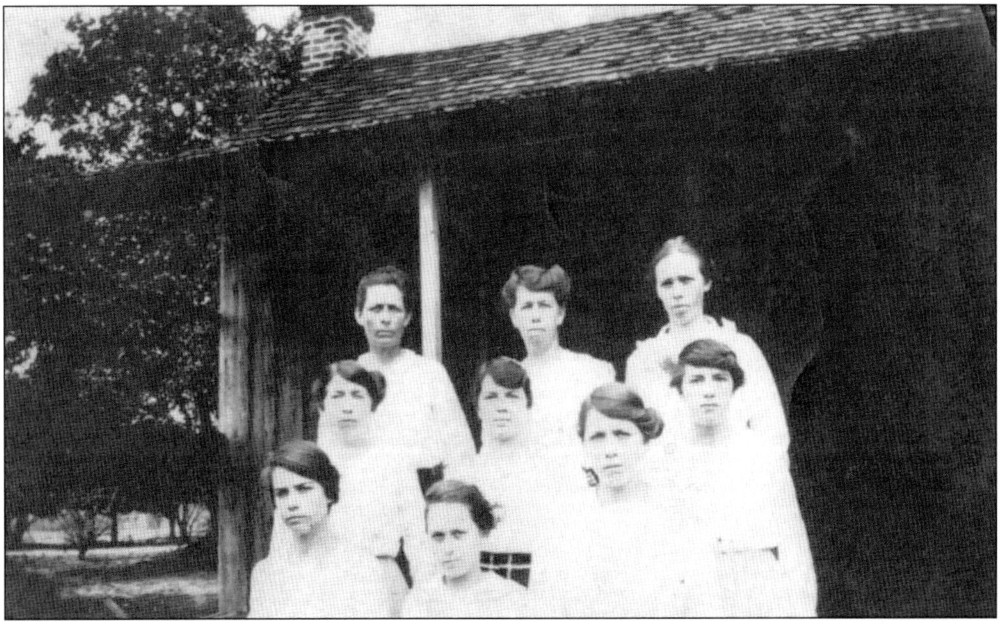

Typical of large families at the turn of the 20th century, Lewis Napoleon Stanley and Mary Alice Tomberlin had 15 children. There were nine surviving girls, pictured at the homestead around 1920. They are, from left to right, (first row) Mamie Lenora, Eleanor Stanley Hill, and Eva "Mae" Stanley Gaskin; (second row) Hattie Elizabeth Stanley Ryals, Louneta Stanley Smith, and Edith Stanley Broecker; (third row) Fannie Lee Stanley Boyette, Dosha Ann Stanley Fagan, and Donnie Ella Stanley Godwin. Fannie was born in 1884 and Eleanor in 1907. (Courtesy of Marco E. Stanley.)

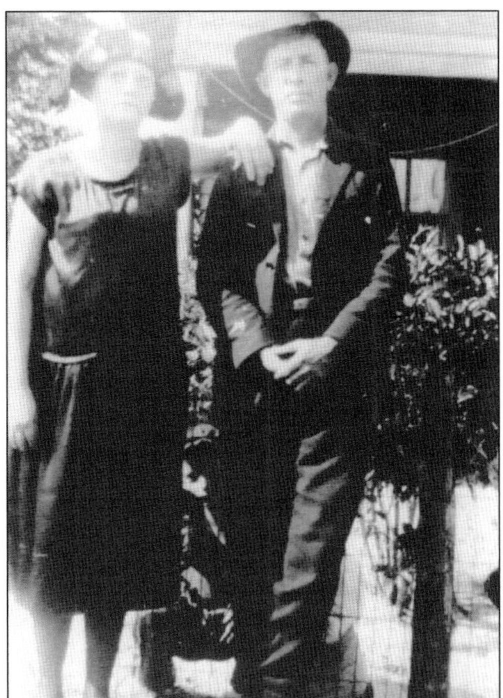

Rollie Stanley was born in July 1888 to Lewis Stanley and Mary Alice Stanley. Rollie married Malinda Jane Gillette, the daughter of Sarah L. McKendree Gillette and Hardy A. Gillette. They were the parents of 10 children, but only three survived birth—Roscoe, Marco, and Sarah Mahaley. Sarah Mahaley, a local version of Rosie the Riveter, worked in the shipyards in Tampa during World War II and married Roy Overstreet. (Courtesy of Marco E. Stanley.)

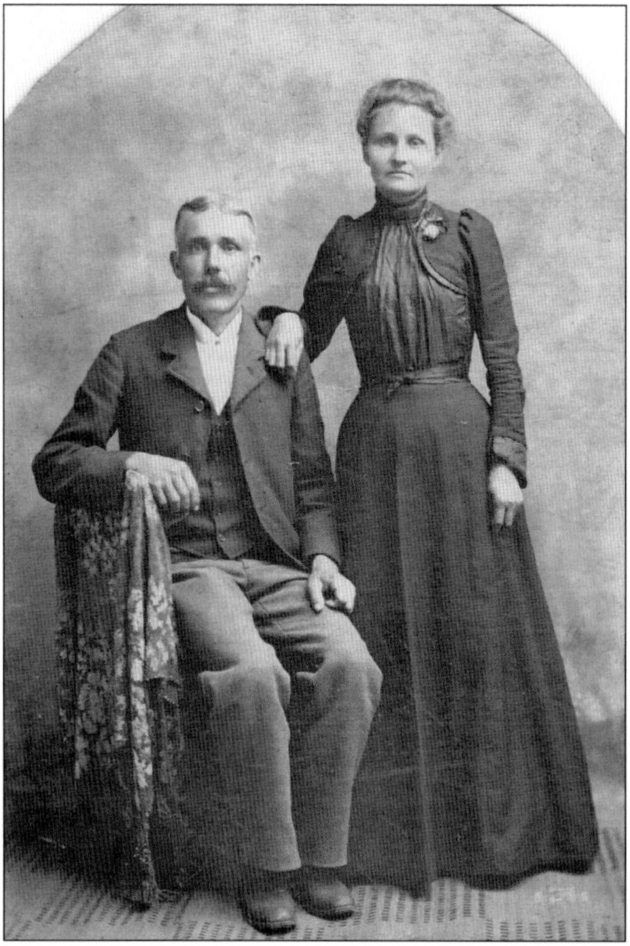

Moray Jackson Kersey and Nancy Emma Studsill pose in 1879. Moray was the son of Libron and Barcilla Boyette Kersey, shown on the 1879 survey map of Wesley Chapel. The Kerseys had multiple connections, including the Boyettes and Ryals. Nancy, daughter of Augustus Studstill and Sophronia Elizabeth Boyette, migrated with her widowed mother. She subsequently married Sherrod Ryals; both are listed in the 1910 census. (Courtesy of Susan Maroney and Beth Kersey Hayes.)

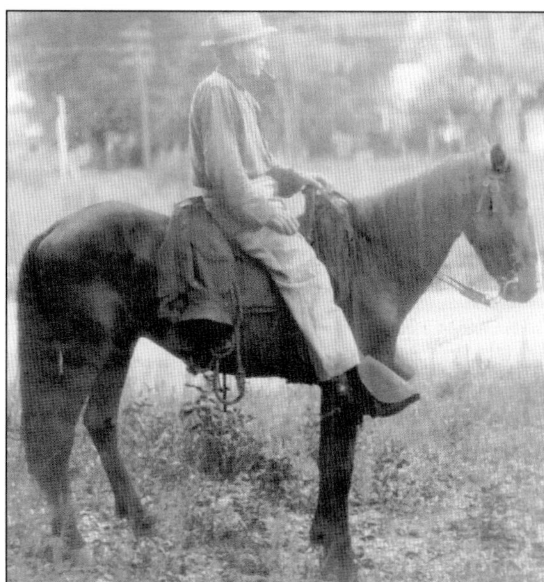

Lewis Reed "Dee" Wells, son of John Wesley Wells and Mary Elizabeth Gaskins, was one of the first of the Wells family to settle in Wesley Chapel. Dee was the Pasco County supervisor of registration. When Dee died in office, the Florida governor appointed his wife, Roxie Ann "Missouri" Spivey Wells, to finish out his term. Dee was previously an impounding officer during the no-fence laws. Grandson Wayne Sweat said, "When the county received a report of fenced livestock that were range cattle or hogs, Dee Wells would confiscate the cattle and put them in a pen maintained by the county. . . . [E]ventually, someone claimed the cattle, and the fee was collected." (Courtesy of Wayne Sweat.)

Roxey Ann "Missouri" Spivey Wells was the wife of Dee Wells. They were married in 1898. She was the daughter of John David Wells and Roxey Ann Wooten. Her children were Roxie Vernon Wells, Delbert Lewis Wells, Louis G. Wells, John Dendy Wells, Nelson Elliott Wells, Norma Juanita Wells, Royce Millard Wells, and Berley Spivey Wells. Missouri served as supervisor of registration after her husband's death in 1933. The supervisor of registration position was the forerunner to the contemporary supervisor of elections position. (Courtesy of Wayne Sweat.)

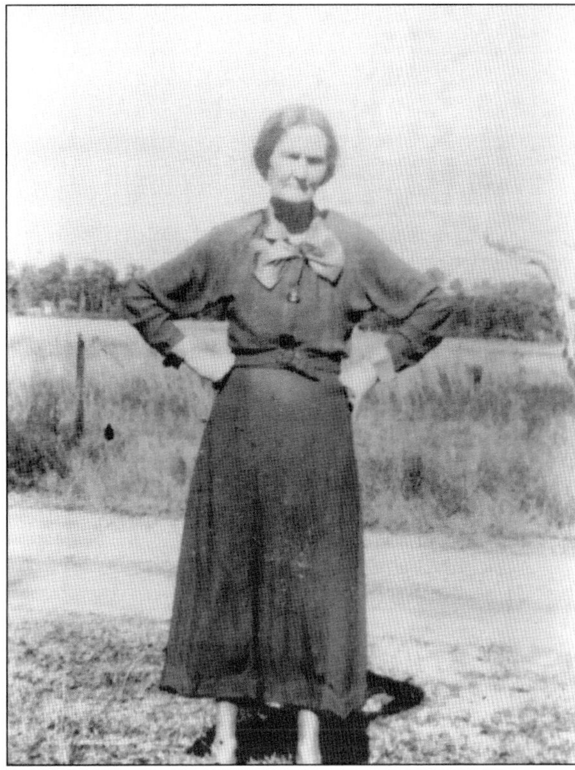

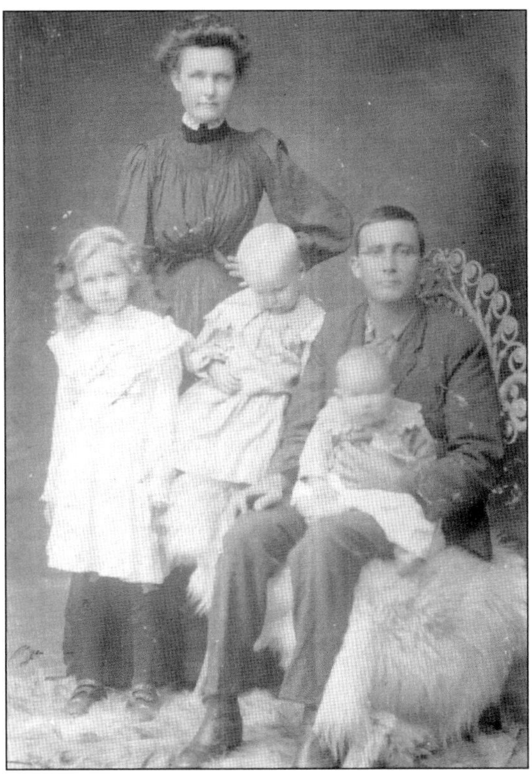

Dee Wells and his handsome family are pictured in 1904. From left to right are Roxie Vernon Wells, Missouri Spivey Wells, Delbert Wells, and Dee Wells, holding John Wells. John became well known in his adult career for developing a dredging company that accommodated government contracts. He dredged the swampland that was to become Cape Canaveral and worked all the way up the coast to Delaware. (Courtesy of Wayne Sweat and Cletia Pierce.)

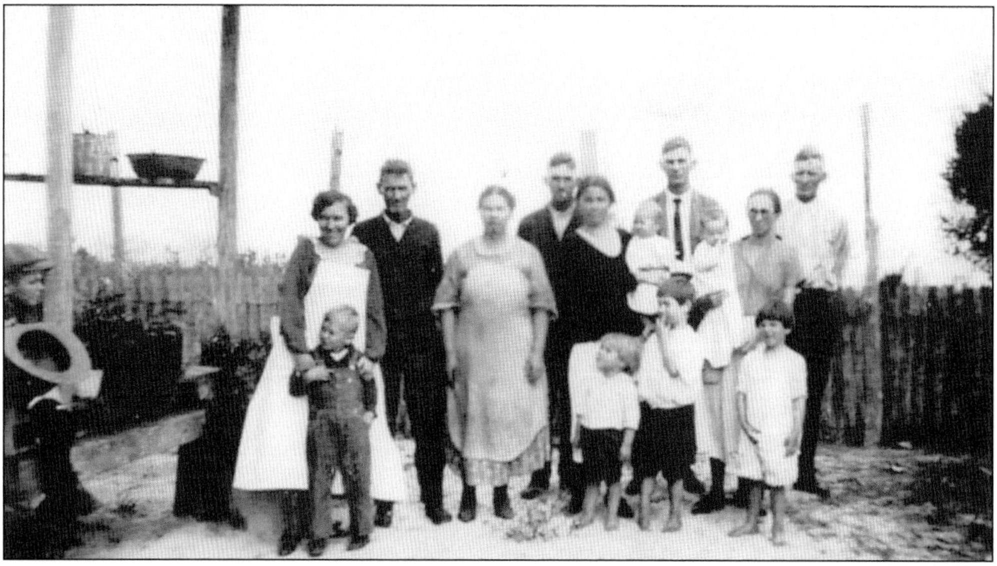

Members of the Wells family in Wesley Chapel have lined up in their backyard around 1927. Family members identified by Charles Estepp include, left to right, (first row) Murray, John, Reuben Lee, and Bernice Wells; (second row) Grace, Lourina, Minnie holding Roy Wells, and a sister of Lourina holding Celestine Wells; (third row) John Reuben, Reuben Wesley, Willie, and Wallace Wells. Lourina had several sisters—Sallie, Mary, Rosa, Ida, and Azeline. (Courtesy of Charles Estepp.)

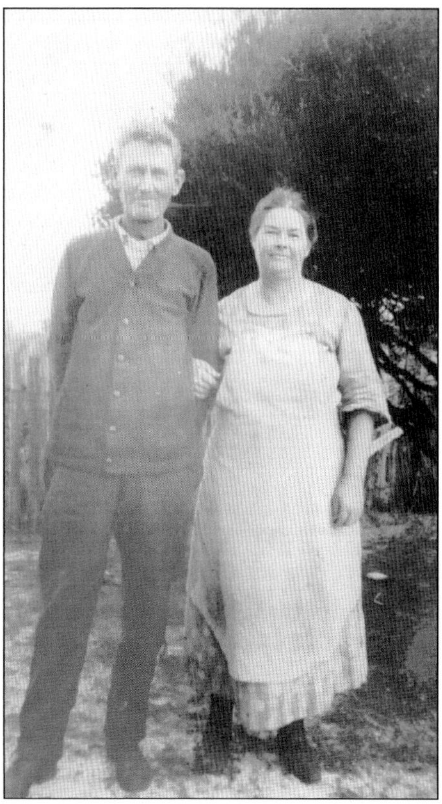

John Reuben "Rube" Wells and Lourina Geiger Wells stop in front of their orange tree. John was the son of John Wesley Wells and Mary E Gaskins. Lourina was the daughter of Jesse C. Geiger and Mary A. King. "Rube," brother of Uncle Coop Wells, plants about two-thirds of a crop of corn, and his cane and velvet beans are looking very lively. Wells successfully grew spring onions and a new variety known as the "Rube Wells" yam, which matures about three weeks earlier than ordinary Puerto Rican yams. In 25 years of farming, there were only three months when Wells did not have sweet potatoes on hand. (Courtesy of Kimber Ann Ferguson.)

Born in 1857 in Levy County, Florida, Mary Etta Gillette, the daughter of Joshua Jackson Gillette and Malinda Rose Morgan Gillette, married James Robert Cooper, who was born in Georgia in 1875. Mary had 14 children. Joshua was one of the first five commissioners for the newly formed Pasco County in August 1, 1887, and later was a trustee of the schools. Mary and James are buried in Holton Cemetery. (Courtesy of Marco E. Stanley and Cletia Pierce.)

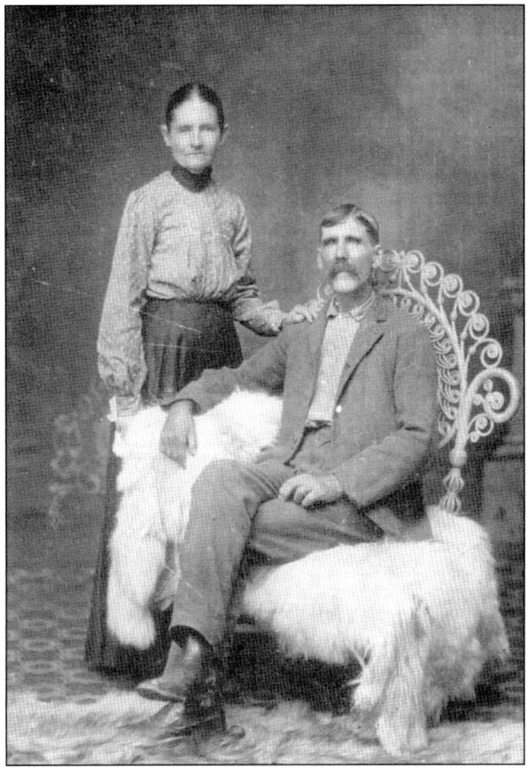

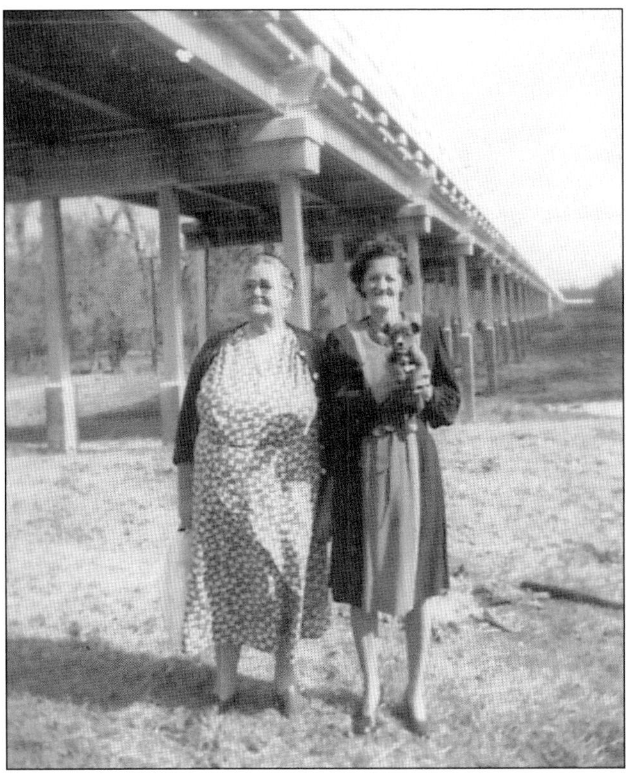

Horace Gillette is listed as an early settler. He and wife, Zelin Grantham, had 12 children. One of the most notable was daughter Maggie Gillette Keen, who was born in September 1903 and passed away in 1973. This photograph is of Maggie and Zelin, daughter of Robert Grantham and Margaret Ann Revels. Maggie became ruggedly independent and was known for her walking trips and outspoken language. She had the ability to negotiate with Wiregrass Porter about livestock space and possessed an instinctive insight into people—along with a few unconventional mannerisms. (Courtesy of Marco E. Stanley.)

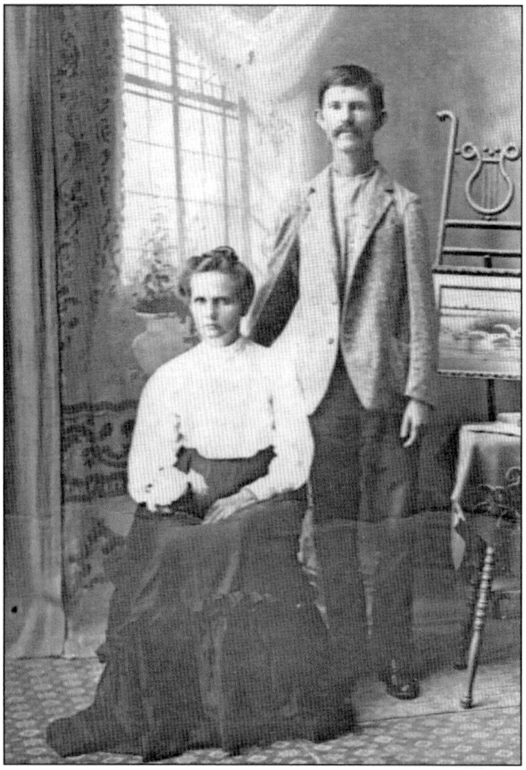

Hardy A. Gillette married Sarah M McKendree in Hernando County on December 29, 1881, when the governing county for Wesley Chapel was Hernando County. By 1887, Wesley Chapel was a part of the new county of Pasco. From around 1881 to 1887, the southern end of Hernando County had been increasingly populated with settlers and traveling the sand trails to the then county seat of Brooksville for business and marriage licenses was rugged. It aroused interest in a county division. A meeting was held with every precinct in the southern section, which included Wesley Chapel, represented. Spearheaded by Jefferson Alexander Hendley and Dr. Richard C. Bankston, the eventual county division facilitated growth. Under Florida governor Madison S. Perry, two counties—Citrus and Pasco—were created from parts of Hernando County. The children of Hardy and Sarah Gillette were George Jackson, Lehilla, Lela, Malinda Jane, Matilda, Viena, and Minnie. (Courtesy of Evelyn Wells Smith.)

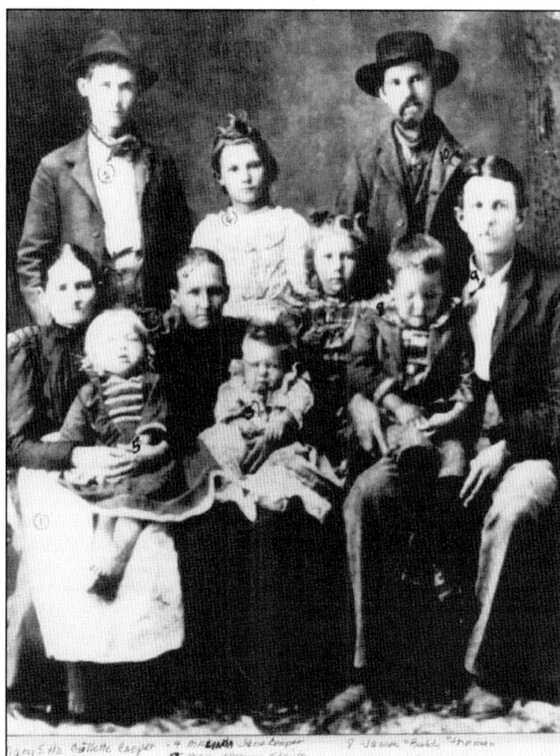

This family photograph was taken around 1902 in Wesley Chapel. From left to right are (first row) Mary Etta Gillette Cooper, holding her granddaughter, Eva Thomas Corley; Malinda Jane Cooper Thomas, holding her daughter, Mary Thomas Stanley; Sally Thomas Gaskins, in the plaid dress; and Sebron "Jim" Thomas, holding James "Buddy" Thomas; (second row) Ephraim Cooper; Malinda Jane Gillette Stanley; and Hardy Gillette. The surveyor in 1879 said traveling through Wesley Chapel was "not an easy passage through . . . the general surface is low, level, and much of it is often covered with water." (Courtesy of Marco E. Stanley.)

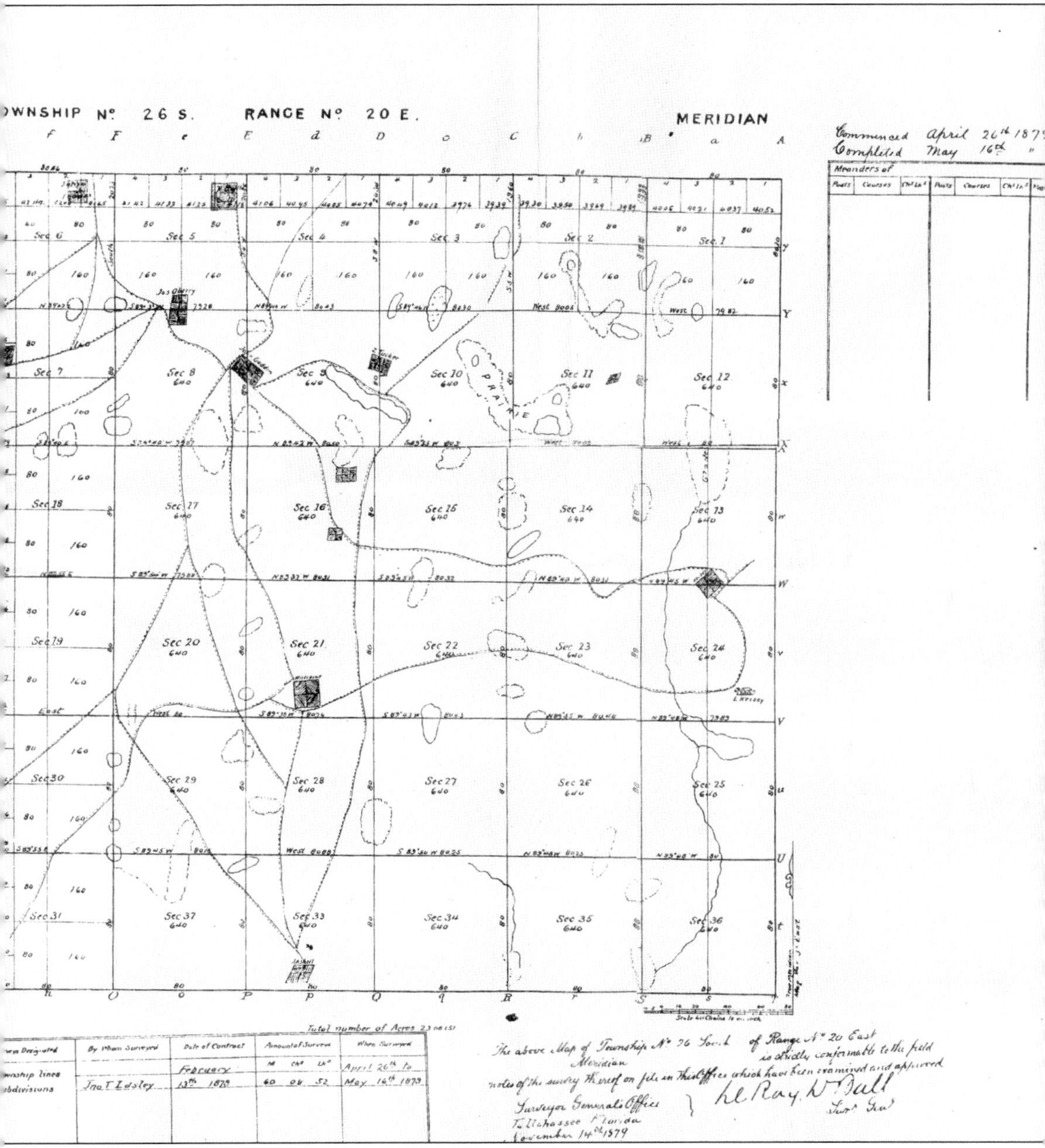

In 1879, the Wesley Chapel area was plotted as Township No. 26 South, Range No. 20 East. This occurred when Wesley Chapel was still a part of Hernando County, Florida. The map lists 12 homesteads from April 26 to May 16, 1879: Jack Asbel, Thomas Ashley Boyette, Jane Godwin, Libron Kersey, James Kersey, James R. O'Berry, William Smith, James Smith, John Thomas, Lucinda Tucker, Z Tucker, and W.W. Williams. Some other settlers documented in the 1880 census were J.L. Branch, Eli Cooper James Cooper, Richard Ellis, Elias Geiger, J.J. Gillette, Berrien Godwin, Jacob Godwin, John Godwin, David Osburn, and T.G. Wells. (Courtesy of David L. Brown and Michael C. Boyette.)

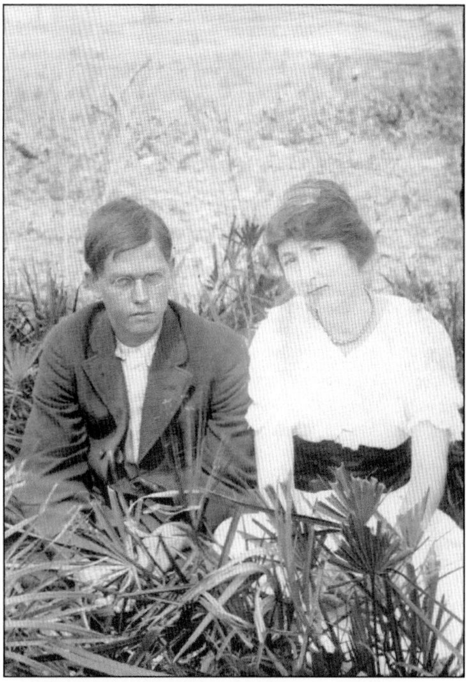

Thomas Jackson Asbel and Pearl Lola Bissett Asbel pose among the native grasses at their homestead. They are the son and daughter-in-law of Jack Asbel and Susan Asbel, who are mentioned on the previous 1879 range map as homesteaders. Thomas and Pearl's children were Carl, Elmer, and Wilbur, as listed in the 1930 census. Wesley Chapel is generally low-lying pine flatwoods and the vegetation includes longleaf and slash pines with an understory of saw palmetto, wax myrtle, inkberry, and various grasses and a variety of oak species. (Courtesy of Cletia Pierce.)

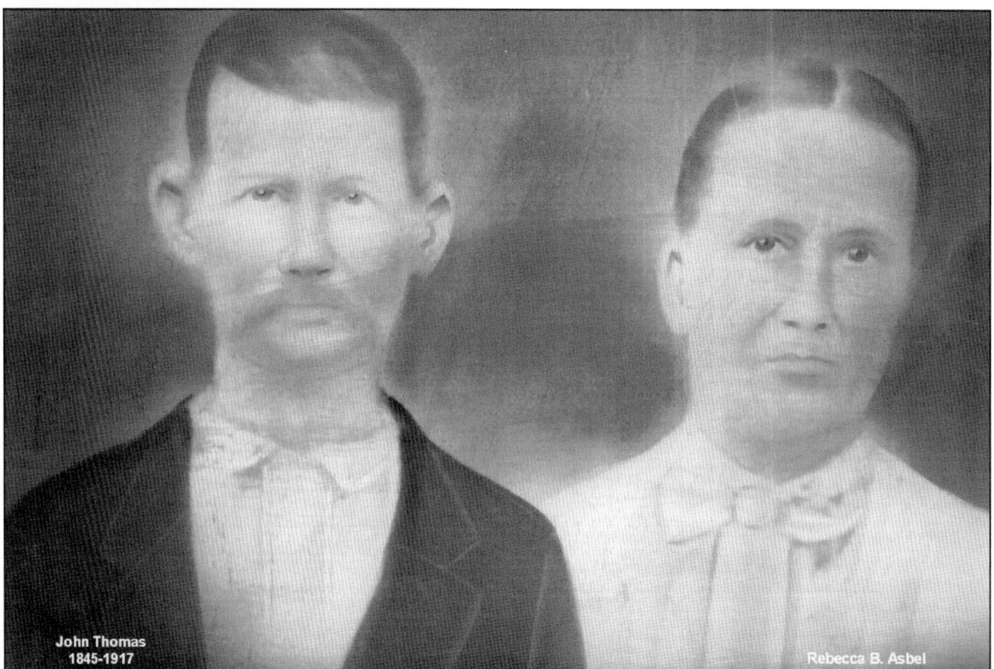

John C. Thomas was married to Rebecca B. Asbel. Their children were Sebran, Andrew, Laura, Charles, Joseph Lee, John W., Jimmie, and Eliza Thomas. They show up consistently in the census records from 1880 to 1910 as living in Wesley Chapel. John was buried in Holton Cemetery. Great-great-grandson Kenneth Stewart has done extensive research on the family, and much of the lineage can be seen in the Stewart line via his great-grandmother Laura, daughter of John and Rebecca. (Courtesy of Kenneth Stewart.)

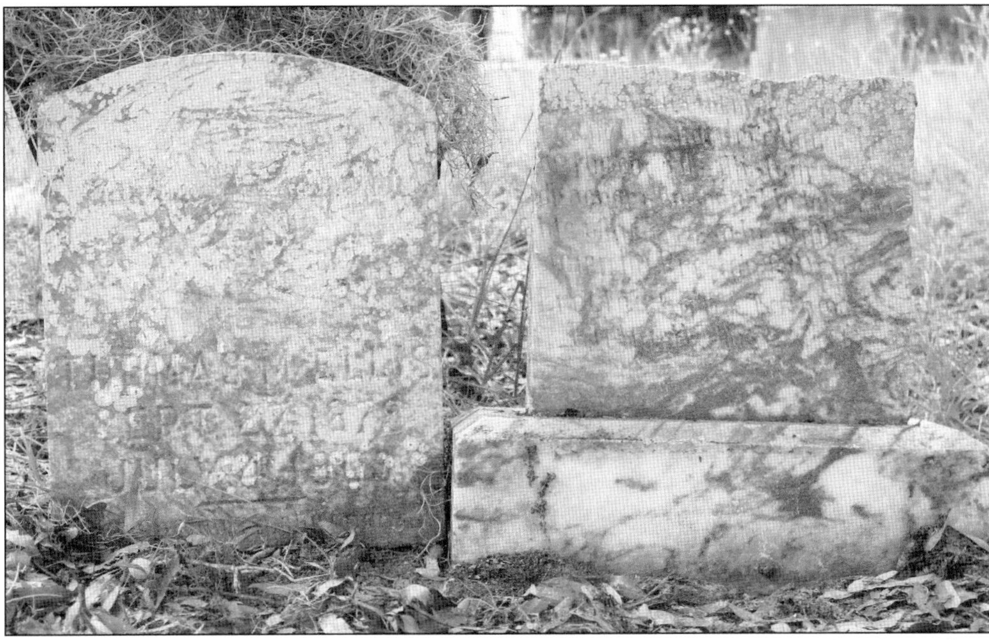

The tombstone of Thomas "Tom" M. Ellis in County Line Cemetery hints at the Ellis-Gillette feud. Tom's brother, Lee Ellis, was married to the beautiful Malinda Gillette, with whom Tom was infatuated. Tom accidentally killed Malinda's brother, Austin, at their home when a bullet went awry. Later, Lee died and left Malinda a sizable insurance settlement. An altercation eventually ensued between Malinda's brother, Preston Gillette, and Tom, in which Tom was fatally shot. Although Pasco County sheriff Bob Sturkie ruled self-defense, the father, Richard Elllis, engraved a lasting 1909 tombstone message: "Mine enemies spoke against me. . . . therefore let them be confounded . . . who sought to take my life which was so brutally stolen by Preston Gillette." Tom Ellis (Dead Man's) Curve sits on Highway 54, just west of I-75. (Courtesy of Ernest Wise.)

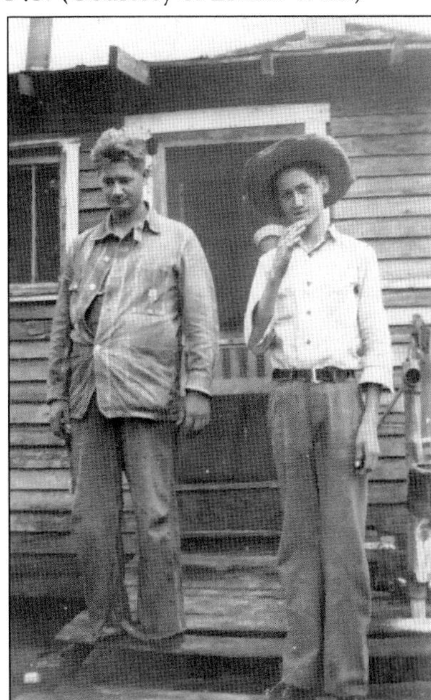

Bryant (left) and James Tucker, sons of James B. and Sarah R. Tucker, stand at the Tucker house in Gatorville around 1926, in the midst of the Great Depression. The name Gatorville perhaps derived from the abundance of bayheads full of alligators for abundant gator hunting. Others believe the name originated from the school newspaper *Gatorville News*. Another explanation is that it comes from the baseball team dubbed Gatorville, which competed with Goatsville in the 1920s. (Courtesy of Anna Jo Bracknell.)

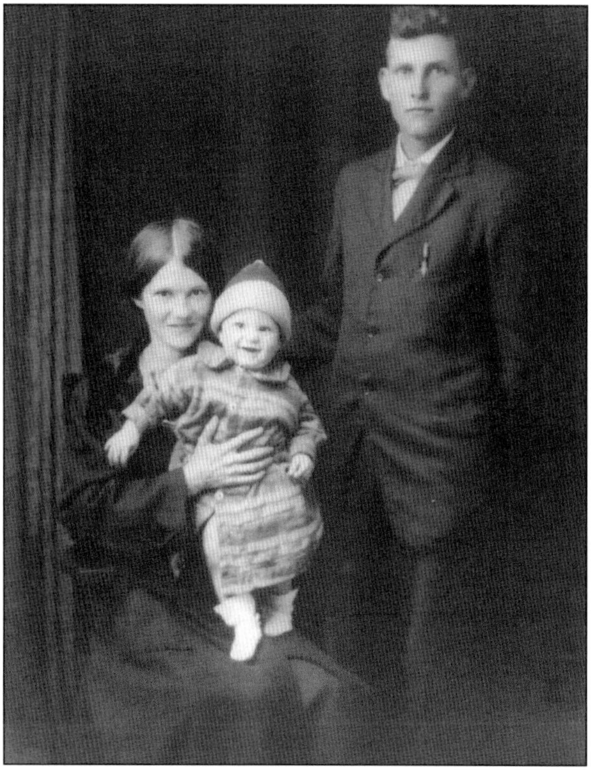

The Dennison homestead was at County Line Road and Bruce B. Downs Boulevard. Beulah Malinda Gillette Dennison, Hursel A. Dennison (Sr.), and Mannie A. Dennison Sr. are pictured. Mannie was born in 1898 to Allen Scott Denison and Martha Ann Hill, who was the daughter of Elisha Allen Hill and Mary Ann Jane Cooper. Allen drove the stagecoach from Fort Brooke to Fort King for the Concord-Apopka Stagecoach Company. "These were rugged times. When Mannie's father was injured after being thrown from a horse, the doctor was summoned via rider, and it took three days for him to arrive, unfortunately too late," said Jim Dennison. (Courtesy of James Dennison.)

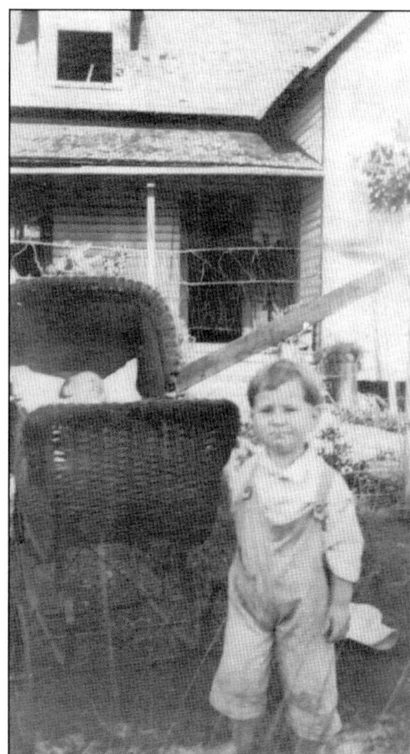

The Wesley Reuben Wells home on Wells Road (at the present-day site of Wesley Chapel High School) was similar in style to other early-1900s frame homes in Wesley Chapel. According to Charlie Estepp, John Reuben "J.R." Wells is pictured here with baby brother Roy Wells in the front yard of their grandparents' home. According to Dawn Wells McMillan, "Uncle J.R. was born in 1922 and Uncle R.W. in 1926." (Courtesy of Marlo Hilton.)

Two

Ranches and Agriculture

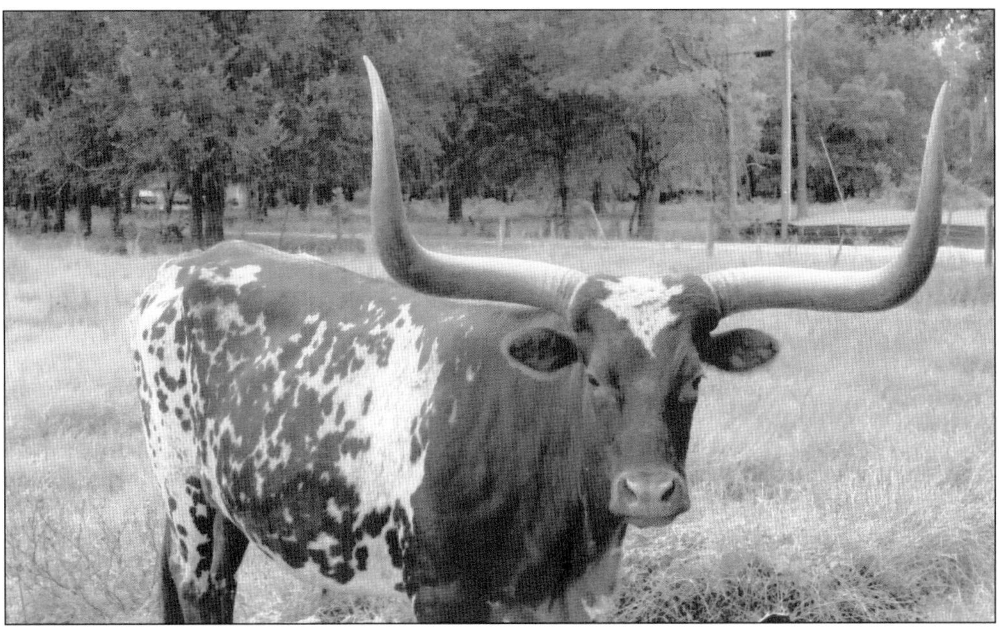

Ranches were a significant part of Wesley Chapel history. An outstanding Texas Longhorn–Ankole bull was 15 years old and had a horn span of 54 inches when he died at the K-Bar in Wesley Chapel. Florida scrub cattle were bred with Charolais, Angus, Ankole, and Brahman mixes. According to Clarence Hale, K-Bar tried to breed workable animals: "If ever a bull produced mean and unruly calves, which we called 'outlaws,' we would switch lineages so they were safe to handle." (Courtesy of Clarence Hale.)

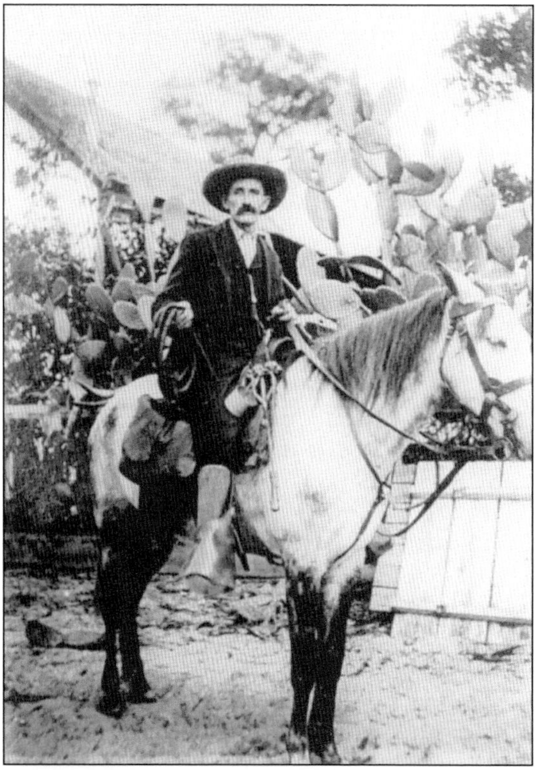

John Samuel Boyette, born in 1865 in Clay Sink, began his cattle business in 1882. He acquired several herds and five brands, and ran cattle from central Pasco to Hillsborough. The railbeds of the Seaboard Coast Line and Atlantic Coast Line Railroads were favorite sleeping places for the cattle because of the heat absorbed during the day. This photograph shows an array of cacti in the background. Wesley Chapel was noted for a 10-to-15-acre cactus farm on Boyette Road, owned by Anthony Tuzzolino from Ybor City and planted between 1940 and 1941. The field became a garden of bright yellow flowers when the cacti bloomed, but the 1962 freeze finished off the plants. (Courtesy of Jeff Miller.)

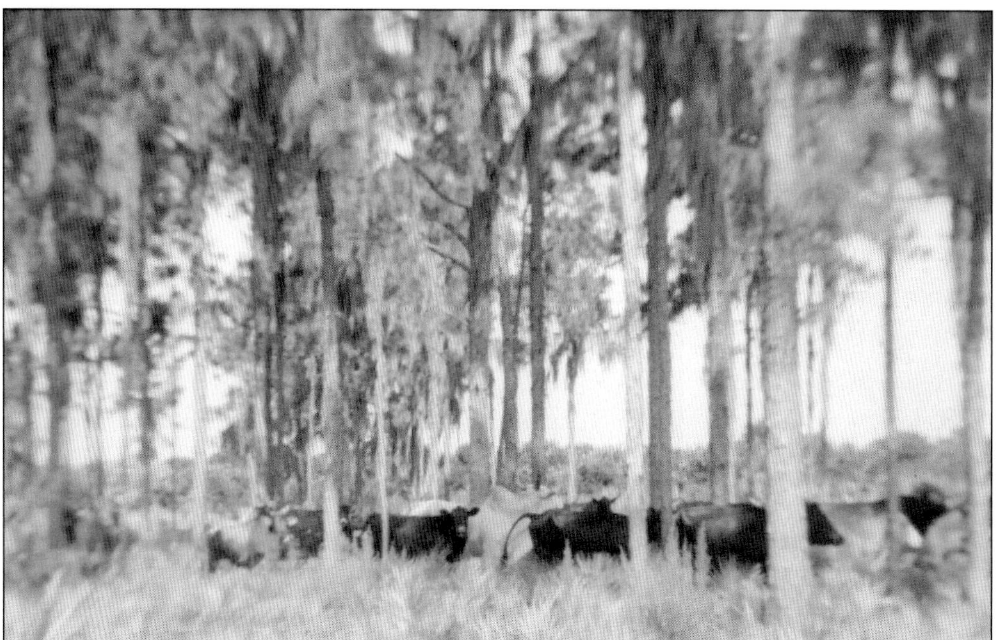

This photograph shows the Ruben Barnes Ranch just east of Curley Road, north of Highway 54. Florida scrub cattle were descended from the criollos originally brought to Florida by the Spanish as early as the 16th century. They were prized for their resistance to parasites. (Courtesy of David L. Brown.)

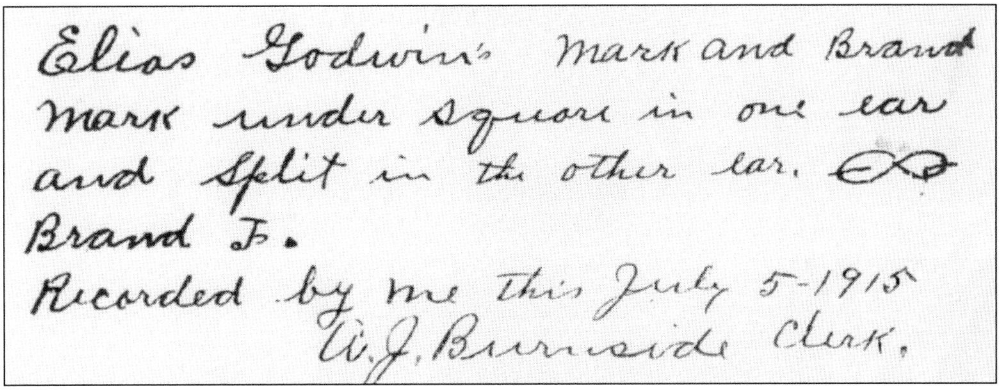

Elias Godwin's mark and Brand
mark under square in one ear
and split in the other ear.
Brand F.
Recorded by me this July 5-1915
W. J. Burnside Clerk.

Born in 1896, Elias Godwin was the son of Lafayette Godwin and Julia Barnes Godwin. His mark and brand were registered in Pasco County Courthouse on July 5, 1915. The clerk's office has an extensive collection of recorded brands and marks on file. Many copies of the brands are also housed at the Mabel Jordan Barn at the Florida Pioneer Museum and Village. (Courtesy of Pasco County Clerk's Office.)

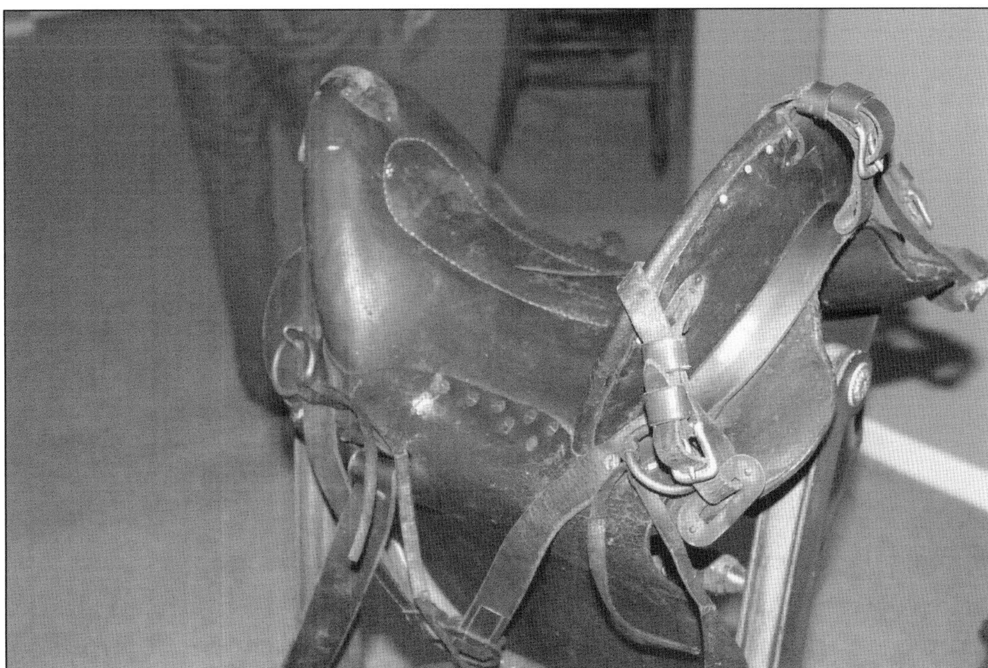

Luther Smith was in the cavalry in World War I. His saddle is preserved and maintained by cousin Roscoe "Rocky" Stanley, who treasures the service. The hornless McClellan saddles were used by Florida cowboys early on. Roping cattle was not used extensively because of the dense scrubland that would snag lariats. Later, when screwworm treatment required that animals be roped regularly, cowboys used lariats and replaced the McClellan saddles with Western saddles that had horns. (Courtesy of Ernest Wise.)

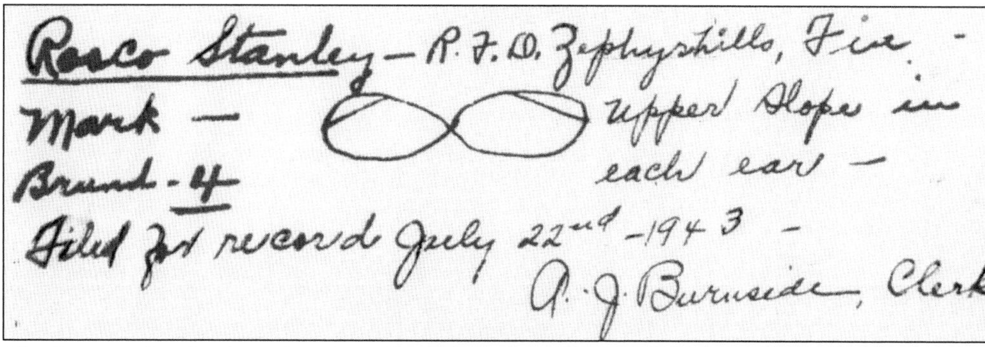

Rosco Stanley—R.F.D. Zephyrhills, Fla.—
Mark — Upper Slope in each ear —
Brand - 4
Filed for record July 22nd - 1943 -
A. J. Burnside, Clerk

The Roscoe Stanley brand and mark were registered on July 22, 1943, at the Pasco County Courthouse. The branding iron for this brand is shown on page 51. Roscoe "Rollie" Napoleon Stanley was born in 1918 to Raleigh and Malinda Gillette Stanley. He died in 2003 at age 85. He was a well-known farmer and rancher for many years and was survived by four children—Raymond Stanley, Frances Overstreet, Malinda Chao, and Roscoe "Rocky" Stanley. (Courtesy of Pasco County Clerk's Office.)

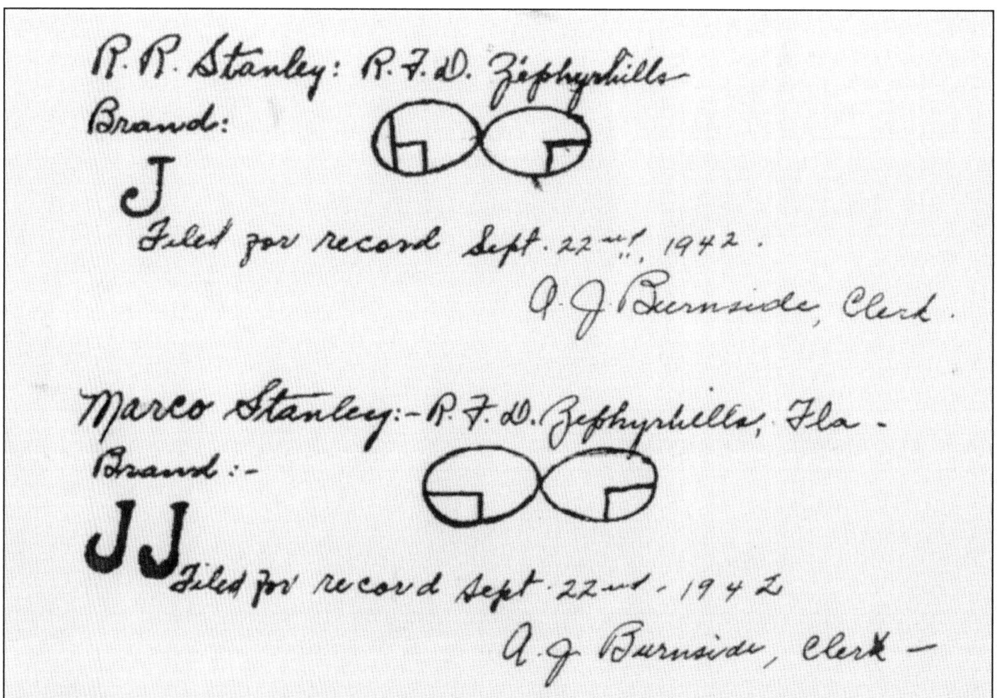

R. R. Stanley: R.F.D. Zephyrhills
Brand:
J
Filed for record Sept. 22nd, 1942.
A. J. Burnside, Clerk.

Marco Stanley:—R.F.D. Zephyrhills, Fla.
Brand:—
JJ
Filed for record Sept. 22nd, 1942
A. J. Burnside, Clerk —

Stanley brands and marks were registered in 1942. Prior to 1951, livestock roamed free, so ranchers identified their livestock (cattle and hogs) via registered marks on the animal's ears and would get together when they wanted to gather the animals. They would saddle up the plow horse and build pens in preparation. "These were wild cattle . . . unlike domestic ones from today . . . kind of like deer. You had to work hard to find them," Cullen Ricardo Boyette explained. After the cattle were rounded up, they were kept in pens for a time to fatten them up. (Courtesy of Pasco County Clerk's Office.)

Luther Smith and son Bill Smith are shown on their ranch around 1940. Community-minded Luther and fellow deacons of Double Branch—Willie Neil McCloskey, James Hill, and Albert Godwin—spearheaded the construction of a new church building, which was dedicated on September 5, 1935, with Ed Bryant as pastor. The attendance had waned in the early 1930s, and prayer meetings were held at the McCloskey residence prior to the new building. (Courtesy of Bill Smith.)

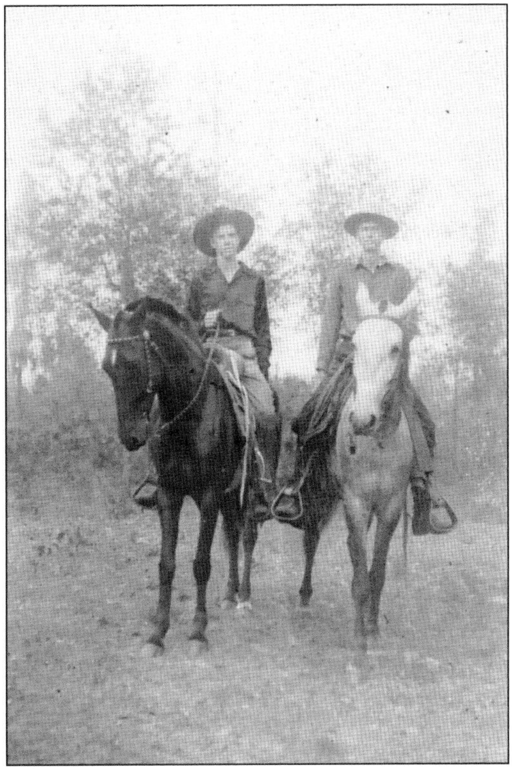

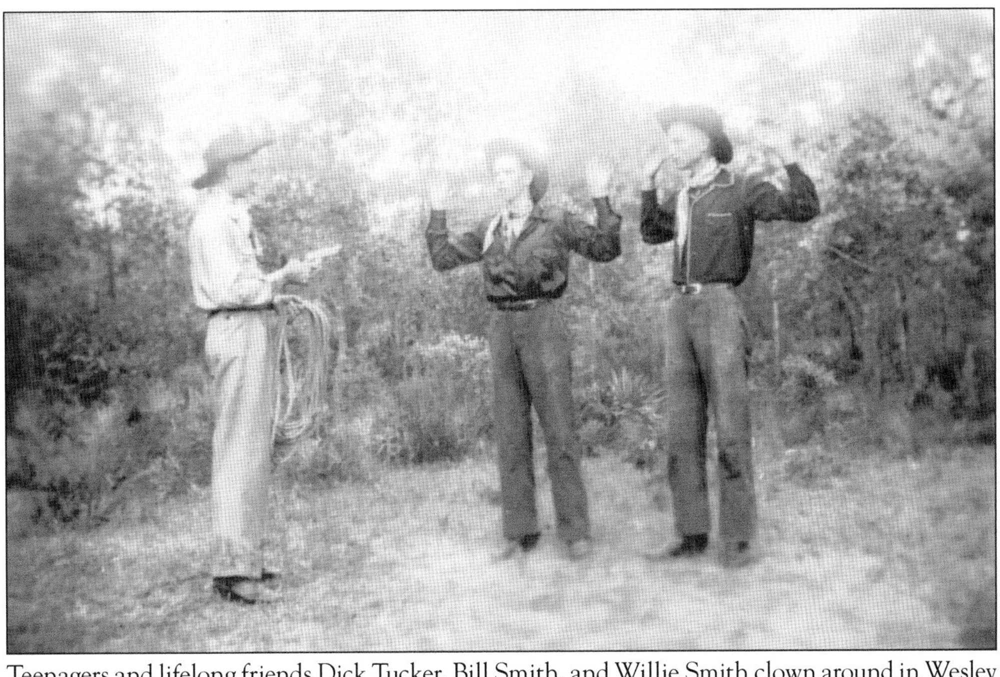

Teenagers and lifelong friends Dick Tucker, Bill Smith, and Willie Smith clown around in Wesley Chapel around 1940. Their comradery lasted and was indicative of the deep friendships in the area. Very cognizant of community values, these three cherish the history of the area. (Courtesy of Bill Smith.)

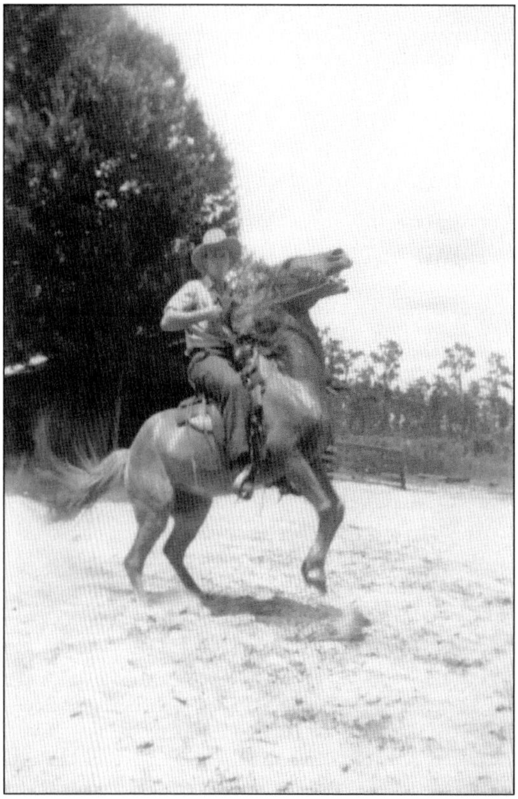

Marco Stanley was fond of horses. One particularly favored horse was Sonny. In the days before abundant horse trailers, Stanley would call to Sonny to load up, and the stallion would then leap onto the flatbed truck with no sideboards. The Stanley family is proud of its frontier history and was recognized as a founding family of Pasco County at the December 1998 dedication of the restored Old Pasco County Courthouse, with the purpose of providing lasting tribute to the pioneer founding families. Plaques are imbedded in the sidewalks leading to the restored courthouse. The inscription on the plaque cairn states: "With sacrifice . . . they applied the labors of love and a steadfast hand. We salute this rich heritage, trusting the pioneers approve, as they reap their final harvest in heaven." (Courtesy of Anna Jo Bracknell.)

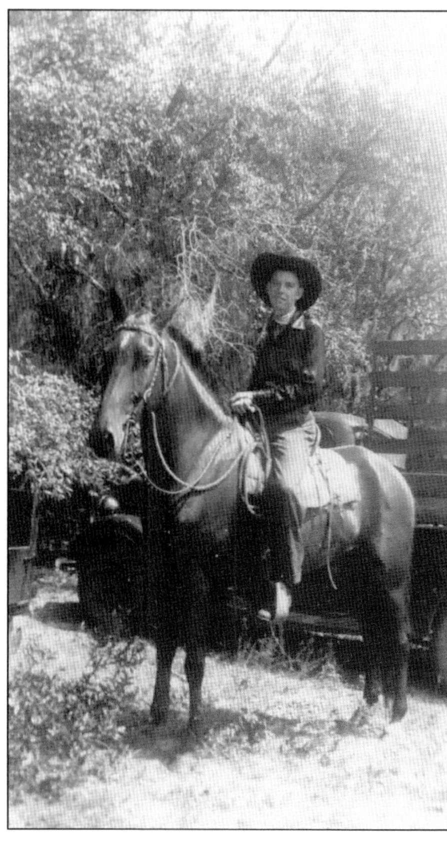

Bill Smith is pictured in 1942. He competed in the local rodeos, which occurred near the Hardy Howell homestead at Boab Gillette field in frontier Wesley Chapel. The location of the local rodeo is shown on page 17. Spectators lined the fence to watch the riders and their broncos. Howell was married to Elizabeth "Lizzie" Godwin, daughter of Wesley Chapel pioneer Jacob Godwin in 1888. The families helped each other with the livestock roundups and working the cattle. Many rode the family's plow horse with a hand-me-down McClellan army saddle that was uncomfortable, although a few did have saddle horses and equipment like lassoes and cow whips. They worked together to round up the livestock and mark the young ones. (Courtesy of Marco E. Stanley.)

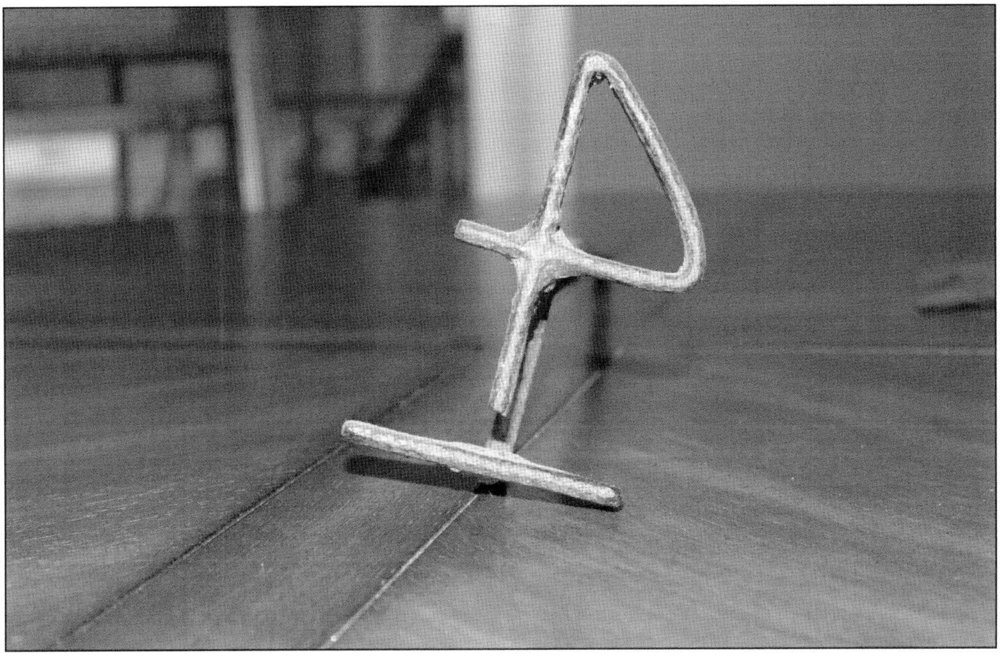

Roscoe "Rocky" Stanley displayed his family's 4-Bar. Hot-iron branding was often done on the flank. Many preferred markings, because they were more readily identified. A rancher could have several earmarks and brands. Contemporary ranchers mostly use plastic ear tags rather than earmarks. The Roscoe Stanley brand and mark were registered on July 22, 1943, at the Pasco County Courthouse. (Courtesy of Pasco County Clerk's Office.)

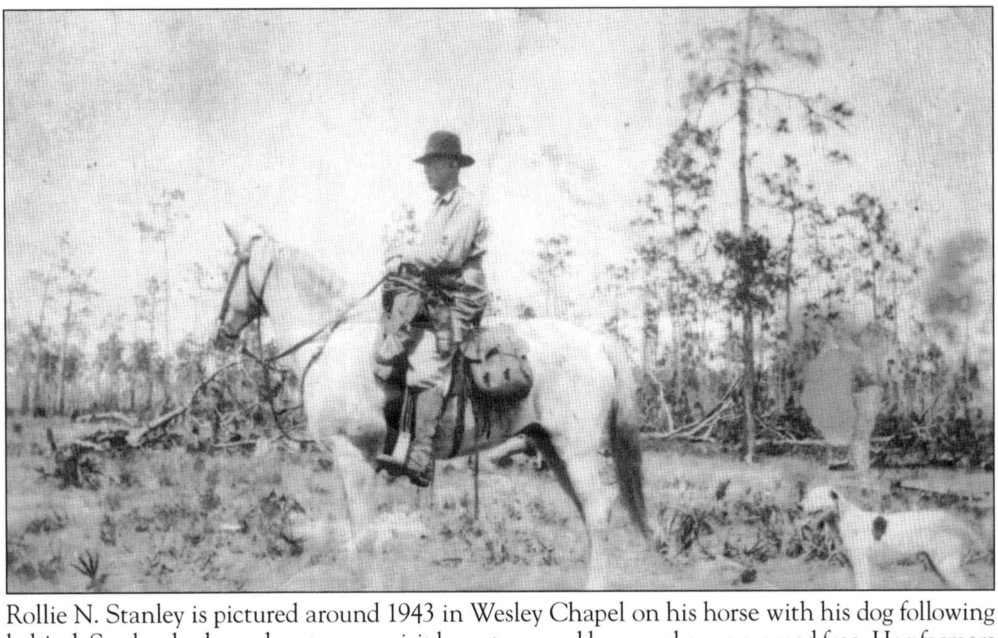

Rollie N. Stanley is pictured around 1943 in Wesley Chapel on his horse with his dog following behind. Settlers had an adventurous spirit by nature, and hogs and cows roamed free. Hog farmers would find places where their pigs could eat acorns, and cattle ranchers would look for areas with native grasses. Brands and markings protected ownership. (Courtesy of William Smith.)

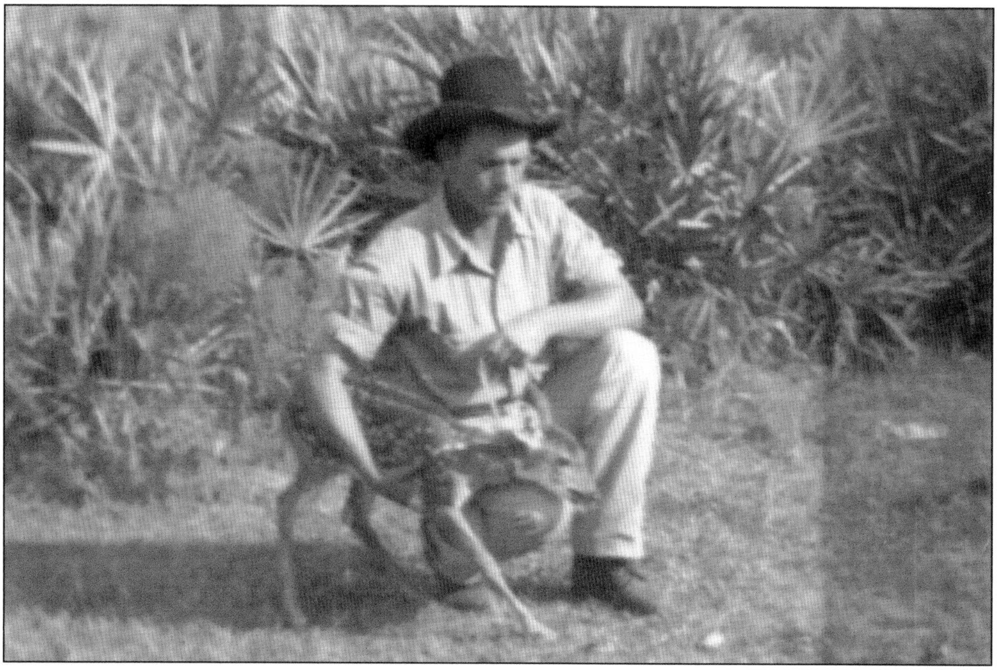

Marco Stanley holds a young fawn. For Shirley Stanley Lanier, there was a lot of hard farm work growing up but also a fulfilling family life. "I had a raccoon as a pet, and one time, Daddy brought home an orphan fawn in 1945 that surely would have died if the old milk cow hadn't nursed her. . . . the fawn followed the cow around and [the cow] even mooed to the fawn just like it was her own," said Lanier. (Courtesy of Marco E. Stanley.)

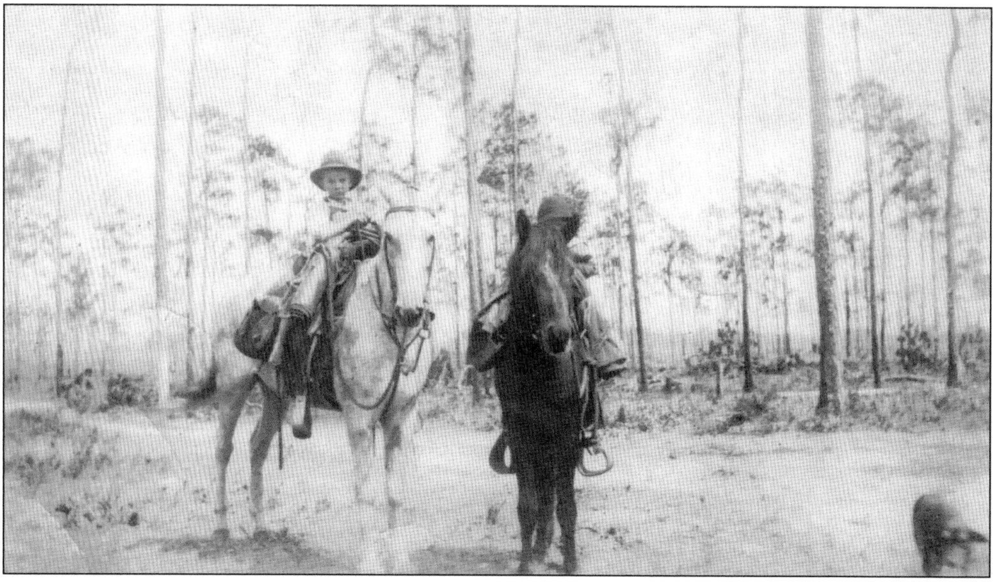

Roscoe and Marco Stanley are out for a ride in Wesley Chapel. "Back then, kids were allowed to stay out of school—as long as they kept their work up—to help out with crops like watermelons and strawberries," said Lillie Stanley. When her son Keith stayed out of classes to help the family out with watermelons or other crops, Lillie helped him get through school. (Courtesy of Marco E. Stanley.)

E.B. Larkin writes in the 1976 *East Pasco Heritage* booklet, "There was abundant open range as the country was sparsely settled. The farms that were fenced and cultivated were very small, primarily places where people raised a garden and things to eat at home. The scrub cattle were small; a grown cow would weigh about 500 pounds." (Courtesy of Florida Library & Archives, Florida Department of State.)

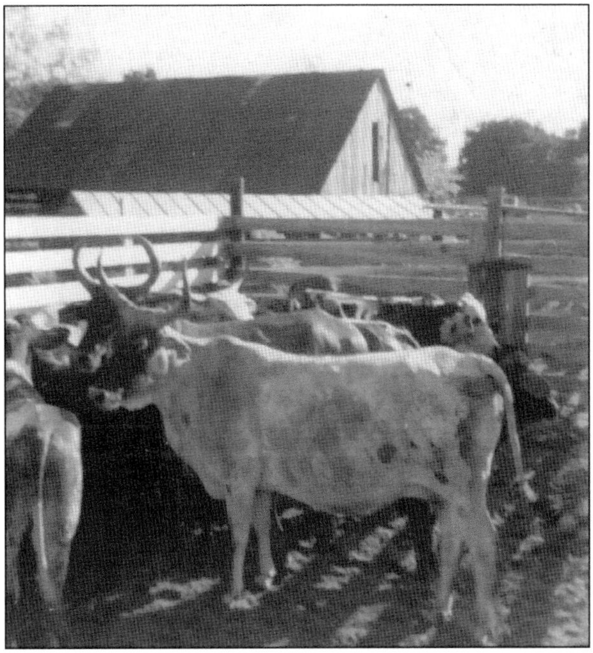

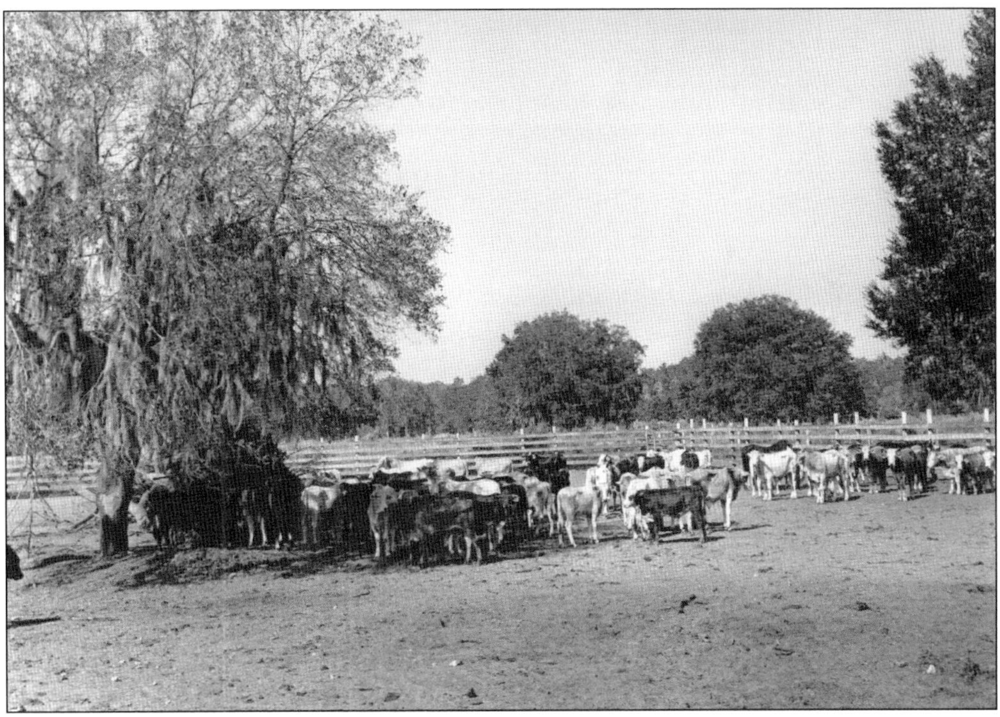

Dan Hale, foreman of the K-Bar Ranch in Wesley Chapel, regularly recruited local boys to assist with branding and roundup. Sonny Branch, Roland "Snooks" Edward McKendree, Vernon Hill, Roscoe Stanley, and Marco Stanley were recollected as skilled horsemen and great workers. Tasks were often shared among the area ranches, and there was a mutual respect. "'Wiregrass' Porter had tremendous admiration for Dan Hale and considered him the quintessential cowboy," said his son, William Porter. (Courtesy of Pasco County Fair Office.)

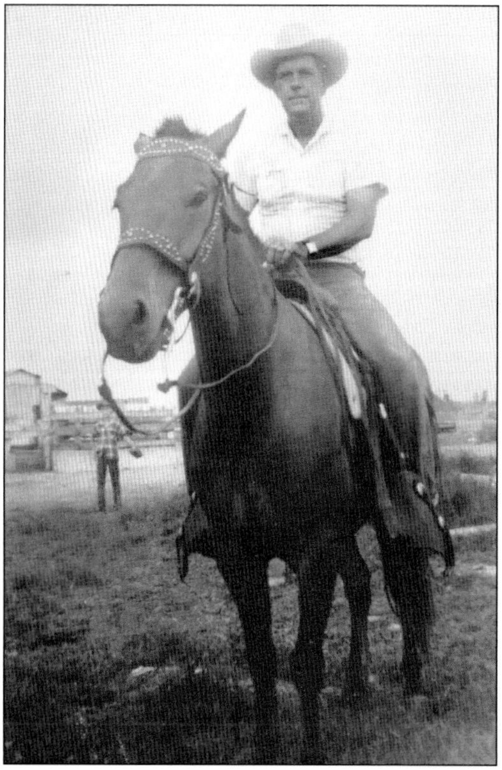

Dan Hale, foreman for I.A. Krusen, managed the ranch for 37 years. The home was about three miles into the pasture, and their sons were born and raised there. The house, built from heart of pine wood, was originally the Strickland homestead (that of James and Alice Strickland) and was a three-bedroom home with a fireplace. Previously, Hale worked on the Harvey Ryals Ranch near Tampa and often assisted the Barnes and Porter Ranches as well. (Courtesy of Clarence Hale.)

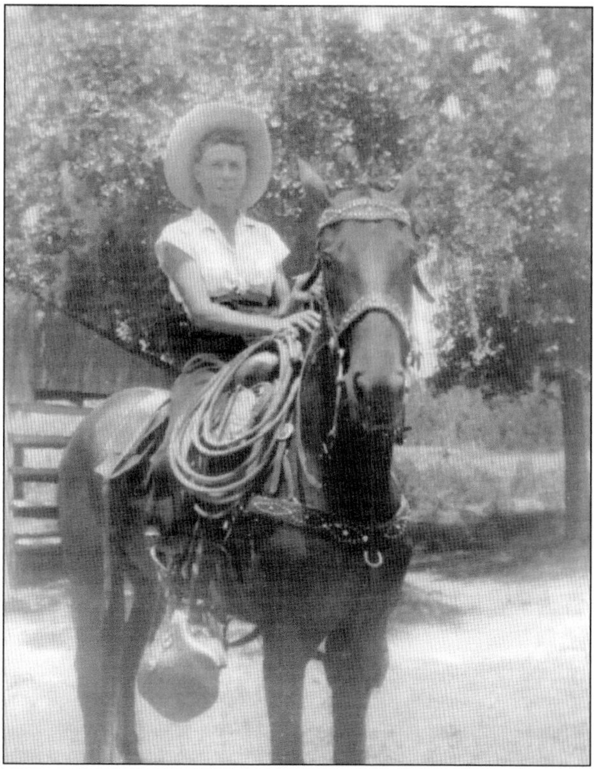

Thelma Hale was born in Georgia and married Dan Hale in Florida. This photograph depicts Thelma with her horse Penny. Thelma cooked for the ranch hands. Son Clarence said, "When we were working cows over on the west side of what is now Bruce B. Downs and elsewhere, she brought dinner to us." Marco E. Stanley added, "She was a great cook!" (Courtesy of Clarence Hale.)

Clarence Cooter Hale (left) is shown with family members, from left to right, Maida, Buddy, Glenda, Thelma, and Doyle Hale. Ranchers Henry Douglas and Wiregrass Porter swapped off to help each other with tasks, and Clarence assisted on Wiregrass Ranch to herd cattle and brand. "Wiregrass was particular about fences . . . didn't want anybody inside his fences," said Clarence, who also assisted at the Oscar Branch and Ruben Barnes Ranches. (Courtesy of Clarence Hale.)

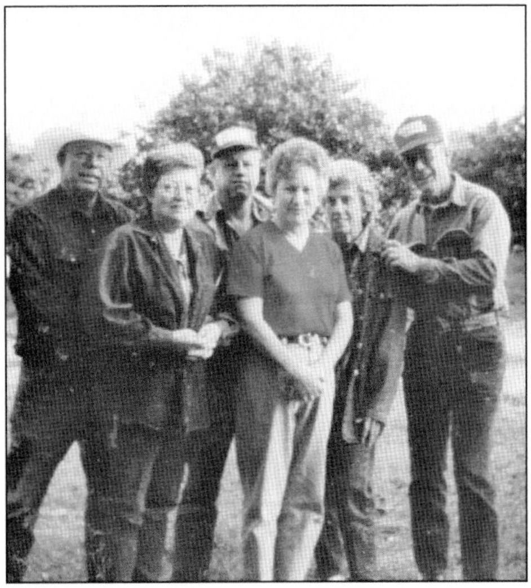

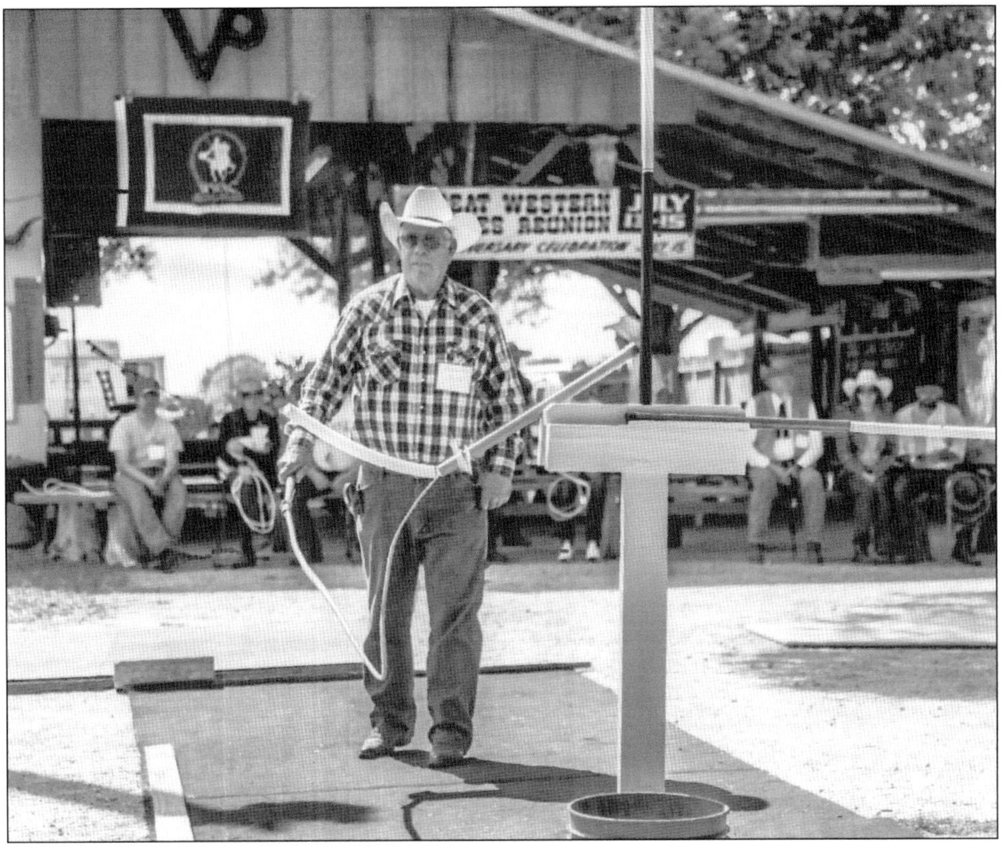

The winner of the Okeechobee Whip Cracking Competition, Clarence Hale is also known for welding and weaving cracker whips, which take about three days to make. In competition, whips range from 12 to 36 feet long with target cutting and bell-ringing. Cracker whips were originally made of hemp and then buckskin, but Hale now uses nylon and hickory handles. Hale has an exhibition whip made out of fireproof Kevlar to snap and ignite a blaze. Whips must be greased to keep them supple, so pioneers used beef tallow and beeswax. (Courtesy of Ernest Wise.)

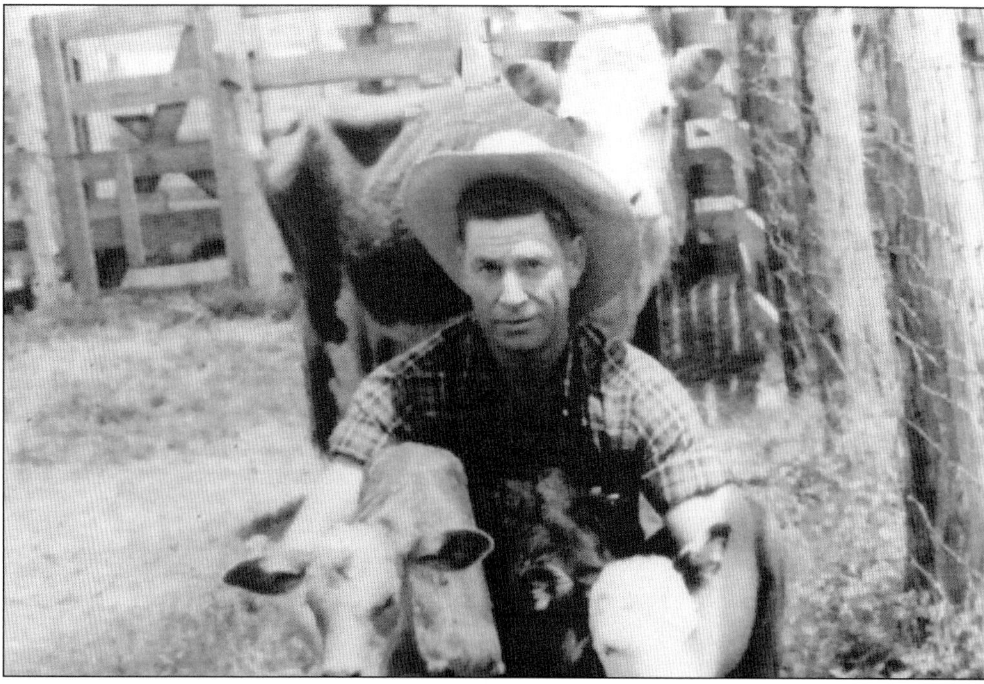

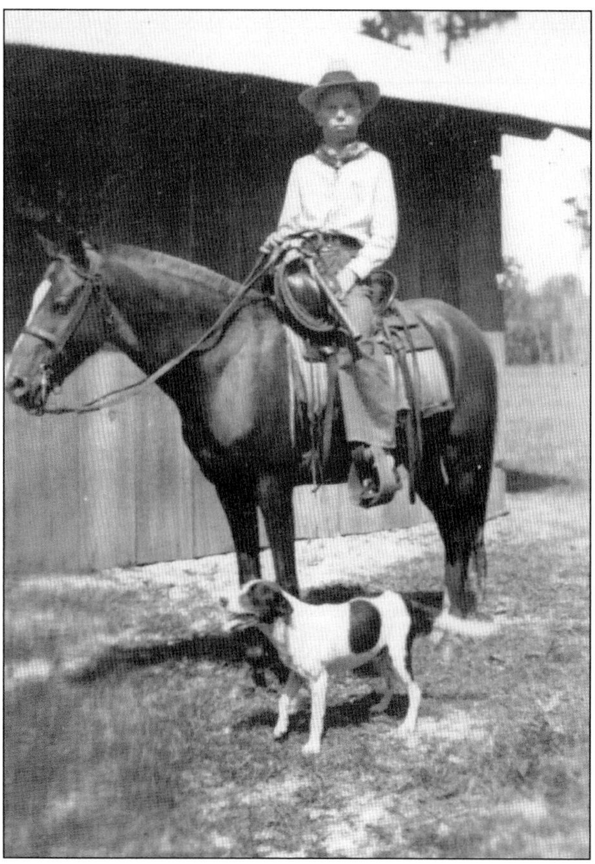

Reuben "Lee" Wells was the son of Police Chief Reuben Wesley Wells and Minnie Wells. He is pictured on the 2,000-acre Immer Ranch with twin calves. The Immer Ranch was founded by Charley Immer and located on the west side of Bruce B. Downs Boulevard, under I-75. Bob Chadwell helped develop the ranch, and William Smith managed it in the 1960s. (Courtesy of Charles Estepp.)

Bill Smith pauses on his horse Dot, with dog Mike. Cattle dogs are prominent in vintage pioneer photographs. They were greatly valued for their ability to locate cows in the swamps and scrub area, where horses could not venture. The dogs also kept the pack in a condensed mass by controlling the sides of the herd. (Courtesy of Bill Smith.)

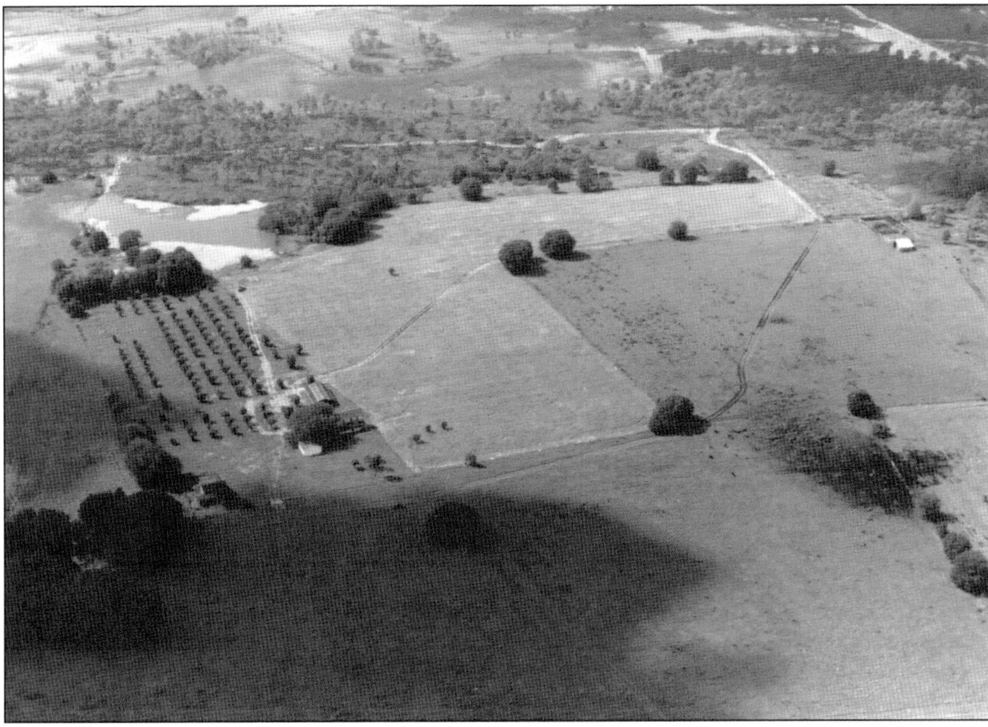

This 1960s aerial photograph, reflective of open land, shows the expanse of the Barnes homestead. Roy Burnside reminisced about Wesley Chapel neighbors Joe and Dawdy Strickland, Cullen Boyette, Fritz Boyette, Jim and Fannie Boyette, Boy Boyette, Frank Tucker, John Tucker, Cohen and Doris Cooper, Joe Cooper, Albert Godwin, John Ellis, the Gillettes, Joe Thomas, Wallace Wells, Dr. Everett, Frank Tucker, Bob and Grace Elam, and Anthony Tuzzolino from his childhood. (Courtesy of Stephanie Brown Benson.)

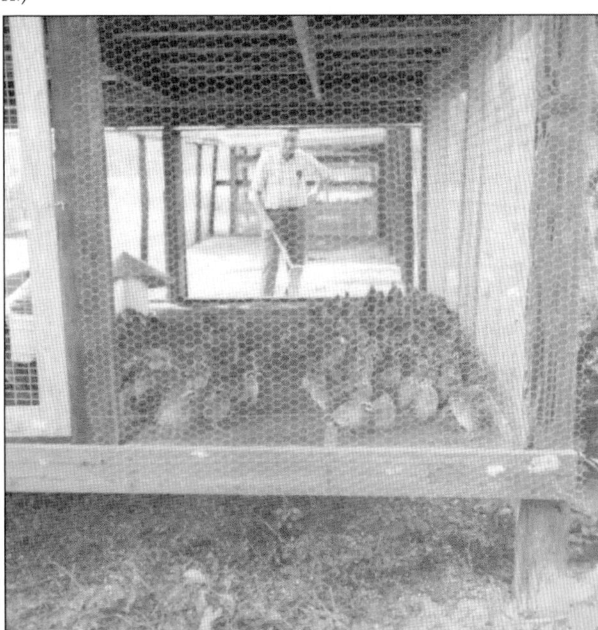

Stanley Ryals and his friend Dr. Lou King, a surgeon at Lakeland General Hospital, raised quail in the 1960s. They kept pairs of quail, collected and incubated the eggs, and maintained brooders for the baby chicks. Grandson Bo Hilton said they became quite proficient in training, even putting a harness on quail. After several years when toxicosis infected the flock, they discontinued the endeavor. (Courtesy of Marlo Hilton.)

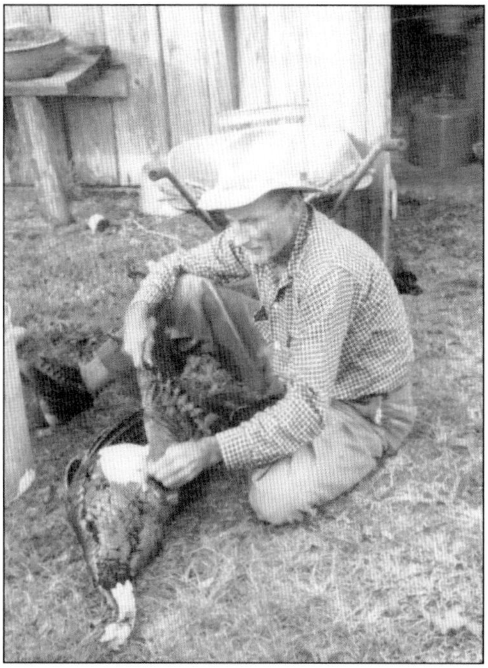

Lauren Morris Strickland was accustomed to living off the land, and wild turkeys like the one pictured are still abundant today in Wesley Chapel. Laci Boyette Stokes, a native of Wesley Chapel, penned a poem entitled "Where I'm From," which includes this excerpt: "I'm from a community that is no longer / From a rich heritage, old timers and moonshiners. / From cattle ranches, farms and orange groves, / Sawmills, ponds and dirt roads. / I'm from unlocked doors / From where your handshake was a bond. / From big front porches, homemade ice cream and catching fire flies." (Courtesy of Anna Jo Bracknell.)

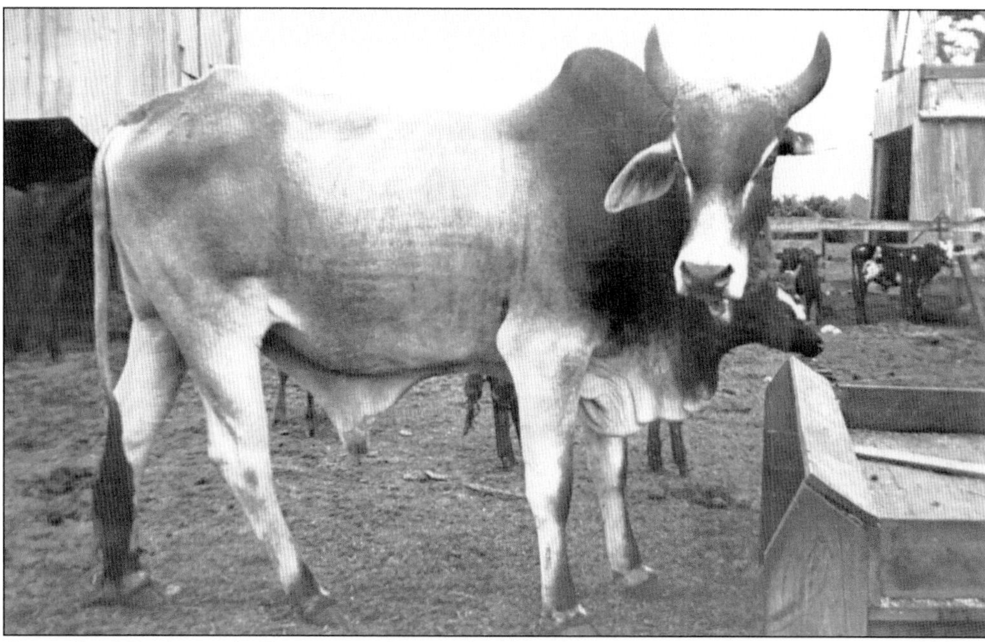

A purebred Brahman bull is pictured around 1939. There was no way to improve the breed of cattle, since only the Florida scrub cow was immune to the fever tick. Angus and other cattle were imported, but they soon became ill and died from tick fever. In 1923, the Florida Department of Agriculture implemented a policy of dipping cattle in a vat; horses and dogs were dipped too. A similar process occurred with screwworms. During the first half of the 20th century, Pasco County cattlemen transformed their scrub herds by crossbreeding with imported beef cattle, which made the cattle business a major source of income. (Courtesy of Krusen Farm, Florida Library & Archives, Florida Department of State.)

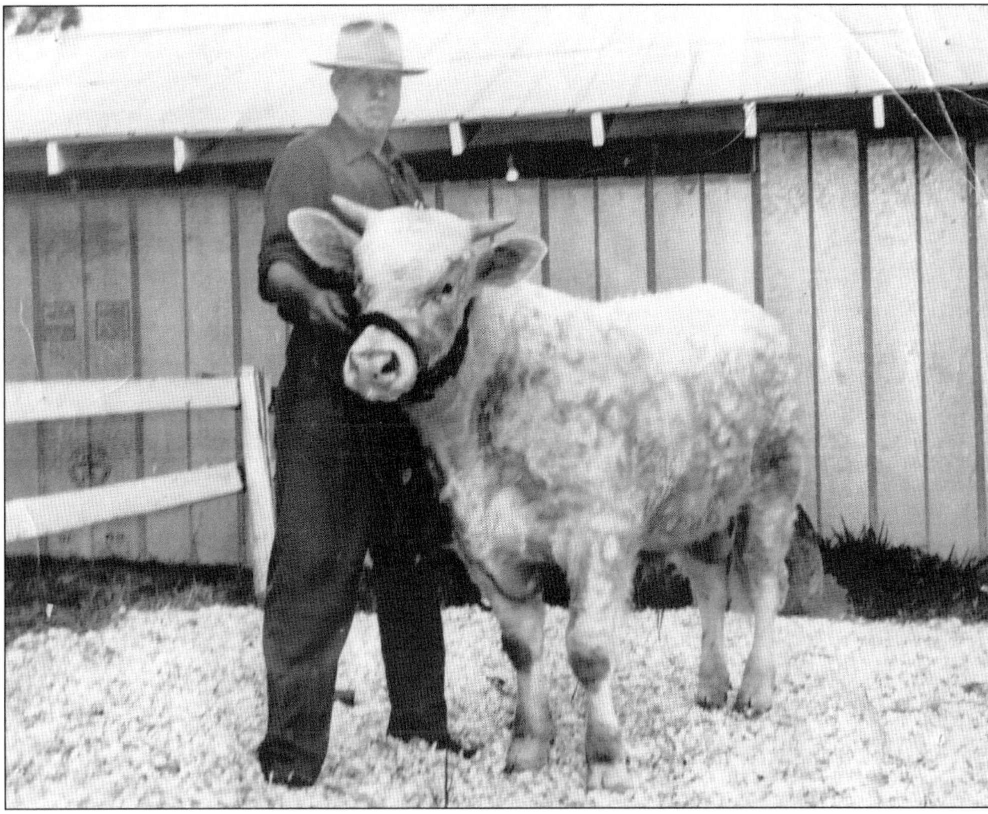

I.A. Krusen stands beside a prize bull at his ranch in 1949. Lonnie Tucker, who worked for Krusen, said, "Mr. Krusen was responsible for a lot of the development. He cleared the land for the airport and gave the government use of that land during World War II. An exceptionally fine person, Mr. Krusen asked me to trap a gator and have it stuffed for the president of the national Chrysler Corporation . . . kind of a symbol of the area!" (Courtesy of Pasco County Fair Office.)

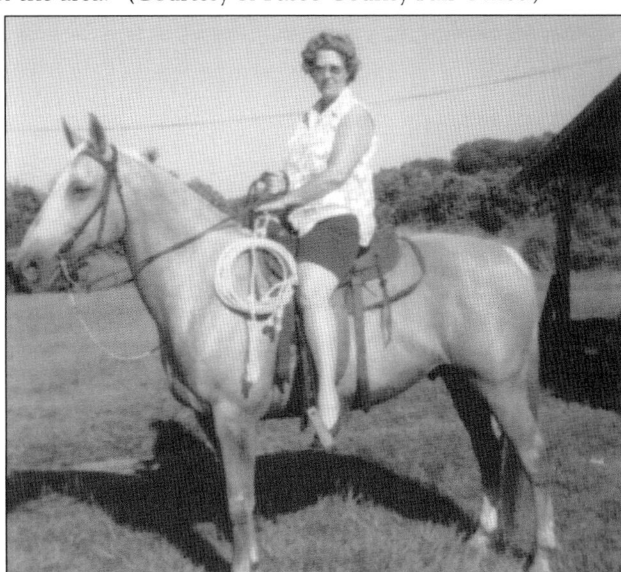

Cracker cowboys were supposedly in Florida 100 years before cowboys were prevalent in the West. From dawn until dusk, ranchers and farmers worked the land. Martha Barnes Brown is pictured on a palomino gelding on the Barnes Ranch. David L. Brown said, "He was a 'beaut' and good-natured too." (Courtesy of David L. Brown.)

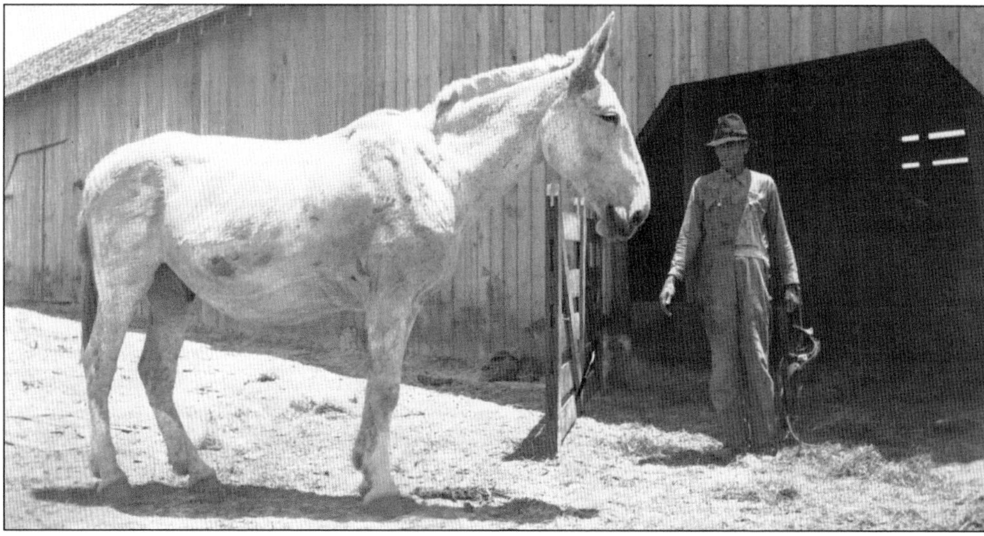

A mule was used on the I.A. Krusen Ranch in the 1930s. Work mules were produced by draft horses—in this case, a Belgian draft horse and a donkey sire. Females are known as mollies and males as johns. The distinctive elongated ears are longer and wider than those of a horse, although not quite as long as those of a donkey. Work mules have larger heads and eyes than horses, and the cow-like tail is a distinguishing feature, as is the vocal cross between a horse's neigh and donkey's bray. (Courtesy of Florida Library & Archives, Florida Department of State.)

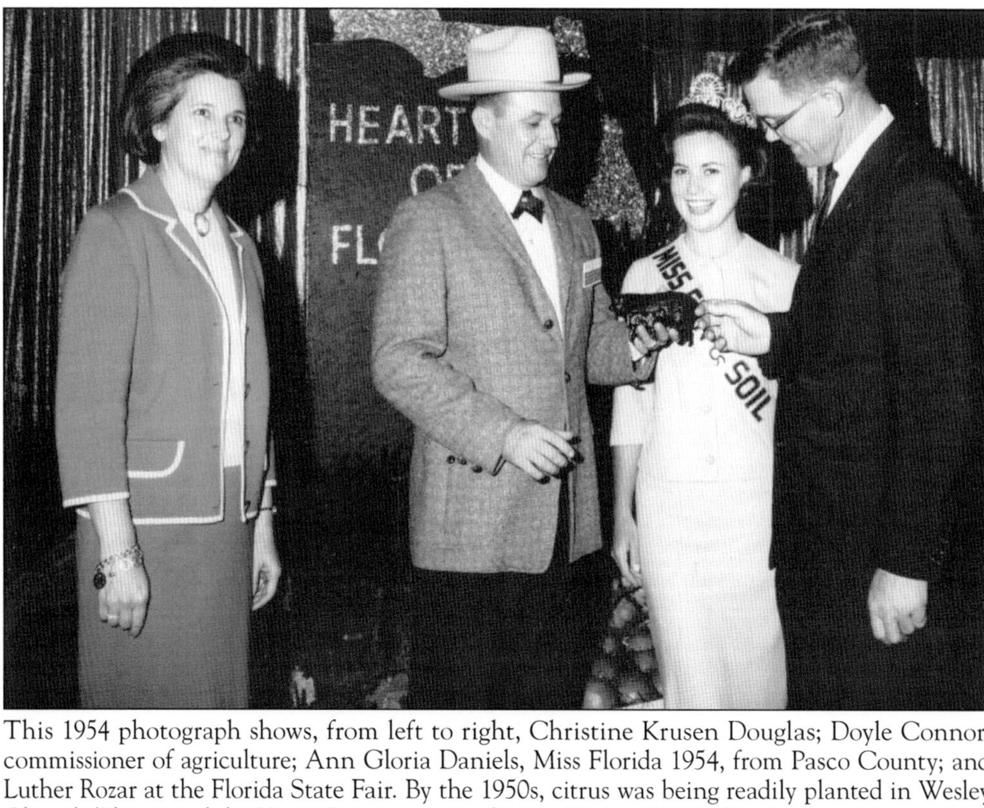

This 1954 photograph shows, from left to right, Christine Krusen Douglas; Doyle Connor, commissioner of agriculture; Ann Gloria Daniels, Miss Florida 1954, from Pasco County; and Luther Rozar at the Florida State Fair. By the 1950s, citrus was being readily planted in Wesley Chapel. (Photograph by Harris Ray, courtesy of Pasco County Fair Office.)

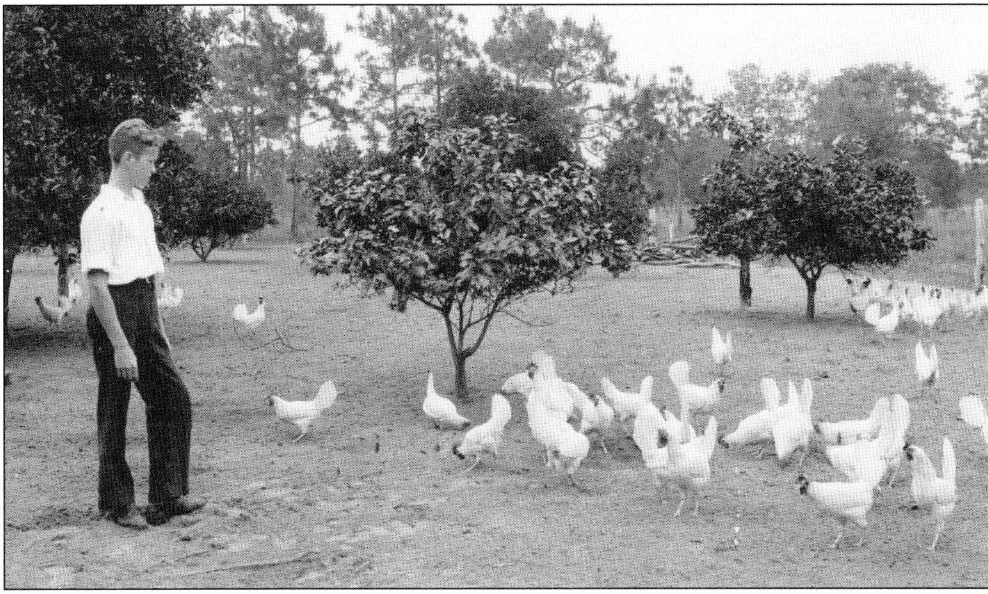

Teacher Emma Lydia Kruse Plank boarded with a family in Wesley Chapel during the week and walked back to Zephyrhills to spend the weekend with her husband and five children. This photograph is of her youngest son, Seth, on April 5, 1937, with his 4-H poultry project near a peach and pear orchard. Edie McGavern said, "Wesley Chapel was out in the boonies in those days. My grandmother Emma Lydia Kruse Plank taught school in a one-room schoolhouse in the 1920s in Wesley Chapel. Many of her older students chewed tobacco." (Courtesy of Florida Extension Service.)

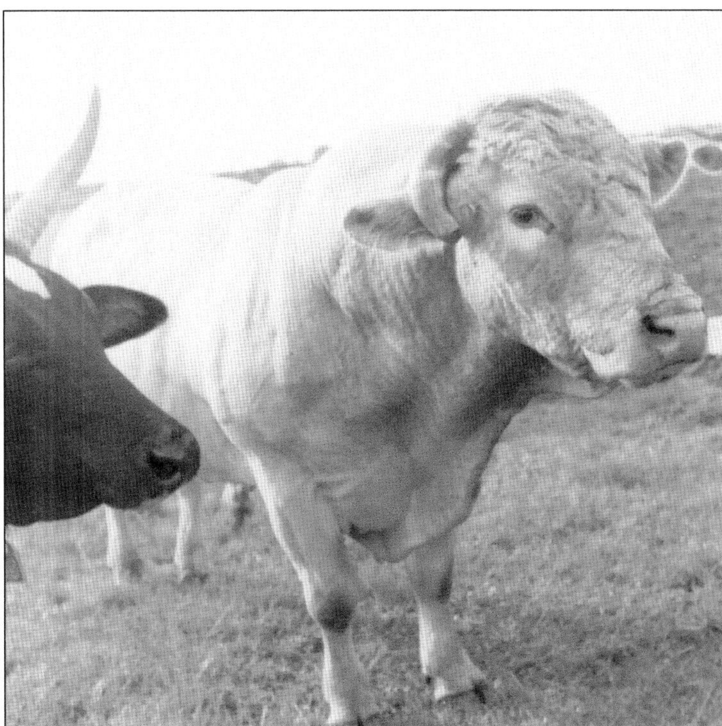

With a goal to eradicate the cattle fever tick, Florida had an aggressive mission to dip cattle in 1910. There were 53 dipping sites in Pasco County, with several in the Wesley Chapel area. The dipping solution was made with arsenic; at the time, ranchers were unaware of the long-term environmental impact. (Courtesy of Marlo Hilton.)

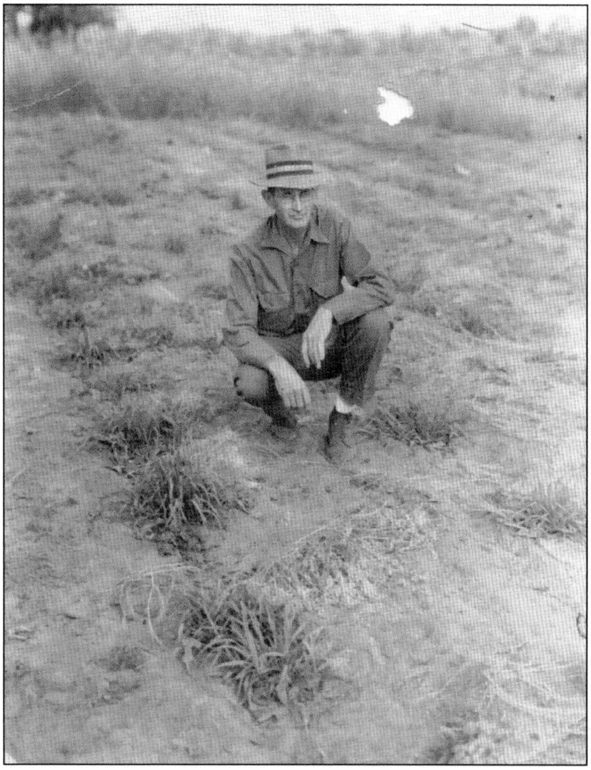

Pasco County extension agent J.F. Higgins inspects crops in this 1940s photograph. Truck patches were typical in Wesley Chapel for many years. The *Dade City Banner* printed a summary of crop-growing in June 1922, praising the velvet beans and cane of T.C. Wells; the orange groves of Sallie Godwin; the okra and peas of J.R. Cooper, F.R. Barnes, J.T. Allen and P.W. Tucker; J.M. Boyette's corn, beans, and melons; P.W. Tucker's sugarcane and guavas; Fritz Boyette's tomatoes; and the sweet potatoes of Albert Godwin, Henry Wells, E.V. Strickland, Rube Wells, and D.H. Smith. (Photograph by Cody Productions, courtesy of Pasco County Fair Office.)

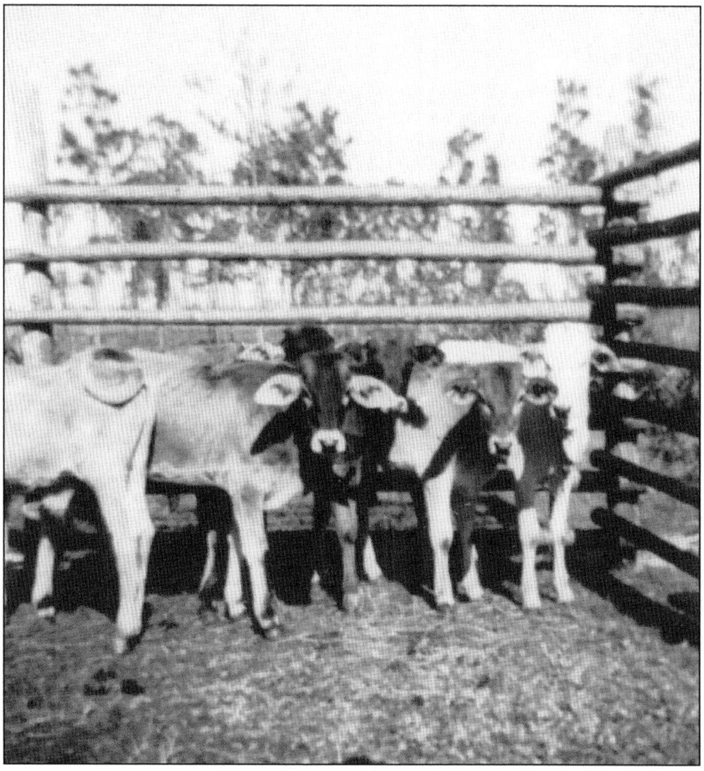

A 1960 photograph on the Ruben Barnes farm shows a metal pen used to hold Zebu cattle, a crossbreed during this time period that was particularly insect-resistant and ranged for great distances. Zebu cattle were an ideal match for Wesley Chapel. (Courtesy of David L. Brown.)

Three

Mid-Century Gatorville Evolving

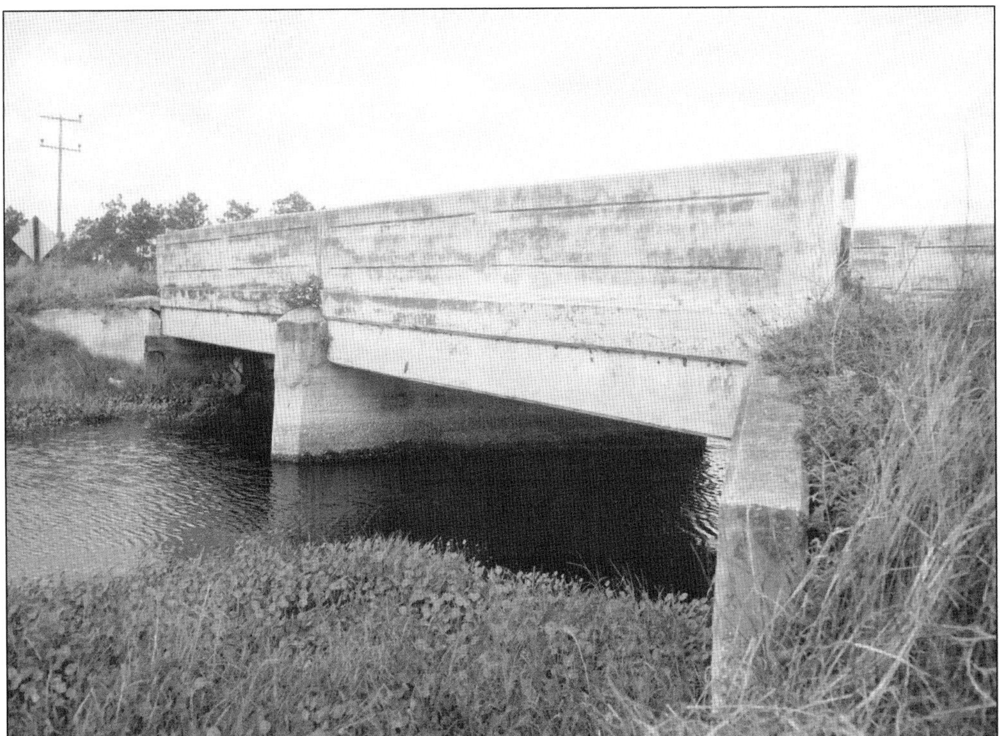

As the 20th century unfolded, pioneer families embraced change. Located west of the Eagles Flea Market, the Highway 54 West bridge was built in 1956. It is near the present-day location of Williams New River Acres. The New River flowed under the bridge, north to the Barnes Ranch, and then into the Hillsborough River. This bridge was used for fishing with cane poles. Wood pilings or support posts are visible under the old bridge in this photograph. The original bridge was built in the 1930s, supported by the Works Progress Administration during the Roosevelt administration. (Courtesy of Florida State Road Department, Florida Library & Archives, Florida Department of State.)

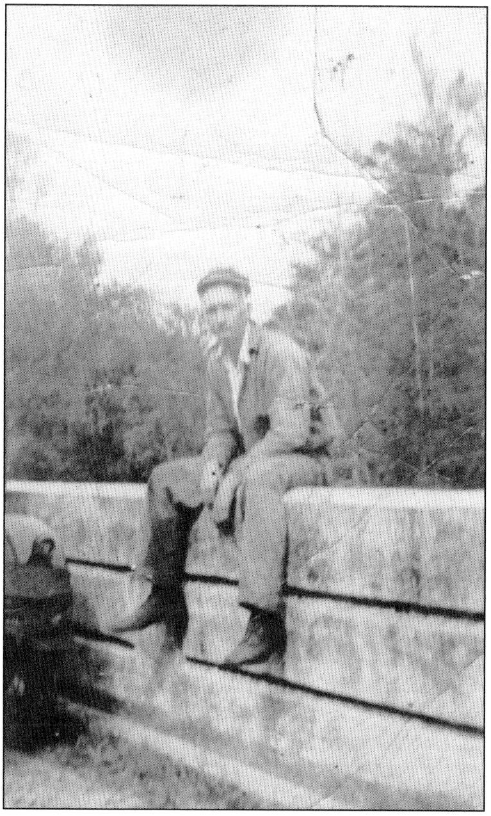

Lonnie Tucker sits on the bridge at New River. The 1879 surveyor reported that the creek known as New River "has no water at this season, except at the deepest places. . . . At many points, it has noticeable banks, holding its course through the ponds and glades and covering in the wet season." Possibly prophetic John Leslie also reported, "The quality of the land in this township is much below the county's average—the soil consists almost wholly of sand. Some of the ponds and swamps, if reclaimed, would produce well; but in their present state are unfit for cultivation." (Courtesy of Anna Jo Bracknell.)

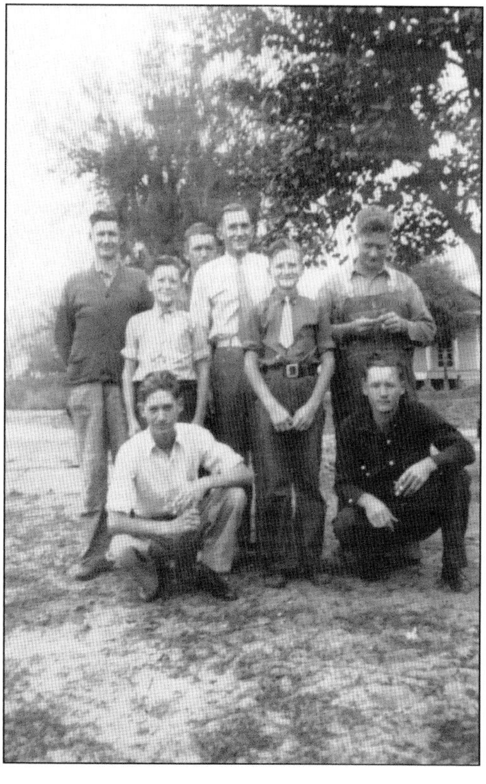

The Tucker Boys are pictured. From left to right are (first row) Jack and Archie; (second row) Dick, Edward, Elton, and Wilbur "Wigg"; (third row) Bryant and Lonnie. According to Carol Overstreet, Lonnie Tucker was a man of his word and had a strong sense of what was right and what was wrong. (Courtesy of Anna Jo Bracknell.)

Luther Smith and his wife, Neta Stanley Smith, are pictured at their house on Smith Road in Wesley Chapel with children Bill and Ruth. Ruth was 18 and Bill was 15 at the time of the photograph. State historic preservation officer Frederik P. Gaske wrote in 2008 that the Smith homestead site is located in the southeast quarter of Section 9 in Township 26 South, Range 20 East. It was once the homestead of William R. Smith, who arrived in the area around 1893, and it was also the location of the Z. Tucker claim as reported in the 1879 government plat. (Courtesy of Bill Smith.)

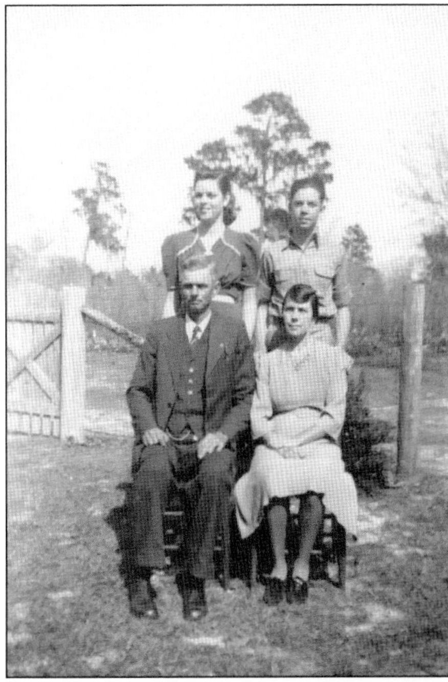

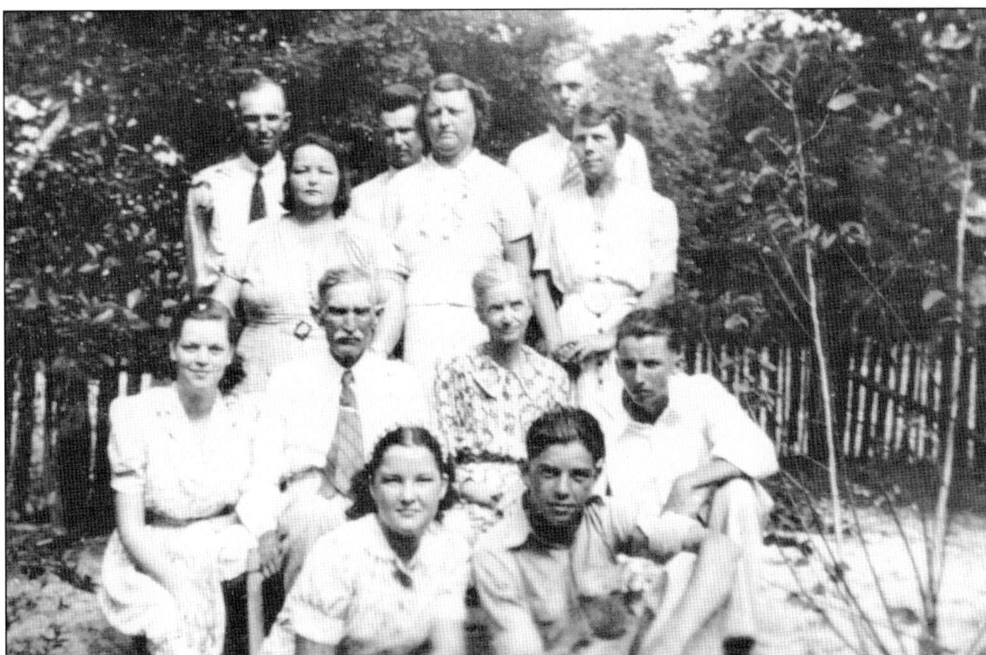

The Smith family was photographed around 1945 in Wesley Chapel. Pictured, from left to right, are (first row) Wanda and Bill Smith; (second row) Ruth Smith Adams, Daniel Smith, Elizabeth Frances Smith, and Genevieve Smith; (third row) Alberta Smith, Olie Smith, and Louneta Smith; (fourth row) Dennis Smith, Milton Smith, and Luther Smith. When Luther returned from the Army in the 1920s, the original one-lane dirt roadway of Highway 54 was being dug with a mule. The more recent paving of County Road 54 occurred in 1942 and 1943, when state prison inmates dug the roadbed by hand. (Courtesy of Bill Smith and Ruth Smith Adams.)

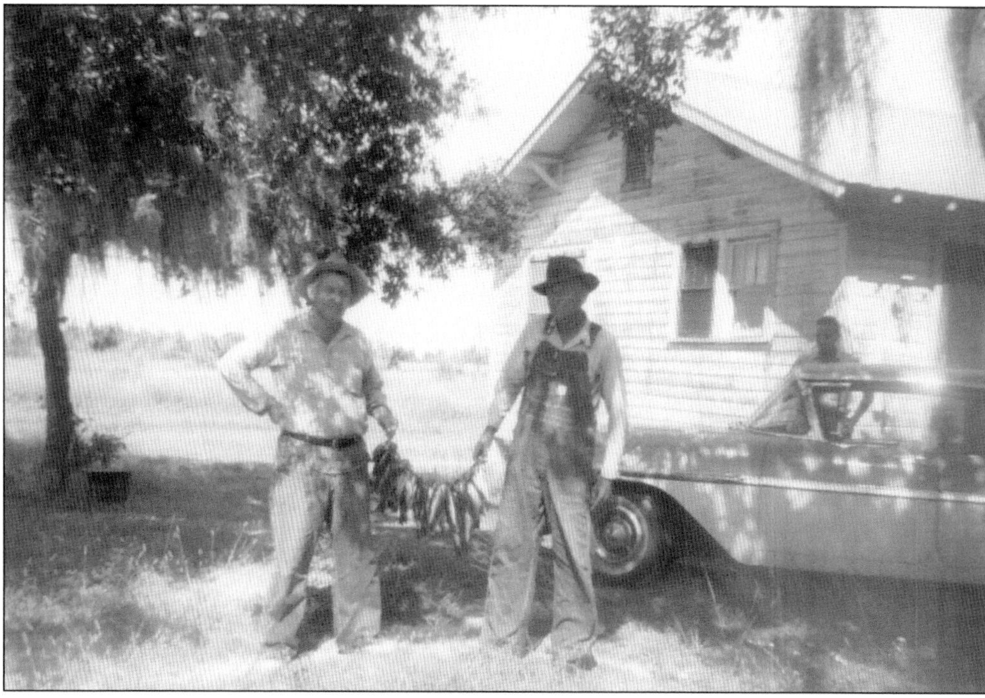

Displaying a string of freshly caught fish, Lonnie Tucker (left) is pictured with Lauren Morris Strickland, posing at the corner of Strickland's house, where River Walk is presently located. Strickland and his wife, Amy Beatrice Helveston, had children Ronald Wayne, Roy Oliver, Lauren Morris Jr., and Edward. Tucker was an avid gator and rattlesnake hunter, and he was never bitten. According to Marco Stanley, Tucker's church attendance would increase after a near miss. (Courtesy of Elisabeth Strickland.)

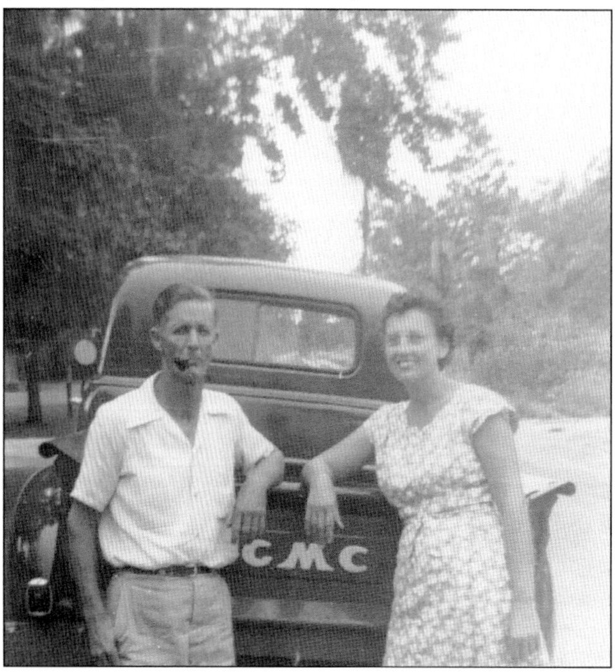

Pictured in Wesley Chapel countryside are James Fernie Cooper and Marjorie Mae Orine Williams, who married in September 1937. Wesley Chapel's population remained low throughout its history. There was a growth spurt after World War II, when people returned home from the military and were able to get low-interest government loans to purchase a house. The community experienced a boom in residential development in the 1970s, which slowed in the 1980s but picked up again in the 1990s and was accelerated before the real estate crash that began in the first decade of the 2000s. (Courtesy of Marco E. Stanley.)

Malinda Jane Gillette Stanley was born in 1892 and died in 1942. Her headstone in Holton Cemetery stands next to six small nameless markers for five daughters and a son. Malinda became a midwife in Wesley Chapel after her children's deaths. In 1900, less than five percent of women gave birth in hospitals, and from the turn of the century until 1930, female deaths in childbirth were at an all-time high, making the services of neighborhood women invaluable. Malinda was the daughter of Hardy Gillette and Sarah L. McKendree Gillette and married Raleigh Napoleon Stanley on April 30, 1907. Marco Stanley added, "My grandmother used to sew all her clothes." (Photograph by Weimer Studio, courtesy of Marco E. Stanley, Marlo Hilton, and Charles Estepp.)

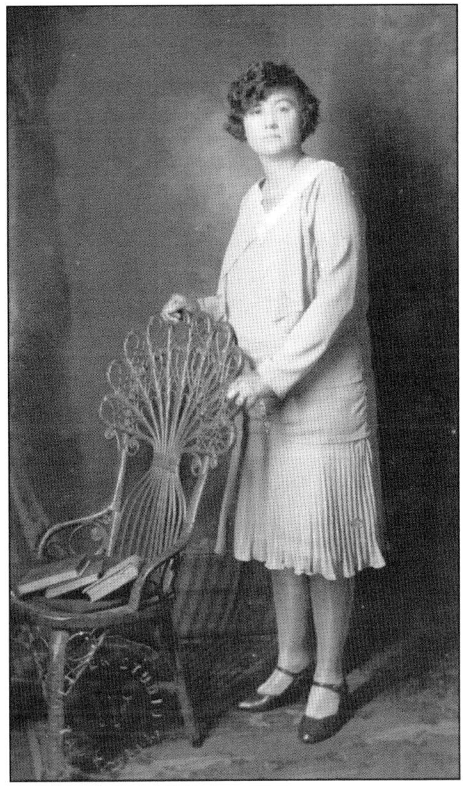

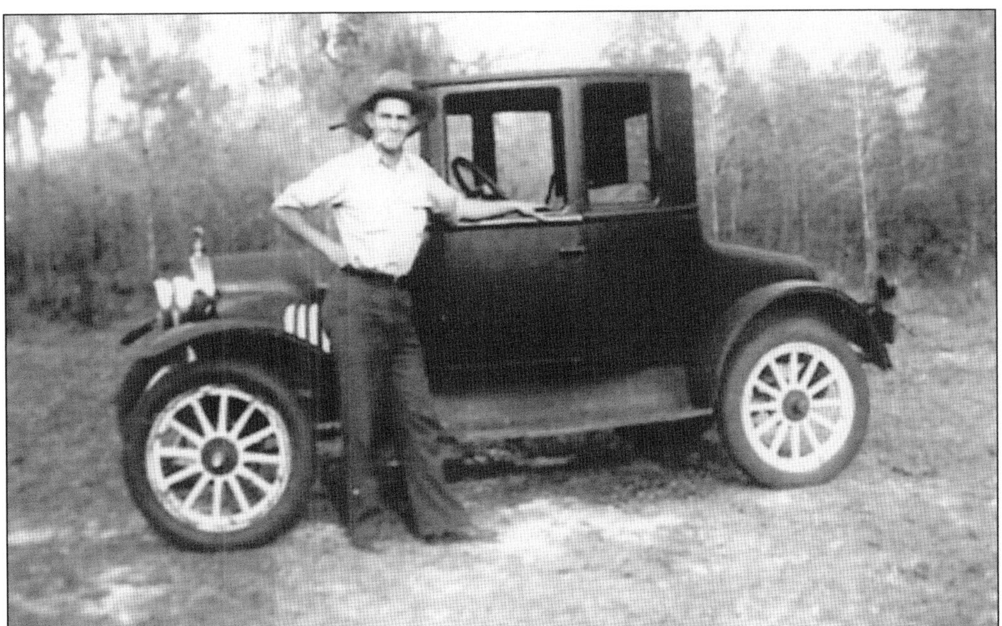

Marco Stanley (pictured) was the son of Raleigh and Malinda Jane Gillette Stanley. He was born in Wesley Chapel in 1921 and passed away in 1966. "My Stanley family is kin to the Gillettes, Boyettes, Godwins, McKendrees, Hills, Bradleys, and the list goes on," said Marco E. Stanley, Marco's son. (Courtesy of Marco E. Stanley.)

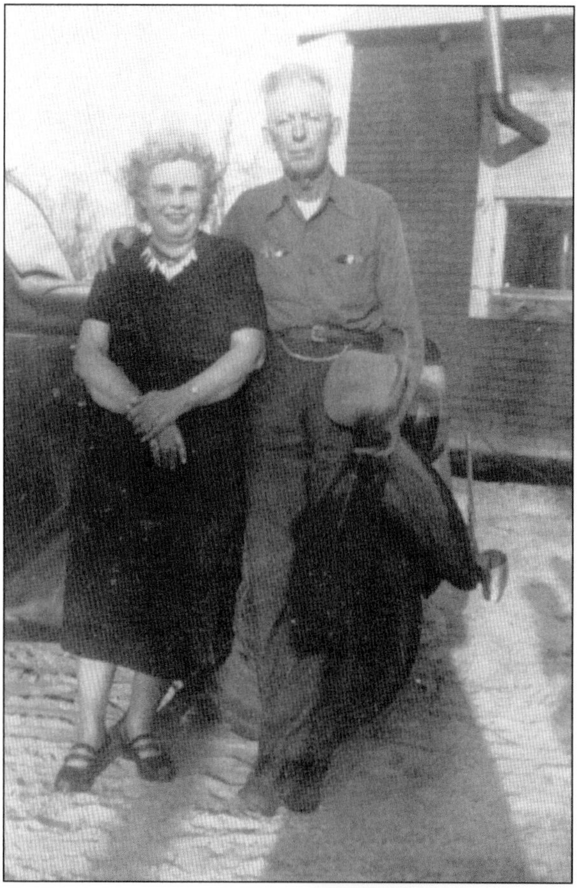

The photograph was taken at the Old Stanley homestead at the end of Smith Road. Raleigh Napoleon Stanley, born on July 31, 1888, and buried in Holton Cemetery in 1973, lived next to Maggie Gillette. The old house burned down a few years ago. Raleigh is shown with his wife, Goldie Locks Williams Stanley, though his first wife was Malinda Jane Gillette (1893–1942). Raleigh was the father of Roscoe Napoleon Stanley (1918–2003), Sarah Mahaley Stanley (1911–1992), and Marco Stanley (1921–1966). (Courtesy of Kimber Ann Ferguson.)

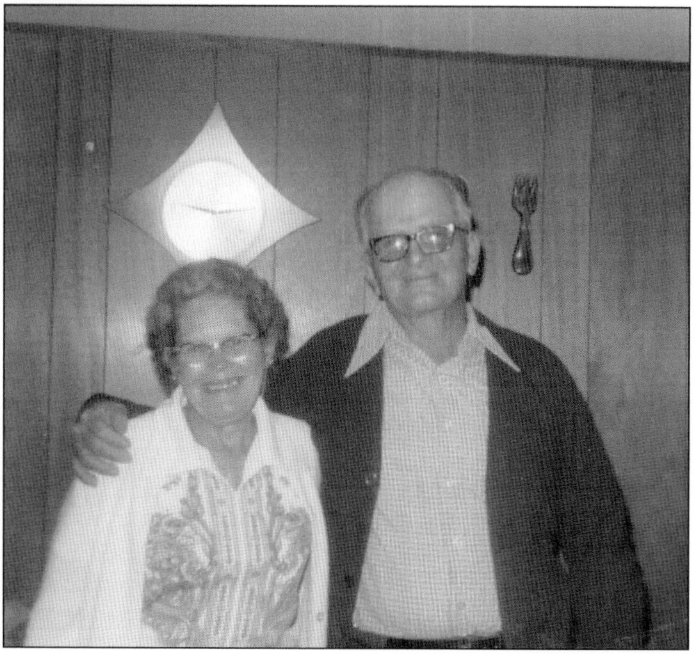

Hazel Weaver Stanley, wife of Roscoe Napoleon Stanley, was an early "school bus driver," who transported students in her own Ford Model A. She was paid per head for transporting the pupils to school. These included neighborhood children along with her own children Raymond, Francis, Keith, and Shirley. (Courtesy of Ruth Smith Adams.)

A 1941 photograph of Gwen Wells Ellerbee and Esther Burnside Boyette at a location off of Ellerbee Road shows them hard at work. Before the washing machine, large kettles of boiling water were poured into the washtub. With homemade lye soap and a washboard, which was set in a wooden frame and a place to rest the bar of lye soap, the clothes and linens were submerged and soaked in warm water in the tub to loosen the dirt. Then the "battling stick" was used to pound the clothes of any remaining dirt, and, by hand, the laundry was rinsed, wrung out, and hung out to dry on the outdoor clotheslines. With the prominence of Florida bugs looming, piercing sun, and inclement weather, it was a cumbersome task that required skill and practice. Monday was the designated washday, and the labor was intense. (Courtesy of Sue Boyette.)

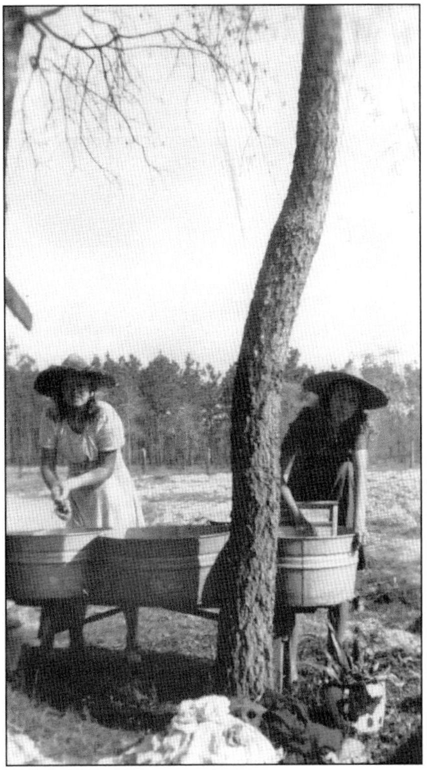

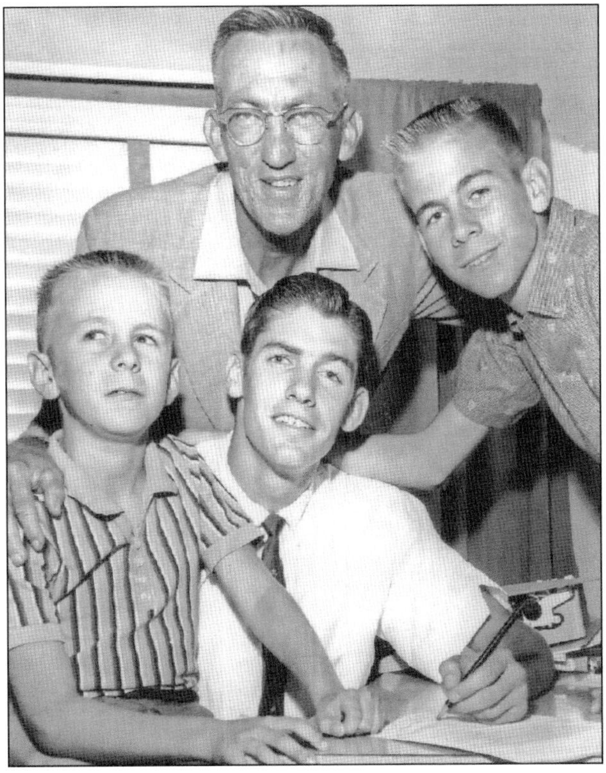

James "Don" Porter signed with Ole Miss to play college baseball around 1958. From left to right are William Porter, James H. "Wiregrass" Porter (father), Don, and Thomas Porter. Don played baseball with Ole Miss and had a professional contract with the Houston Colt .45s, one of two teams added to the National League before the 1962 season. However, with two years of military service, Don had to put the baseball career on the back burner. He managed Wiregrass Ranch later and passed away in 2014. (Courtesy of Quinn Porter Miller.)

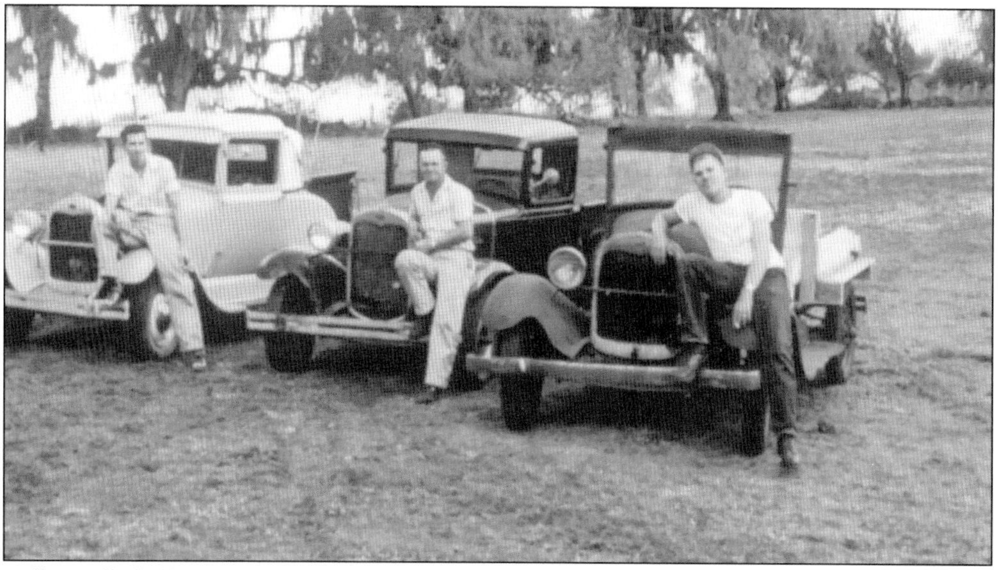

Rollie Wells (left), James Hilton (center), and Ferman Geiger pose with vehicles on the Ryals farm. Automobiles often graced the "Road to Nowhere" in Wesley Chapel, which held iconic memories for natives. Now Bruce B. Downs Boulevard, the Road to Nowhere was a desolated area that ended abruptly at County Line Road and just stopped at the Porter pasture. Some years earlier, Hillsborough and Pasco Counties had agreed to collaborate on the paving of Morris Bridge Road. Pasco paved part of it, and when Hillsborough left the area from the river to Fletcher Avenue as dirt road, a conflict originated. The ill feelings continued when Hillsborough County decided a hurricane evacuation path from Tampa was needed and built what is now Bruce B. Downs Boulevard. Again, part of the road was finished, but a large section of it remained unpaved and dead-ended for many years. (Courtesy of Marlo Hilton.)

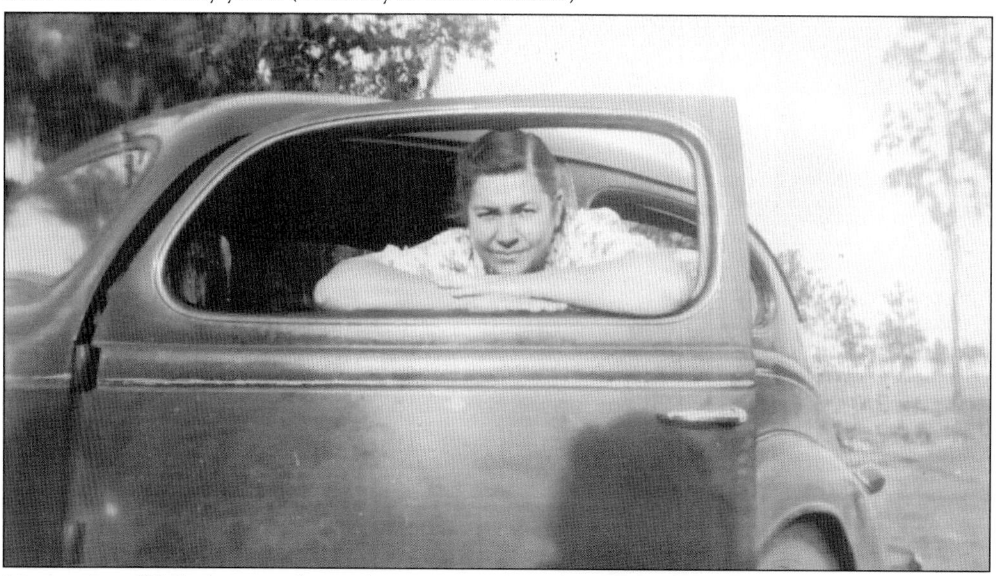

Minnie Lee Wells (pictured) was born in Wesley Chapel in 1901 to Hardy A. Gillette and Sarah McKendree Gillette. She married Reuben Wesley Wells, who became the police chief of Zephyrhills. The car in the photograph was used as a Zephyrhills police car before an official one was purchased. (Courtesy of Marlo Hilton.)

Delbert Lewis Wells and his first wife, Lillian Irene Cooper, are pictured here. Delbert owned a small general store in Wesley Chapel. Lillian was the daughter of Hardy Cooper and Sabra Boyette Cooper and a sister of Fernie Cooper. After Lillian passed away in 1936, Delbert married Ella Mae McKendree. The general store was a small space for congregating and buying a few supplies, with a gas pump out front. The farmers and ranchers depended on the general store, which had a limited stock. With fewer towns and a significant traveling distance to Tampa where larger stores were located, it was not practical to make multiple trips for a needed canned good, kerosene, or miscellaneous items. The store was a gathering point to chat, pass around a newspaper, and share gossip and politics. "You would wind the gas pump one full round for each one gallon of gas," said Wayne Sweat. (Courtesy of Cletia Pierce.)

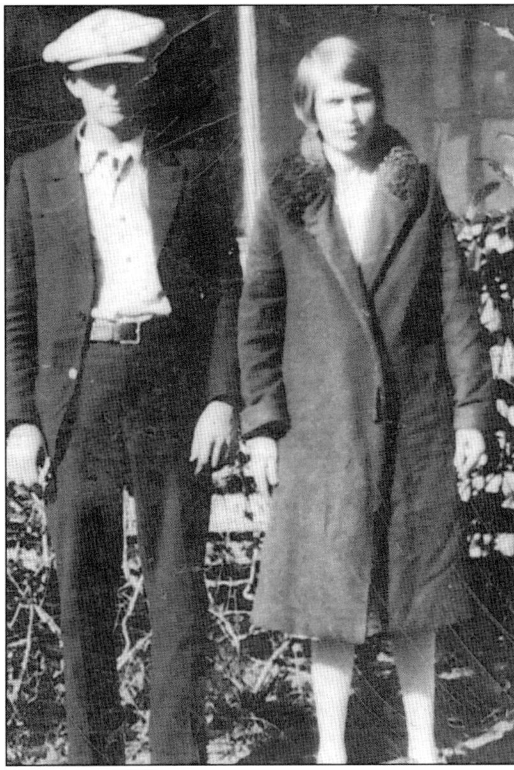

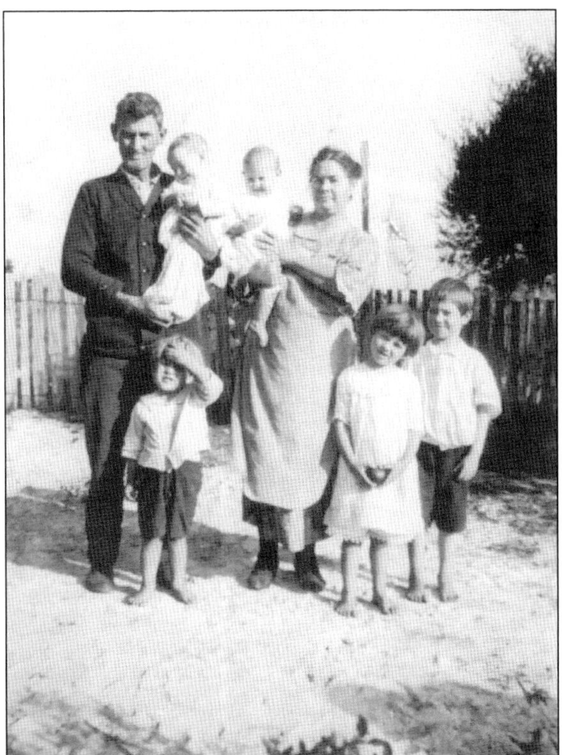

Lorena Geiger Wells and her husband, John Reuben Wells, are pictured with their grandchildren. They are, from left to right, (standing) Lee, Bernice, and John R.; (being held) Celestine and Roy. The photograph was taken in 1927 at the present-day site of three schools—Thomas E. Weightman Middle School, Wesley Chapel High School, and Wesley Chapel Elementary School—that occupy a campus on Wells Road. (Courtesy of Charles Estepp.)

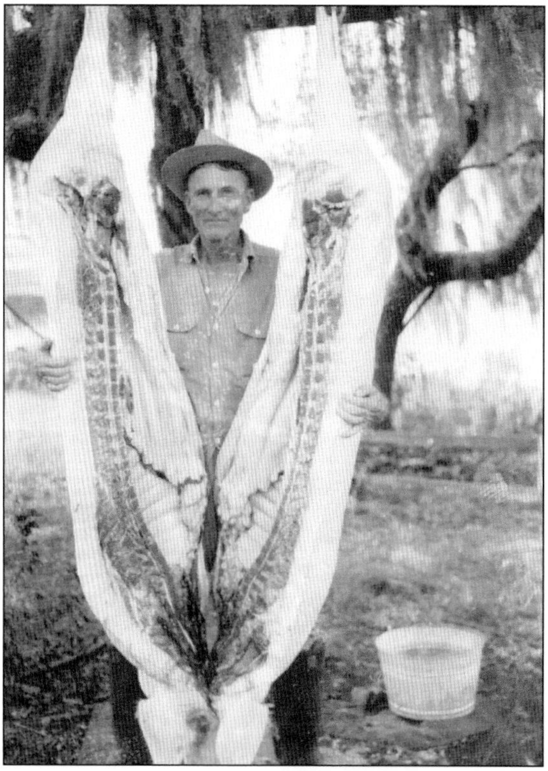

Lauren Morris Strickland proudly displays a hog carcass after a successful hunting trip. He and his wife, Amy Beatrice Helveston, were parents to Ronald Wayne Strickland, Roy Oliver Strickland, Lauren Morris Strickland Jr., and Edward L. Strickland. Wesley Chapel pioneers David Brown, Anna Jo Bracknell, and Marco E. Stanley gave Morris's nickname as "Worm Drive," which came from the driveshaft of the Ford he drove for many years. Another of his nicknames was "Chum Pie." (Courtesy of Anna Jo Bracknell.)

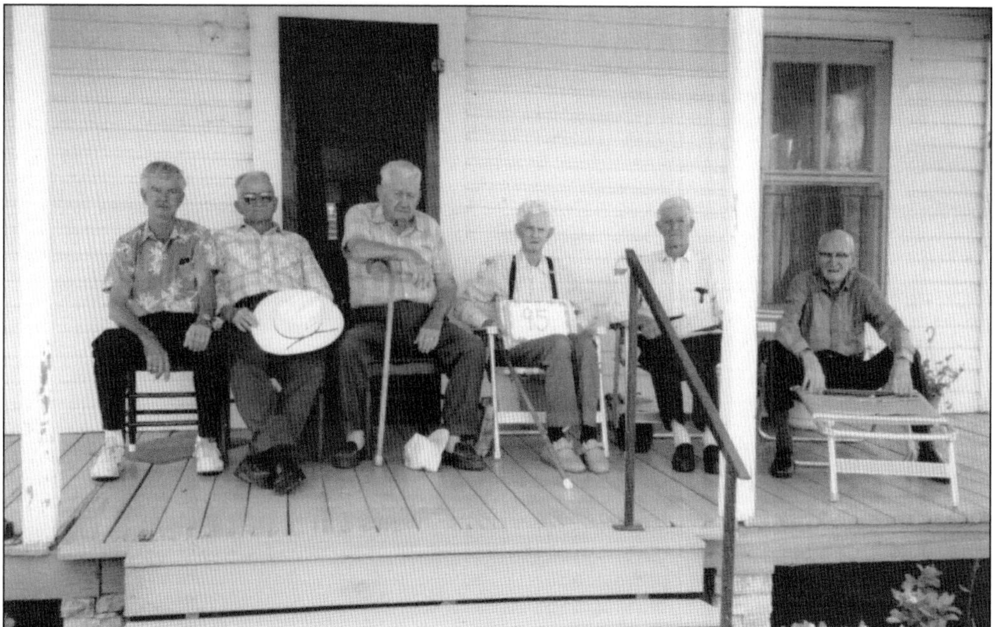

On June 24, 1991, Luther Smith's 95th birthday included a celebration at his home. From left to right are William Smith, Roscoe Stanley, Lonnie Tucker, Luther, Fernie Cooper, and Dennis Smith. In December 1987, Luther was honored along with three other near-centenarians by Mayor Robert H. Johnson. (Courtesy of Anna Jo Bracknell.)

Joseph (left) and Fernie Pasco Cooper were sons of James Robert Cooper and Mary Etta Cooper. Their other siblings were Ephraim, Hardy, Laura, Mary J., Stretie, and Percy. Fernie explained early-1900s turpentine-making: Chipping boxes were used while scoring trees with axes, and turpentine gum ran into "cuppers" and was collected. As the gum became plentiful, a team of mules or a wagon would collect the barrels with skids and empty them into the turpentine stills for distilling. Subsequently, when the gum was boiled, wood chips and debris were skimmed off. Workers, mostly African Americans, also hoed around the trees by hand in the summer to prevent fires. (Courtesy of Cletia Pierce.)

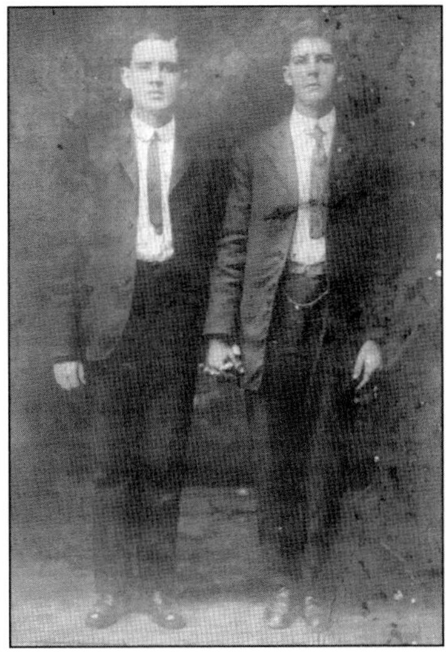

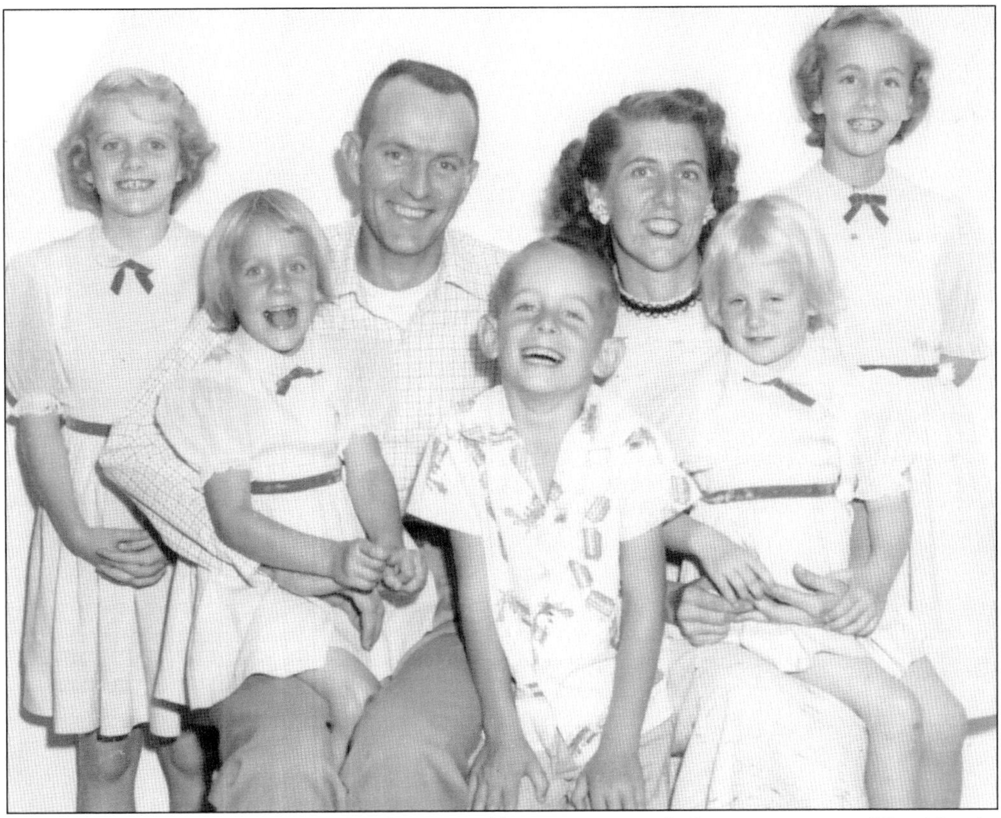

The Edward L. "Slim" Strickland family, pictured here, represented a later generation of Stricklands. From left to right are Vickie Lee, Mary Alice, Slim, Steven Roger, Elisabeth, Lynne Marie, and Karen Elisabeth. The photograph was taken just after Slim, son of Lauren Morris, returned from duty at Westover Military Base in Turkey in 1962. As a master sergeant, Slim was stationed throughout the world as a career soldier and worked in photography for the military; he photographed returning astronauts and presidents. He was offered the position of Lyndon B. Johnson's photographer with the Secret Service. (Courtesy of Elisabeth Strickland.)

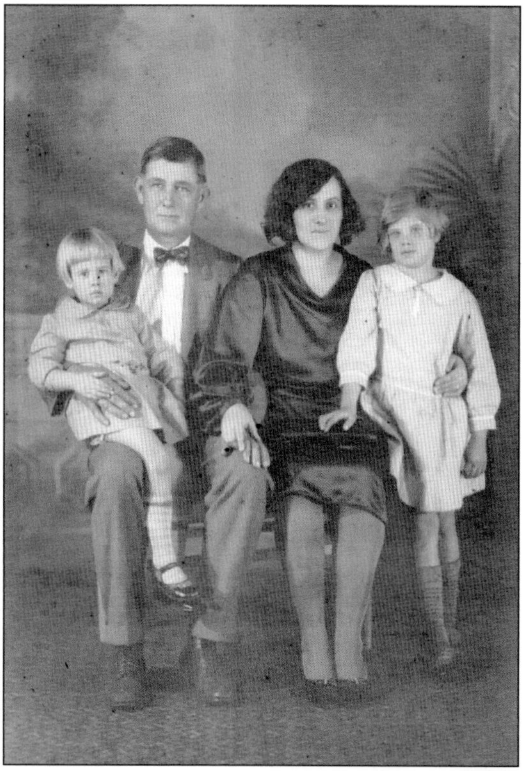

From left to right are Martha Barnes Brown, Ruben Barnes, Clara Baines Robinson Barnes, and Vida Clara Barnes Depue. Both daughters, Martha and Vida, became renowned ranchers. Reminiscing about childhood in Wesley Chapel, Roy Burnside reflected on families: "There were three things you were expected to do as a child in Wesley Chapel. First, you went to school. Second, you performed your chores. And third, you attended church." The Wesley Chapel School operated until the 1950s, and the Double Branch Church purchased the school property in 1956. (Courtesy of David L. Brown and Stephanie Brown Benson.)

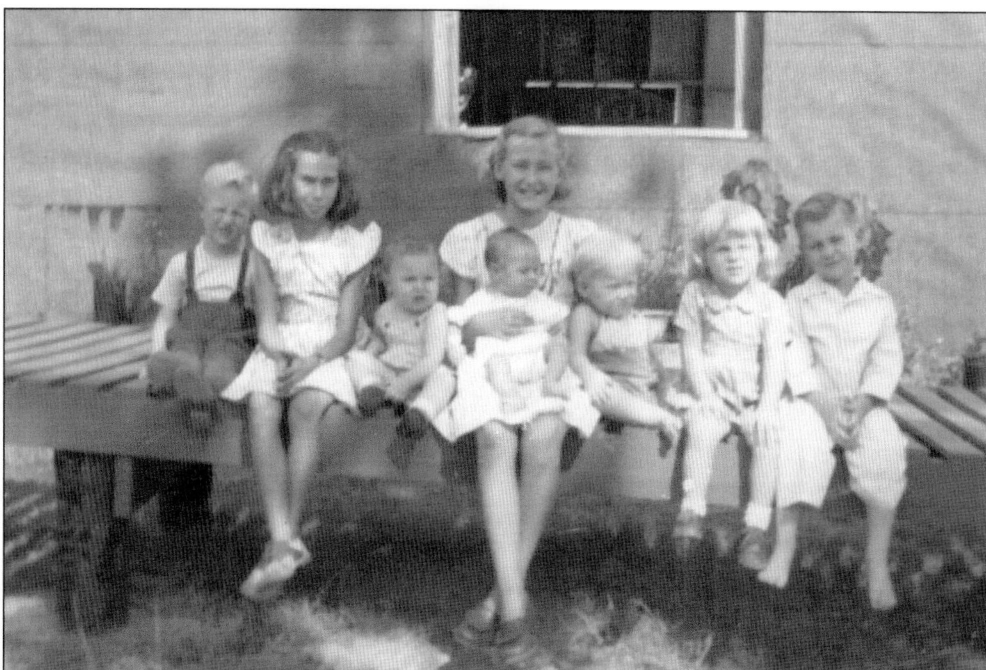

Reuben Wesley Wells and Minnie Lee Gillette Wells visited their grandparents around 1934. From left to right are Walter "Bill" Scott, Eunice Ryals, John A Scott Jr., Loretta Ryals (holding Terry Scott), Reuben Wells, Janet Wells, and Terrell Lee "Buddy" Wells. (Courtesy of Marlo Hilton.)

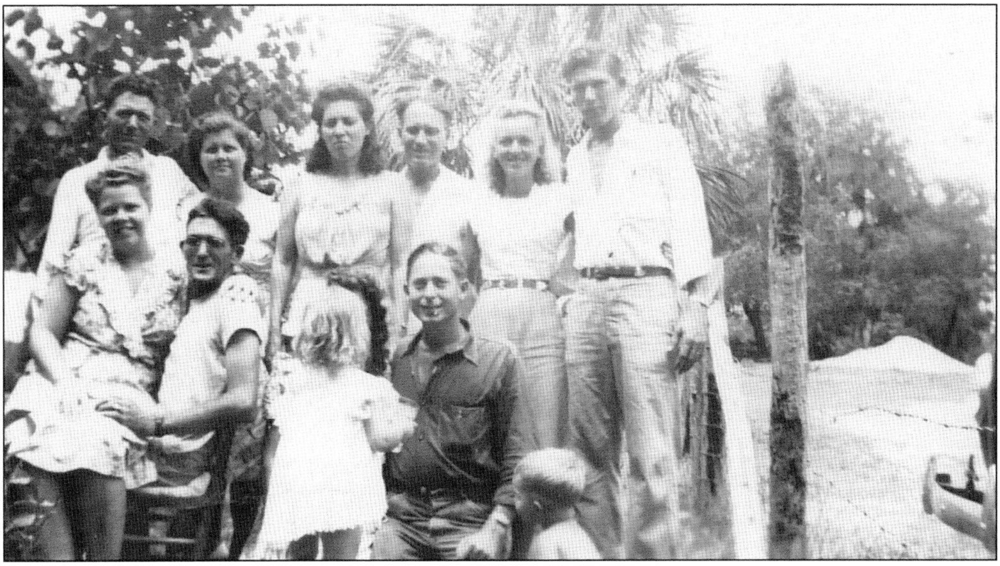

The five children and spouses of Fritz Beauregard Boyette and his wife, Roberta Ruth "Bertie" Gaskin Boyette, gathered for a family reunion in 1948. Pictured are, from left to right, (first row) Sylvina and Lorenzo Bradshaw "Pete" Boyette; Beth Boyette (face obstructed) and Fritz Beauregard "Joe" Boyette Jr., with children Elizabeth Bertha Boyette and Fritz Beauregard Boyette III; (second row) Virgil Lewis Boyette and his wife, Betty J. Boyette; Doris Lorene Boyette Cooper and Cohen Cooper; and Tom Boyette and Ida Godwin Boyette. (Courtesy of Deborah Boyette.)

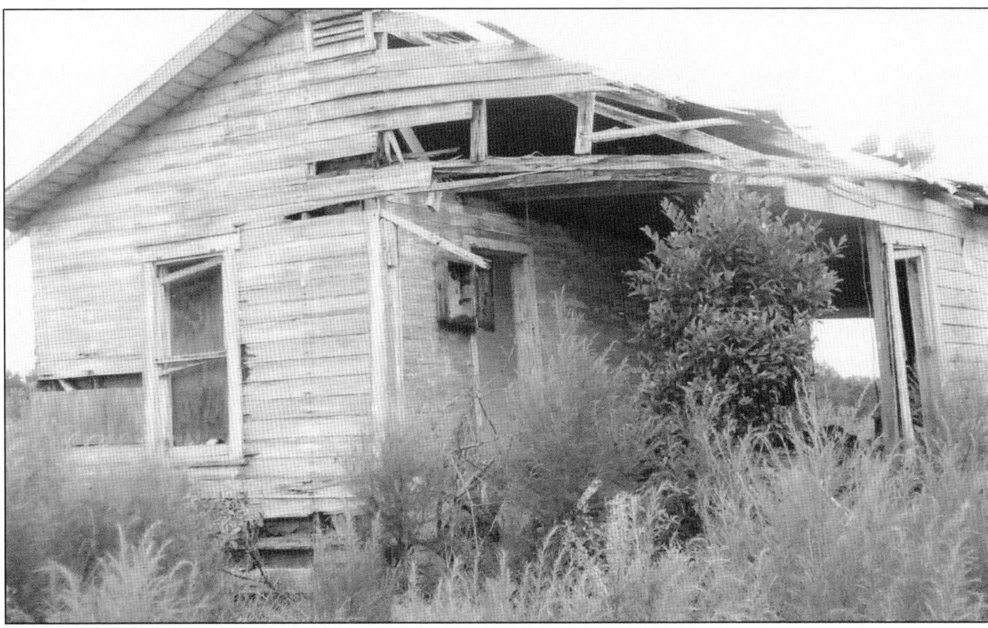

The Widener house sat on the Stanley Ryals place. The family was composed of Luke Wells, his wife, Nellie, and their children Juanita "Nita," Colleen, and John "Johnny" Wayne Widener. At age 69, Johnny said, "My daddy was a sharecropper in Georgia, and after we moved to the area, he worked for Owen Gall and later for Elsie and Manola Hill on their chicken farm. Those were the good days in Florida . . . not so populated. You could fish everywhere, and there was an abundance of wildlife . . . rabbits everywhere." (Courtesy of Marlo Hilton.)

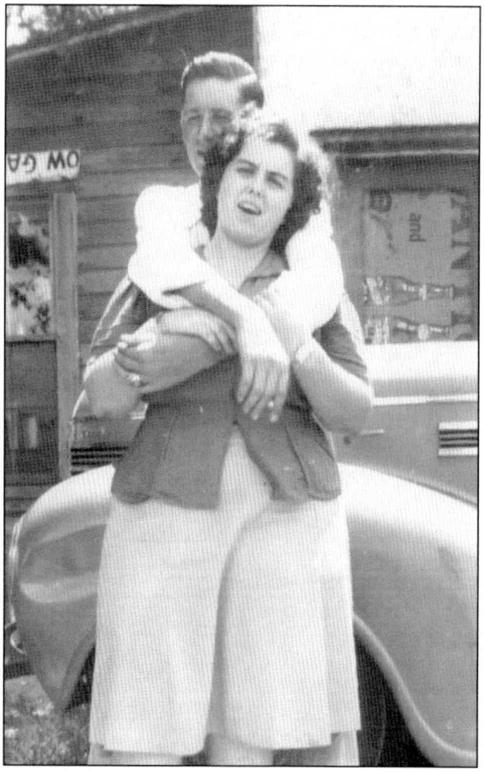

Lonnie Tucker gives a bear hug to his wife, Rebecca Juanita Davis. Lonnie began working at age 13 and earned $1 a day plus dinner for labor on Luther Smith's farm. He worked in building roads. Later, he worked in timber at I.A. Krusen Logging, Larkins Logging Company, and Clarence Strickland Logging. Finally, Lonnie worked at Moody's Hardware for over 31 years. A rugged outdoorsman, he also provided for his family by providing fish and game. Lonnie's only daughter, Anna Jo Bracknell, said, "On one of many hunting excursions with his good friend Morris Strickland, my dad said that he was bewildered that Morris was not actively hunting, and upon investigating, Morris exclaimed that he figured my dad would get enough for both families." (Courtesy of Anna Jo Bracknell.)

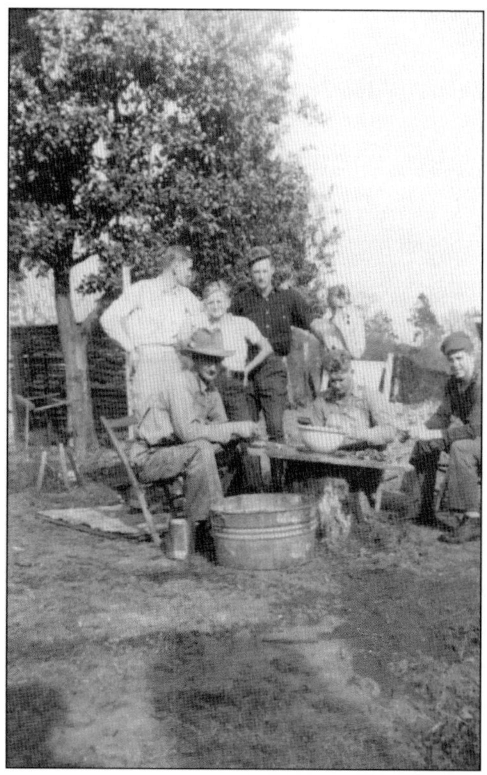

The 1930s were tough years in the midst of the Great Depression. Ingenuity and the willingness to do odd jobs helped. Six of the eight Tucker boys of Wesley Chapel are doing just that in their yard. They could be cleaning fish or frog legs, contemplating a moonshine still, stirring up some grub, or considering a host of other tasks in frontier Florida. (Courtesy of Anna Jo Bracknell.)

David L. Brown's family home is pictured at Christmas around 1962. In the photograph are Billy Ruben Brown, Robert Ernest DePue, Mary Francis Depue, Bill T. Brown, Vida Clara Barnes DePue, Brenda Sue Brown, David Lee Brown, Ruben Barnes, and Vida Ann Brown. (Courtesy of David L. Brown.)

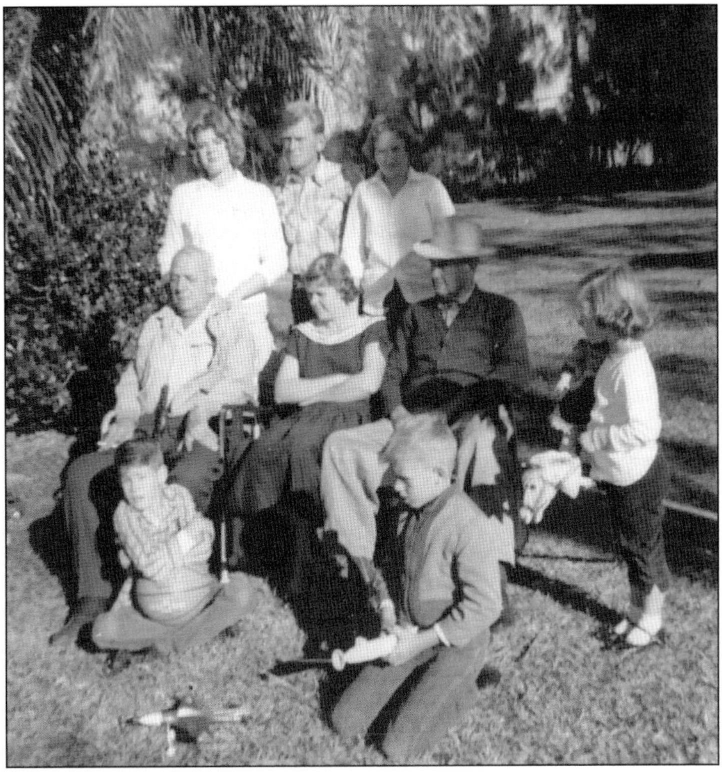

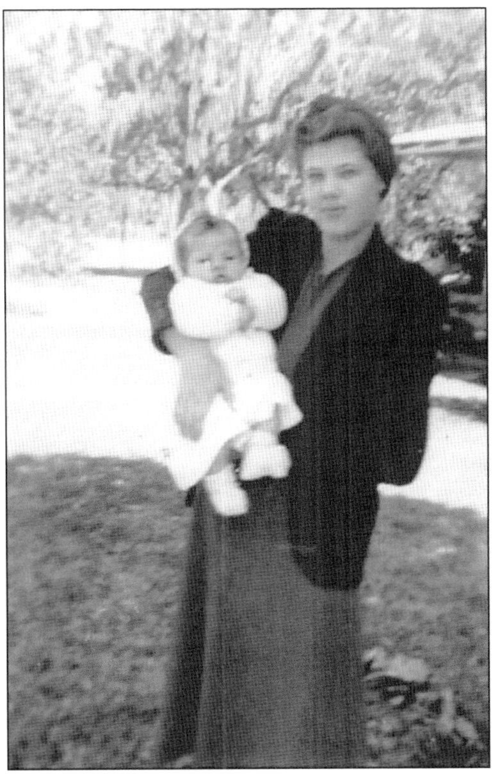

Vida Clara Barnes DePue is holding Mary F. Depue Nutt at the Barnes Ranch. Born January 27, 1922, Vida was the daughter of Ruben Barnes and Clara B. Robinson Barnes. She was married to Robert Earnest Depue and lived and worked in citrus, cattle, and lumber on the ranch in Wesley Chapel until she was 88 years of age. Her nephew David L. Brown said, "Remnants of the tram roads are evident from Handcart Road to Curley Road through the entire pasture. They were narrow-gauge rails and used primarily for the purpose of transporting turpentine. In the middle of the ranch is the family cemetery, which was originally the turpentine community where the workers lived with commissary, homes and well (which is still there)." The loading area in front of the turpentine still on the Barnes property was known as Stanley Station. (Courtesy of David L. Brown.)

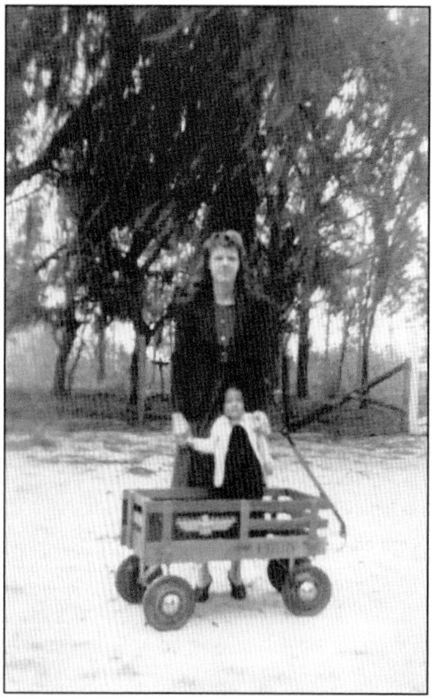

Vida Clara Barnes Depue (standing), daughter of Ruben Barnes, and Clara Baines Robinson are shown with a wagon. The Barnes family's history is rooted deep in the history of Pasco and Hernando Counties. The Barnes and Brown families are both related to the fellow pioneer families of Strickland, Redbrook, Godwin, Leggett, Smith, and Hill, just to name a few. Ruben Barnes had two children, Martha and Vida. (Courtesy of David L. Brown.)

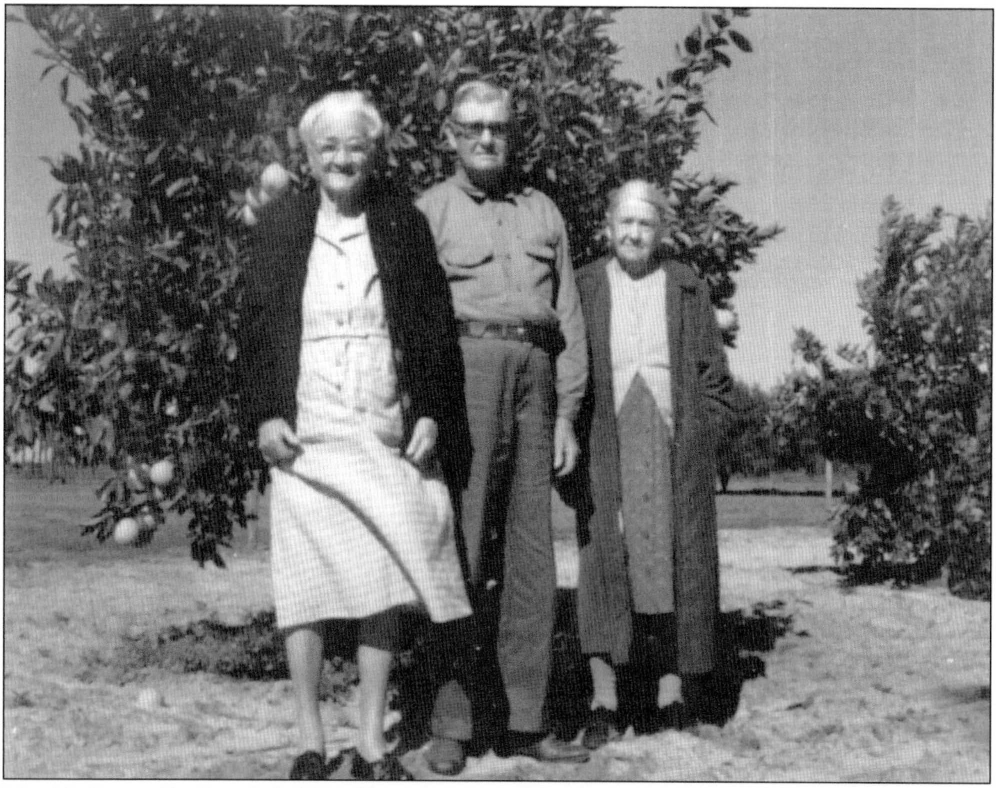

Matilda Barnes Redbrook (left) and her sister Lucy Barnes Leggett are shown with Ruben Barnes in front of the Barnes home in Wesley Chapel around 1960. The photograph shows off the ripe citrus in the luscious grove. Citrus groves were prominent in Wesley Chapel for many years, and Pasco Packing Plant in nearby Dade City (the county seat) originated in 1936 and was the largest single citrus packing plant in the world. After a series of freezes in the 1980s, citrus production moved south. (Courtesy of David L. Brown.)

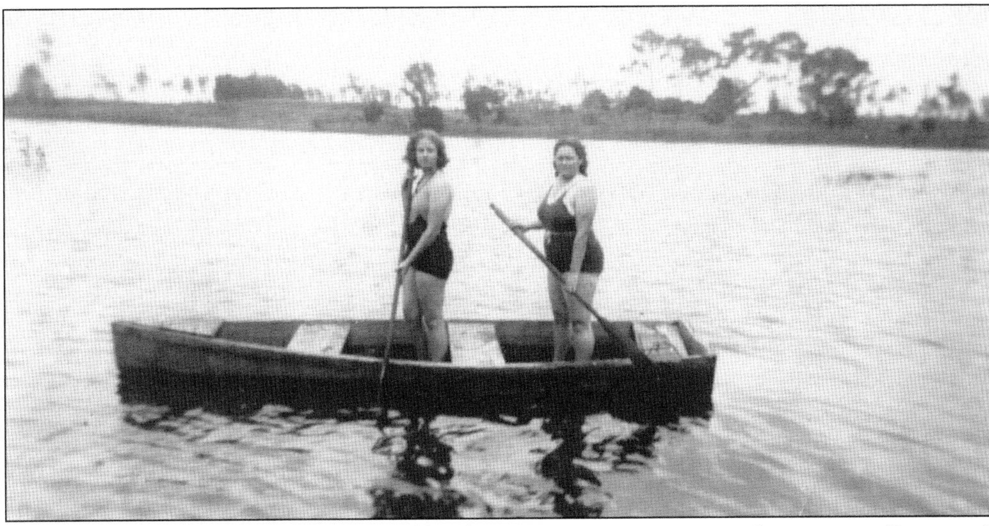

Martha Barnes Brown and Belma Strickland Dennison enjoy a canoe adventure on Gooseneck Lake, north of Highway 54 and just west of Land O' Lakes. Outdoor entertainment in the Wesley Chapel area included communing with nature via canoeing, swimming, and fishing. Other forms of entertainment included the occasional excursion to Zephyrhills for a movie and the monthly trek to Tampa for shopping. (Courtesy of David L. Brown.)

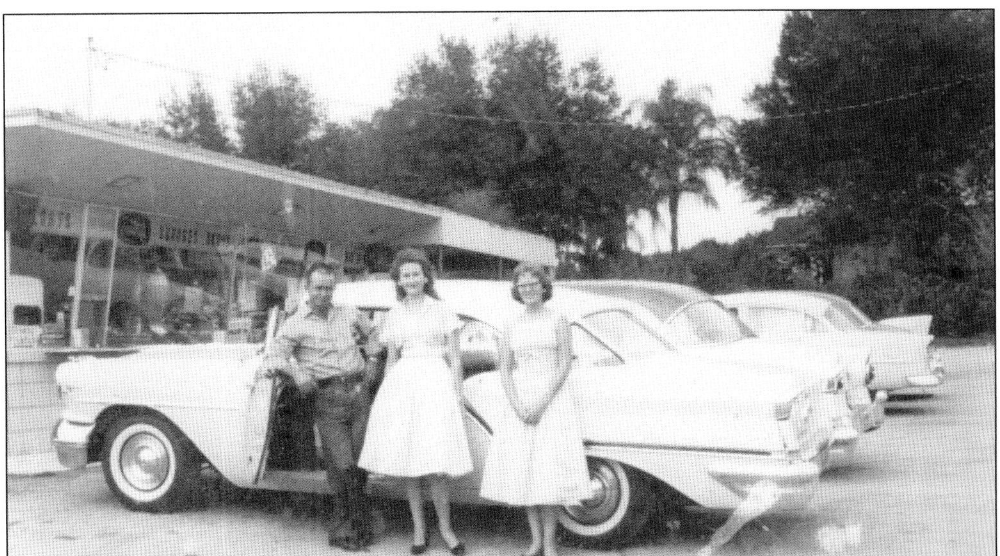

Many Wesley Chapel residents spoke of mid-1960s recreation, which included activities at Zephyrhills High School and the Freezette Drive-In off Highway 301, where James Hilton, Loretta Ryals, and Sandi Surratt are photographed by their car. (Courtesy of Marlo Hilton.)

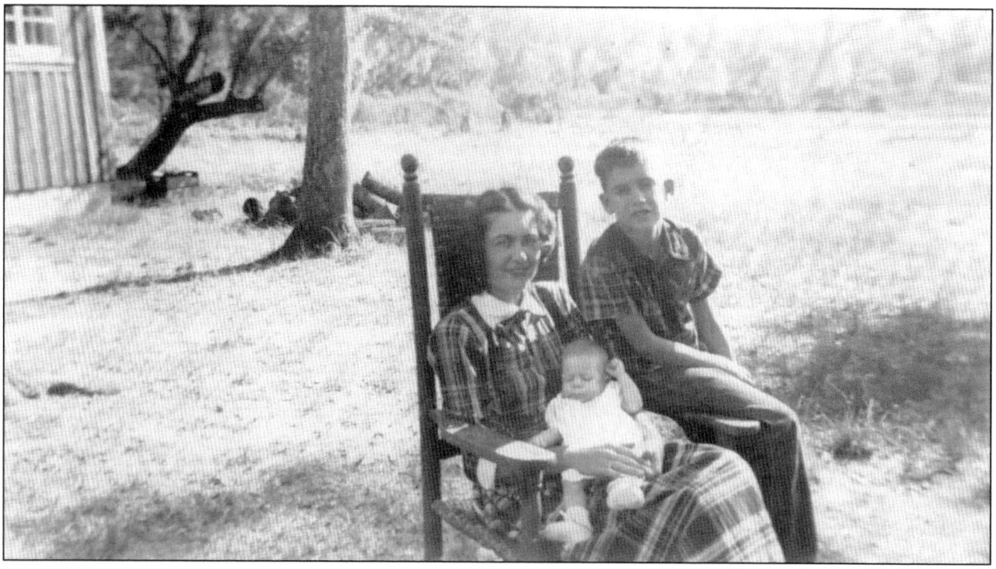

A November 27, 1948, photograph shows Martha McDonald Porter, wife of James H. "Wiregrass" Porter, with children James "Don," 8, and Tom McDonald, 3 months, in front of the family home in Wesley Chapel. Family members recalled Martha's quiet responsibility. She was able to whip up a feast for cowhands with little notice, and they quipped that she could have been a short-order cook. She pursued a nursing career before marrying Wiregrass and adjusting to a rural life. "She could work at the ranch all day and then attend a garden club event in Tampa that evening," said her son William. (Courtesy of Quinn Porter Miller.)

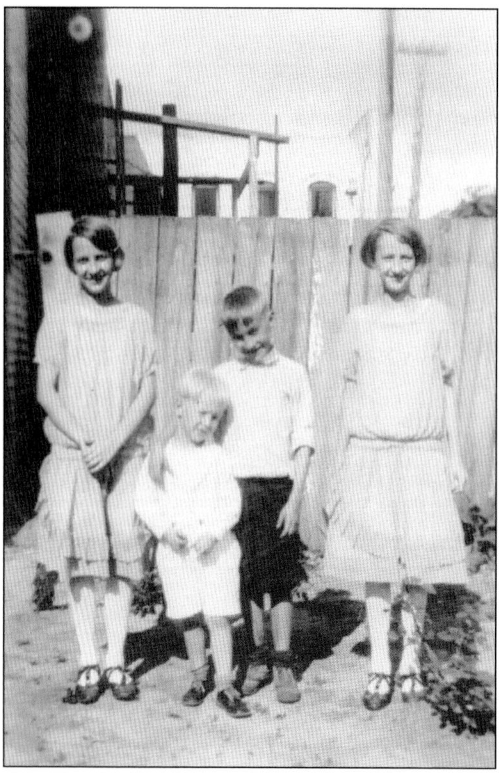

The children of James Barney Porter and wife Kathryn Hatcher Porter are pictured around 1921. From left to right are Martha, Robert Paul, James Hatcher, and Margaret. Four generations of the Porter family have worked the land in Wesley Chapel. They sold land for Saddlebrook Resort and later Meadow Point. They also donated land for Pasco-Hernando State College (Porter Campus at Wiregrass Ranch), Florida Hospital Wesley Chapel, and several public school sites. (Courtesy of Quinn Porter Miller.)

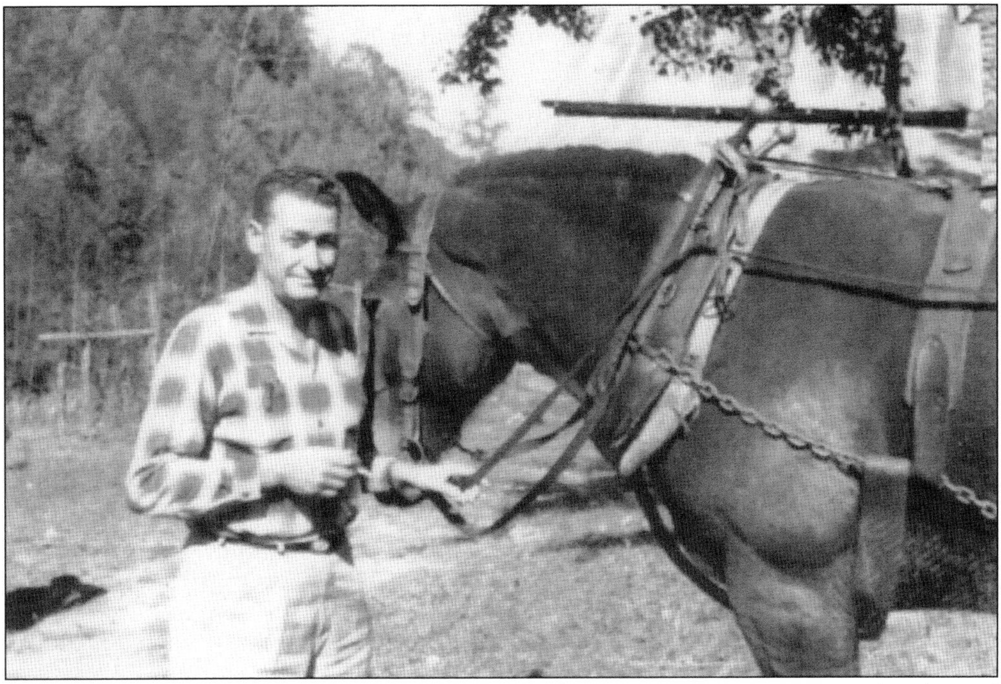

Stanley Ryals, at age 45, stands with a draft horse in the 1960s. In a 1990 interview, Stanley said he met his wife at a square dance. "She [Bernice Wells] lived out in Wesley Chapel in the woods, about halfway between Highway 52 and 54 . . . just where you turn off to go into Saddlebrook, about three or four miles. Her family home was situated in an orange grove. Her daddy worked for an old sea captain. In fact, after we married, we had the same job . . . working for $25 a month and a house. That is what we were getting by on. I paid $25 for an old Model T too." (Courtesy of Marlo Hilton.)

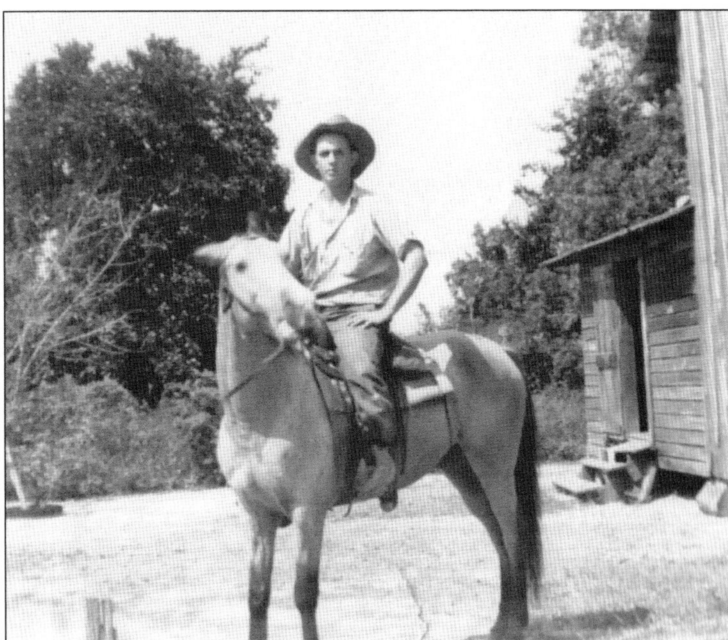

Marco Stanley, an expert horseman, is shown around 1942, riding a steed owned by Gordon Hill. He is at Louis Napoleon Stanley's home in Wesley Chapel. The house included a loft area, depicted at far right, that was used for sleeping. Lore is abundant, with stories of Marco's horses and his wrangling skills. (Courtesy of Marco E. Stanley.)

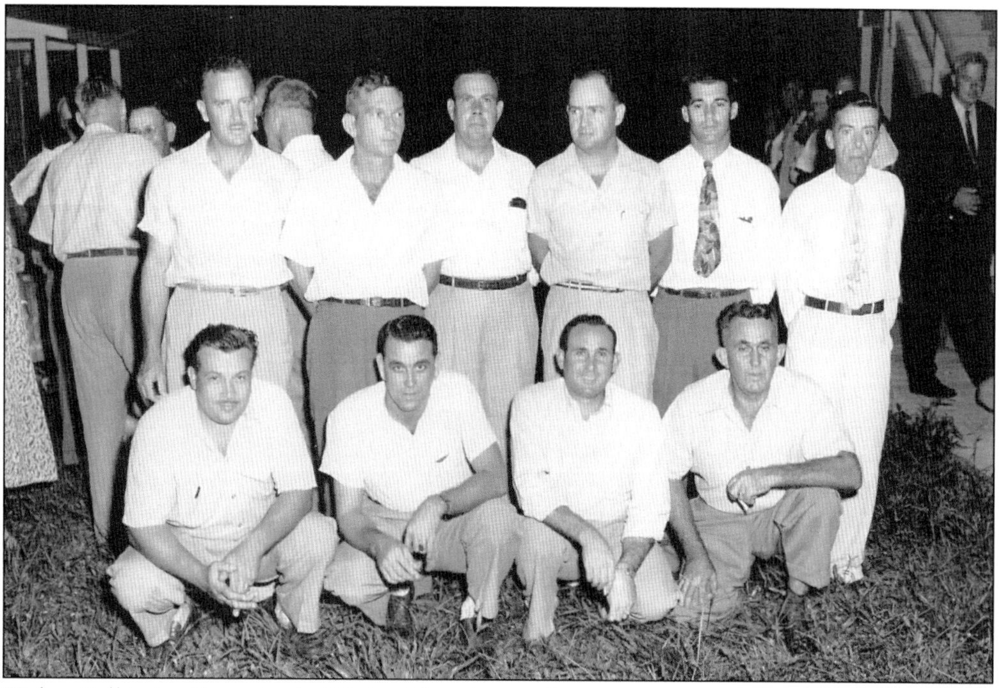

Walter Gall is significant in the Wesley Chapel area. He was instrumental in selling land from the Rockefeller trust to the Porter family. He was also a leader in neighboring Zephyrhills, including his civic service as a Mason. Pictured are, from left to right, (first row) Jesse Kaylor, Philip Guy, Boyd "Bud" Massey, and Isaac Massey; (second row) Ralph Lair, Paul "Jiggs" Schmidt, Dave Vestal, Owen Gall, Vance Forbes, and Harry Bletcher. At far left, the lady in a flowered dress is believed to be Lorena Royal, attending along with her husband. In the upper right corner of the photograph is the stairway to the Masonic hall. (Photograph by Joseph E. DeAngelis, courtesy of Vance Forbes.)

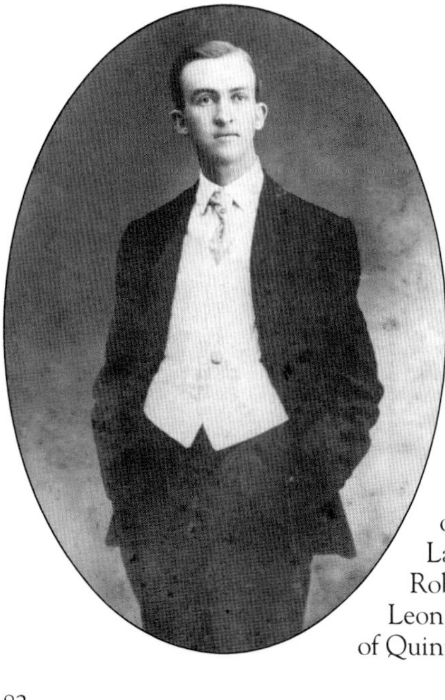

James Barney Porter was involved in the hotel and ice plant businesses in Balsam, North Carolina, before moving to Florida and working in Lake City and then Plant City. His grandson Bill said that Porter bonded with the land and built a family cohesiveness that instilled a sense of stewardship. He owned thousands of acres south of Highway 54 from the mid-1940s on. Large parcels of land were given to sons James H. and Robert. Robert later sold his land after World War II to Leon Bishop, who owned Jack's Cookie Company. (Courtesy of Quinn Porter Miller.)

A photograph taken in 1938 shows four generations. Pictured are, from left to right, (first row) Eliza Gaskins McKendree and Muriel Merritt Sessoms with baby Judith Sessoms; (second row) Sarah McKendree Wilson and her daughter, Gladys Wilson Merritt. Sarah McKendree and Augustus Addair "Gus" Wilson celebrated their golden anniversary in 1946. (Courtesy of Elisabeth Strickland.)

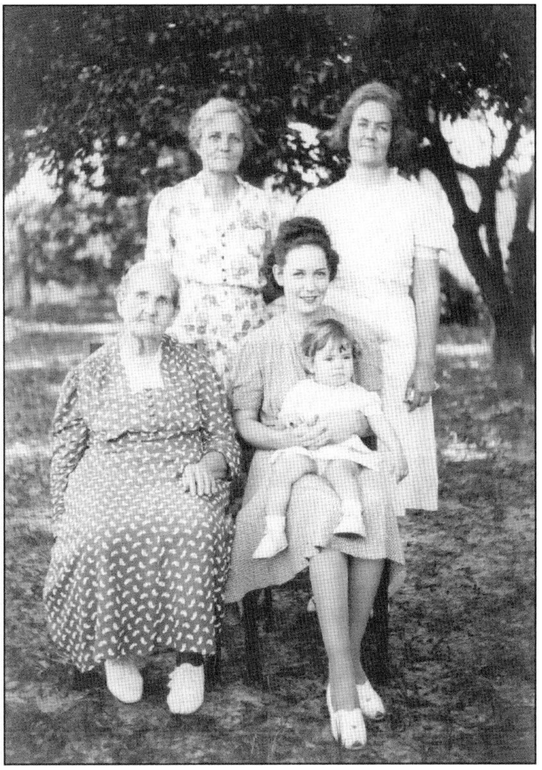

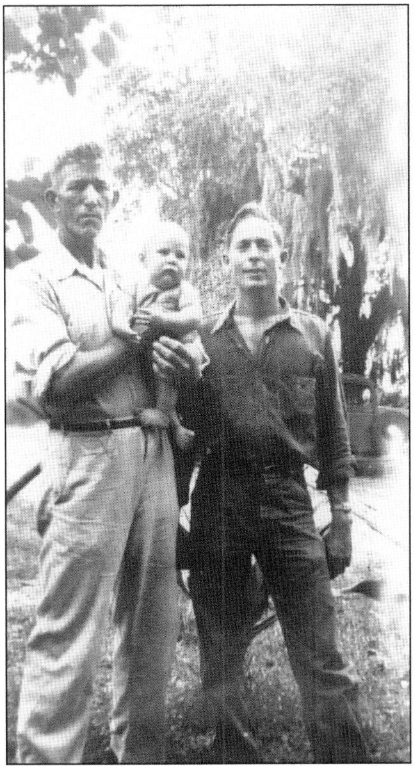

Fritz B. Boyette Sr. and Fritz B. Boyette are pictured with one of Fritz Sr.'s grandsons in 1945. Fritz was appointed to the county commission by the governor in 1921, and the *Dade City Banner* reported on November 24, 1922, that "the people of Wesley Chapel are in better hopes of getting road No. 9 now that Commissioner Boyett has told them that Engineer Turner has assured him that the work will begin in a few days." Most agree that the construction of I-75 and the development of the Quail Hollow Golf Course were turning points in Wesley Chapel. When Saddlebrook Resort opened in 1981, an international emphasis was brought to Wesley Chapel. (Courtesy of Deborah Boyette.)

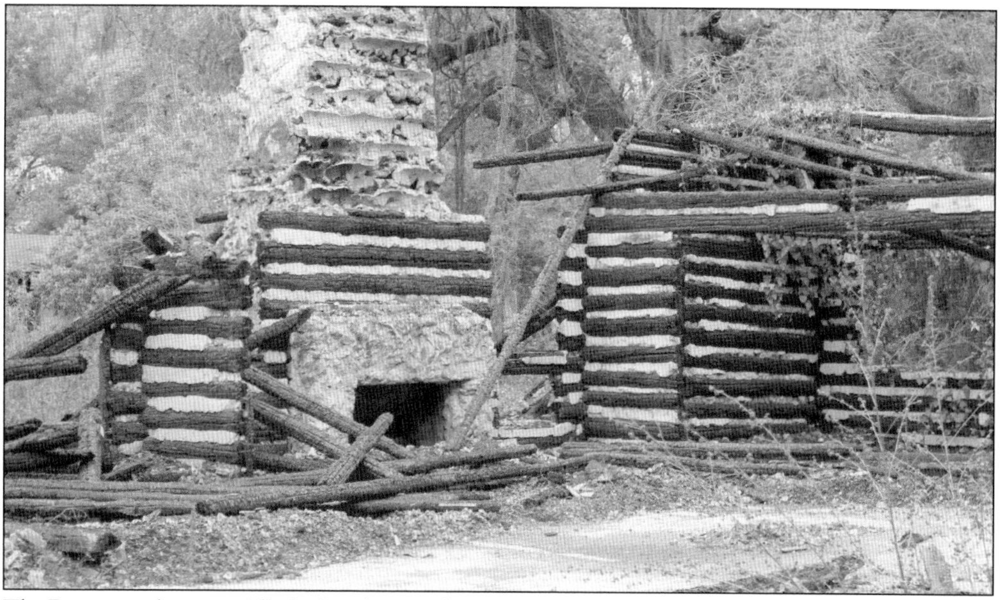

The Ritterman home on Ellerbe Road in Wesley Chapel was constructed around 1940 by veterinarian Dr. Ed Everett and later owned by Dr. Stuart and Sharen Ritterman. The two-story, cypress-chinked log home is significant for its architectural style, reminiscent of hospitable older Florida dwellings. Its native rock fireplace in the spacious living room and "pecky cypress" (distressed and wormholed wood—once the cheapest available lumber and now highly prized) has been effectively used throughout for interior walls, ceilings, and floors. (Courtesy of Ernest Wise.)

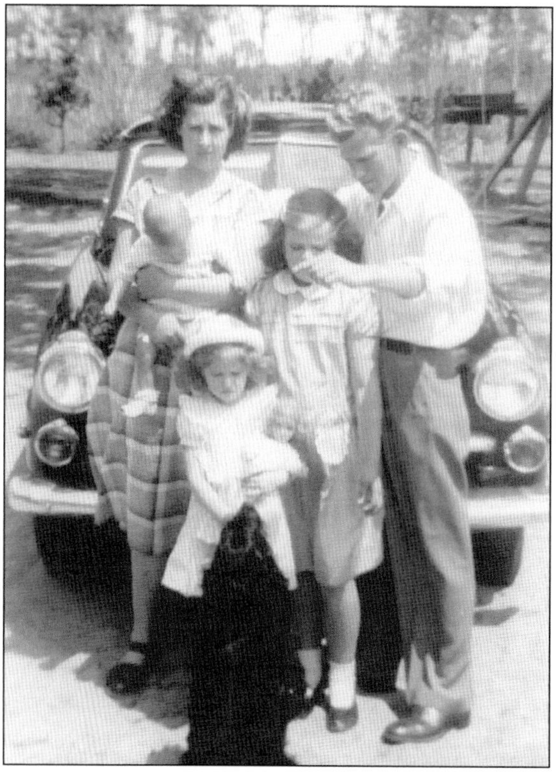

Martha Barnes Brown is shown with her husband, Bill Brown, and three children. Her son David recalled that Martha started teaching in nearby Zephyrhills as a single woman after graduating from Florida Southern College in Lakeland. "Her father thought it was too far for a young woman to drive alone to work from Wesley Chapel, so he built her a house near the school and bought her a car," said David. She later managed the Ruben Barnes Ranch and was known for her exemplary ranching skills. (Courtesy of Stephanie Brown Benson.)

Four

Economy

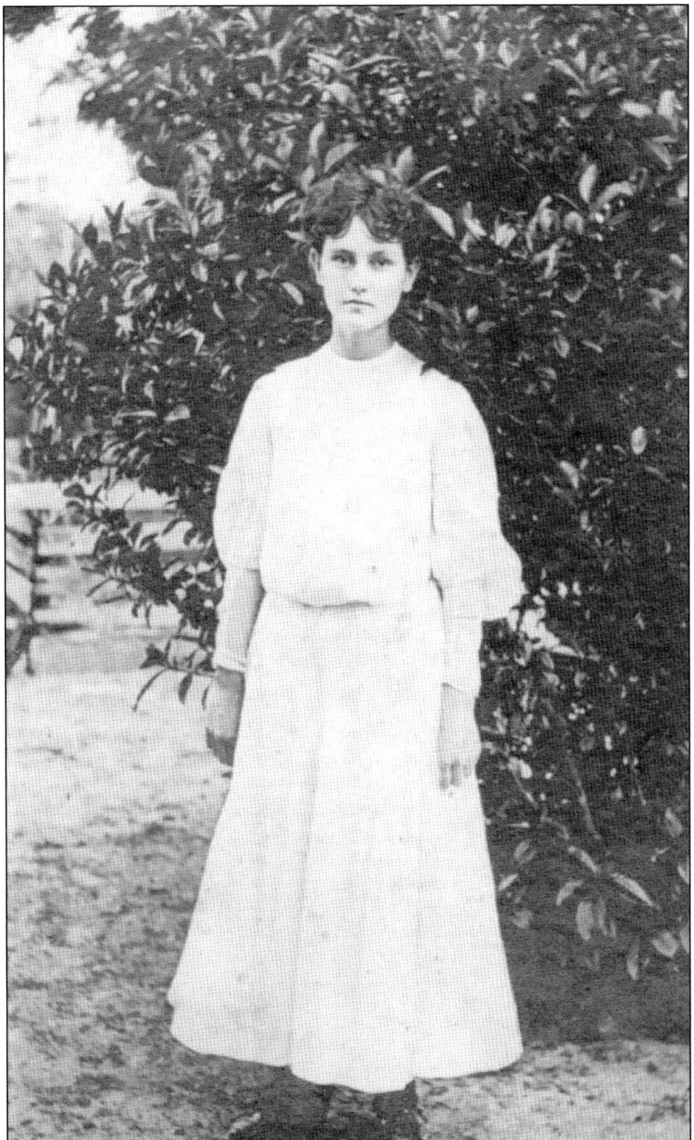

Mittie Lula Wells, pictured next to an orange tree, was the daughter of Mary Elizabeth Gaskins Wells and John Wesley Wells. Lula married Fernie Pasco Cooper in 1908. Lumber trusts, including that of J.D. Rockefeller, preceded the large ranches in Wesley Chapel. Pasco Cooper cut lumber on the Rockefeller land, while Walter Gall served as the land agent. (Courtesy of Cletia Pierce.)

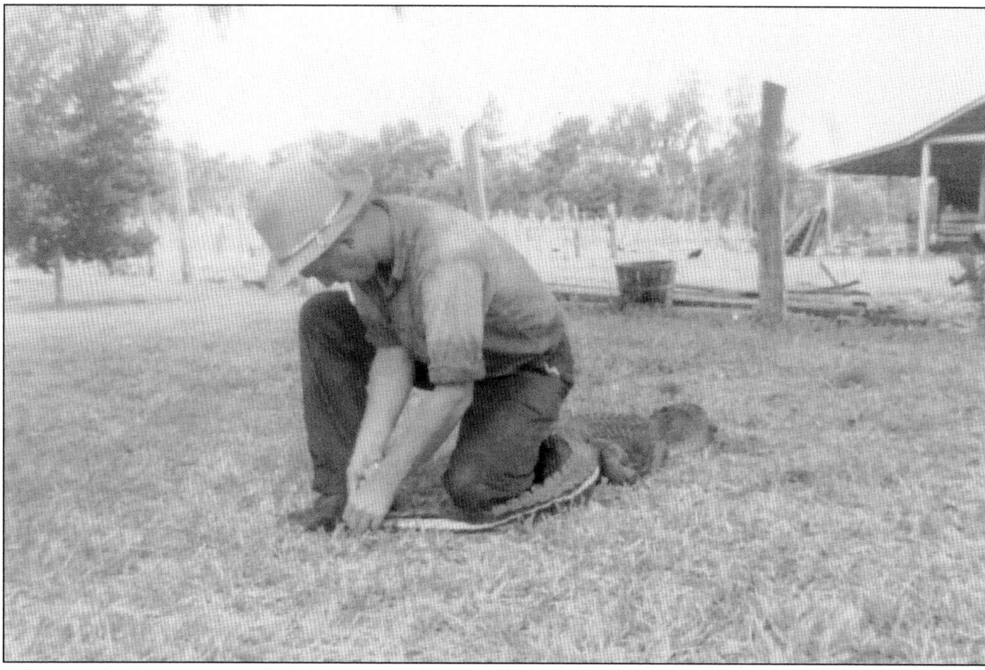

Alligator hides were a valuable commodity and a source of income in Wesley Chapel. On the old Stanley homestead, Roscoe Stanley skins an alligator. A family member reported that hides sold for $30 per foot. (Courtesy of Marco and Roscoe "Rocky" Stanley.)

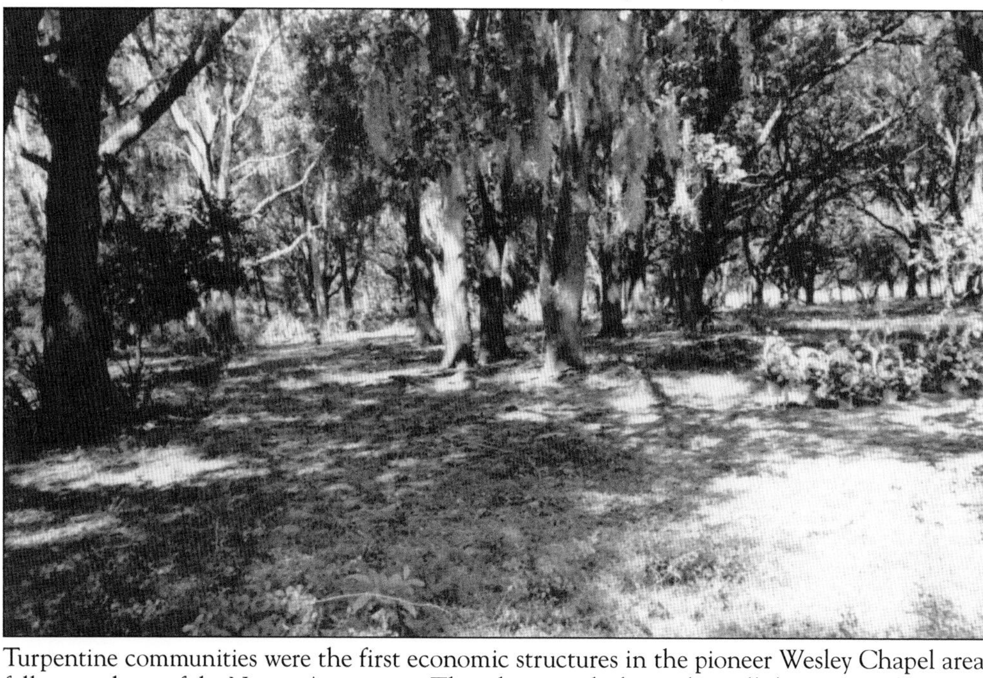

Turpentine communities were the first economic structures in the pioneer Wesley Chapel area, following those of the Native Americans. This photograph shows the well that was in the center of the turpentine community, which occupied an area of the Ruben Barnes Ranch. Remnants of the tram roads can also be found throughout the area and were used for transporting lumber and turpentine. (Courtesy of David L. Brown.)

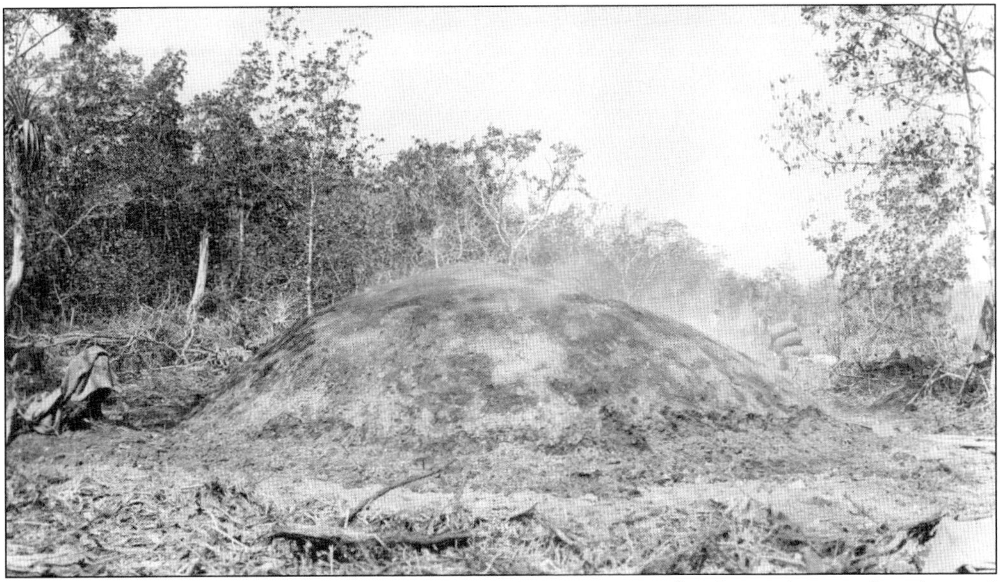

As the Wesley Chapel historical marker reads, "When times were hard, people turned to charcoal making and even moonshining to survive." A charcoal kiln is shown in this 1925 photograph. (Photograph by John Kunkel Small, John K. Small Collection, courtesy of Florida Library & Archives, Florida Department of State.)

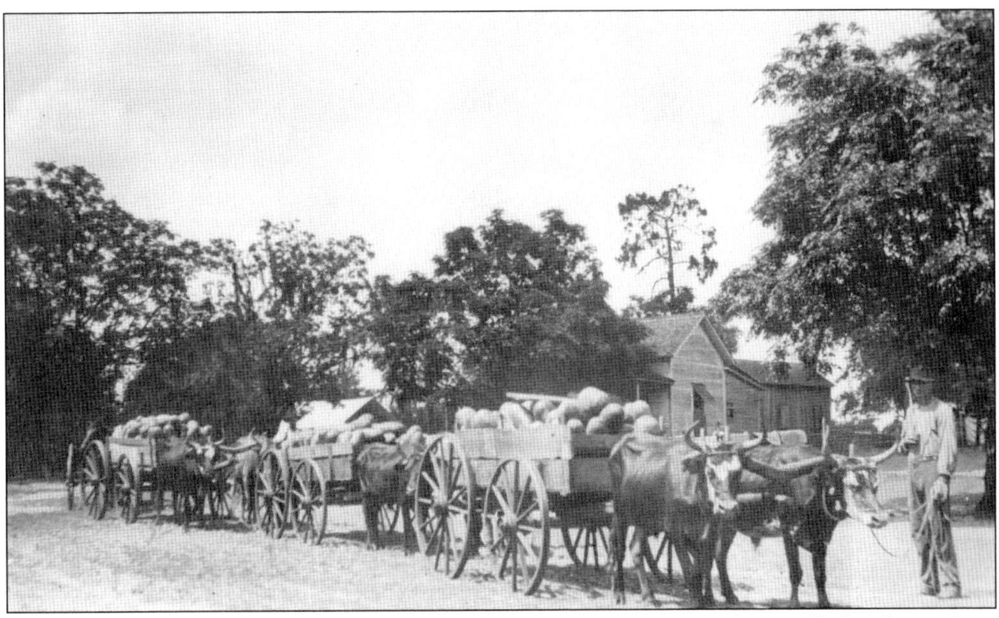

A large load of watermelons is being taken into Zephyrhills. Marco Stanley recalled melon picking many years later in the 1960s: "We would split the middles and load melons and then haul them to the train depot and pack the melons in the boxcars. We used hay on each layer to keep from bruising the melons. We would ship to a buyer in New York City. Dad [Marco Stanley] would get 8¢ a pound," recalled Marco. (Courtesy of Dr. Ronald A. Goerss.)

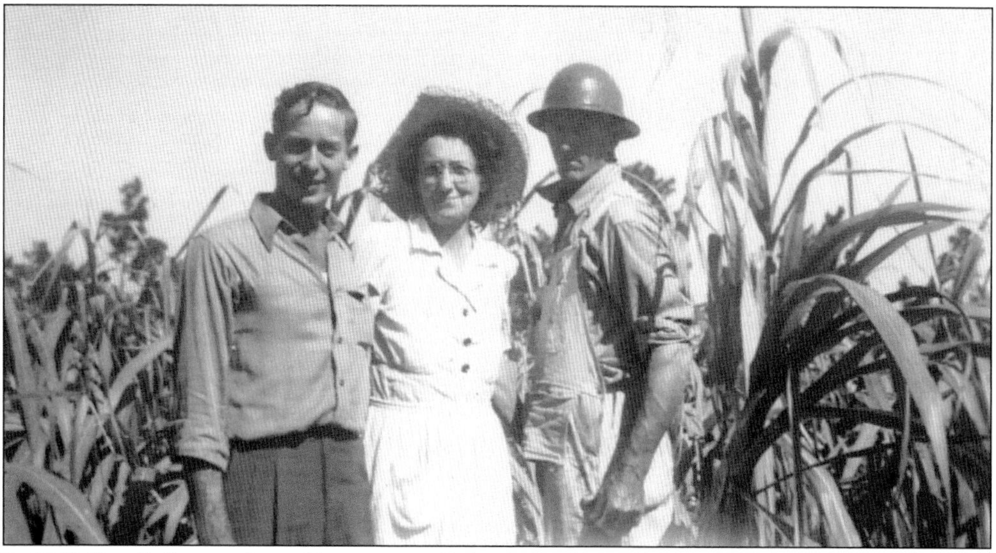

In 1940, Fritz B. Boyette Jr. and his parents, Roberta Gaskins Boyette and Fritz B. Boyette, proudly show off their sugarcane field at the corner of Boyette and Wells Roads. Monroe Boyette said, "I went to lots of cane grindings at Uncle Fritz and Aunt Bertie's and down the road at my grandpa's in the early 1940s." Deborah Boyette added, "Grandma 'Bertie' made my first pork chitlins too." (Courtesy of Deborah Boyette.)

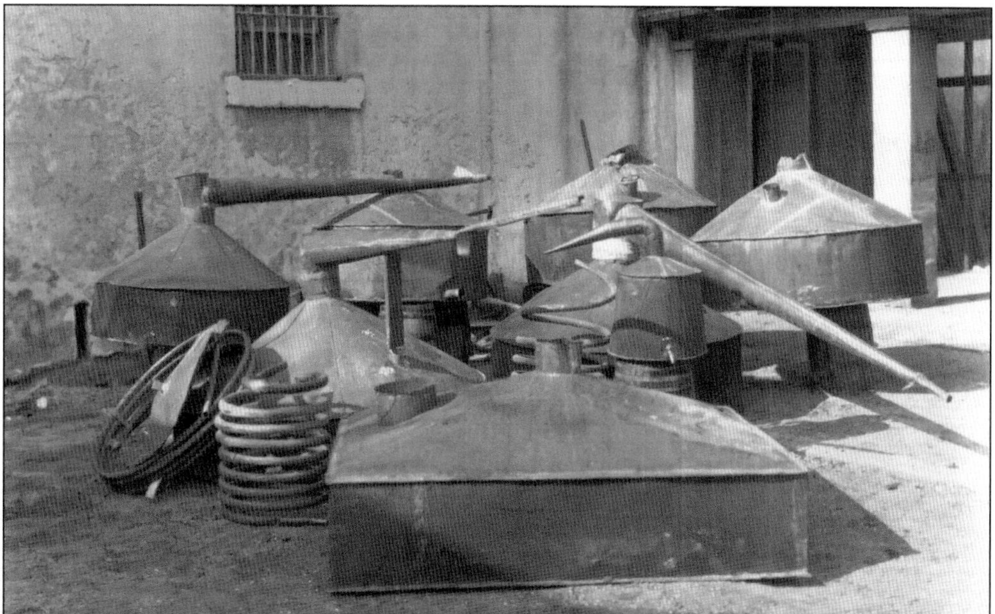

Pictured is moonshine still equipment. On December 18,1926, pistol shots were exchanged in one of the still raids in the Wesley Chapel district just before dawn. Angelo Sangiorgi, 29, was arrested and charged with operation of a 200-gallon copper still, which was seized with 3,500 gallons of mash and 50 gallons of liquor. Two others escaped amid a hail of bullets. There were shots fired in a raid on a 75-gallon still near the J.H. Gillette and Sangiorgi residences, and 10 gallons of moonshine and 2,000 gallons of mash were confiscated. (Photograph by John Gordon, Spottswood Studio, courtesy of Florida Library & Archives, Florida Department of State.)

Around 1931, nineteen-year-old Lonnie Tucker watches for revenuers. He is pictured with his moonshine still in Wesley Chapel. Daughter Anna Jo said the still was located just outside of present-day Saddlebrook. She recalled the surprise 90th birthday celebration for Lonnie. "His elderly pals were the honored guests, and someone smuggled [in] a jug of moonshine, which they exclaimed was 150 proof," laughed Anna Jo. Knowing all of the gentleman were on medication for frailties of advanced age, she gasped at the thought of moonshine, and inquired how they knew that the brew was 150 proof. They replied, "From the frog's eyes [bubbles on top]!" (Courtesy of Anna Jo Bracknell.)

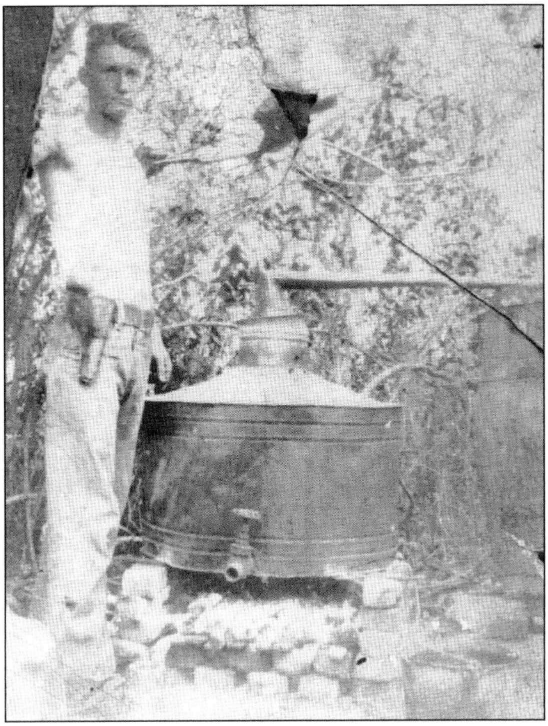

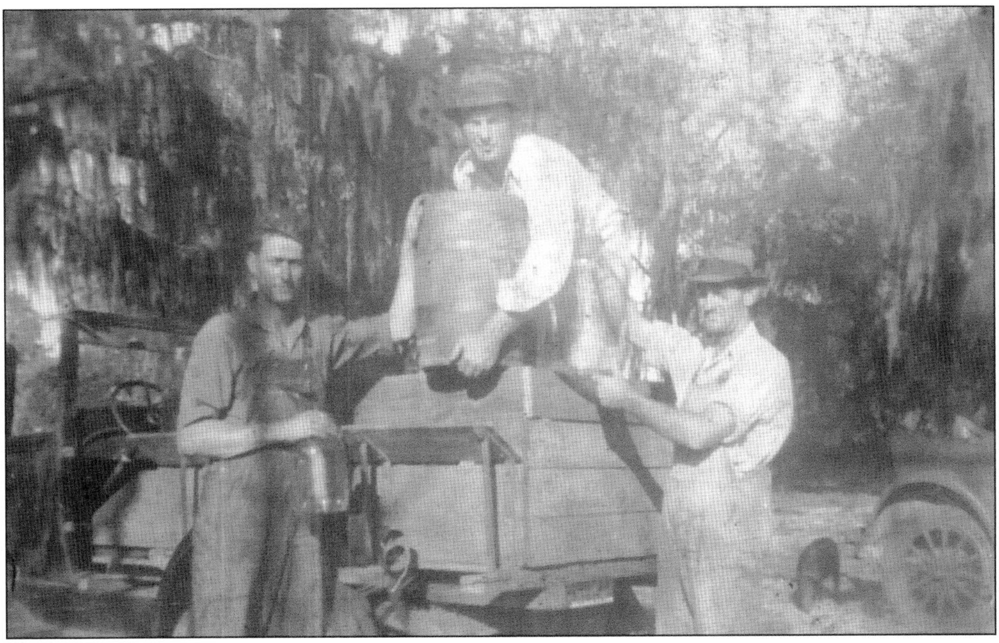

Stanley Ryals (left), Wallace "Willie" Wells (center), and Reuben Wesley Wells were identified by Charles Estepp. Stanley Ryals recalled, "I came up one night through the woods, and there was a revenuer. I just went on home and told my wife, Bernice. . . . We had sugar and whiskey in the house. We didn't sleep that night. About 2:30 a.m., we got up to check on the car again, and it was gone. That next morning, I said, 'I'm quitting,' and we got rid of everything. Well, I might have used the rest of that sugar up, but I was done making whiskey." (Courtesy of Marlo Hilton.)

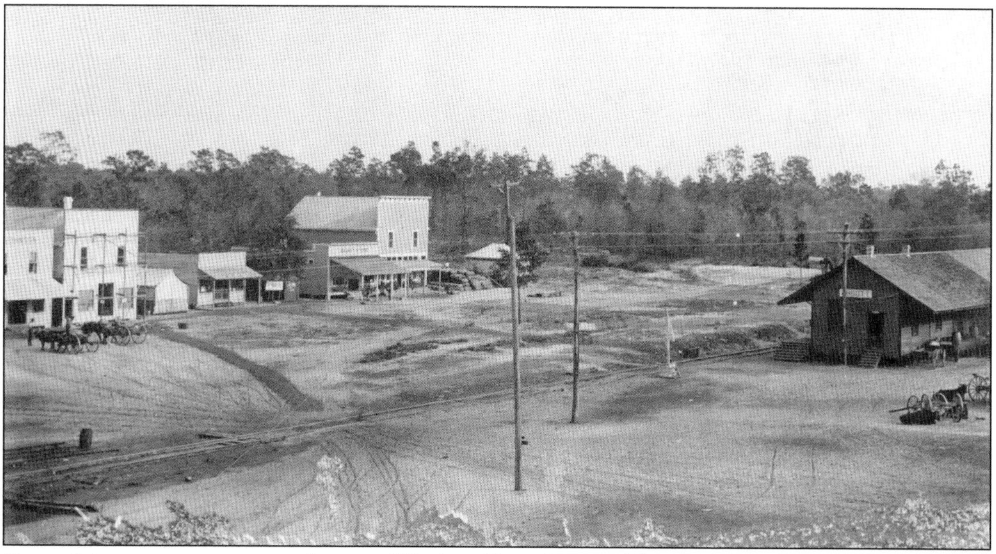

One of the nearest towns to frontier Wesley Chapel was Abbott. It also was a rugged frontier settlement, as shown in this photograph with a view looking south, which was taken on Seventh Street in Abbott. Abbott, also known as Abbott Station, later became Zephyrhills. (Courtesy of Dr. Ronald A. Goerss.)

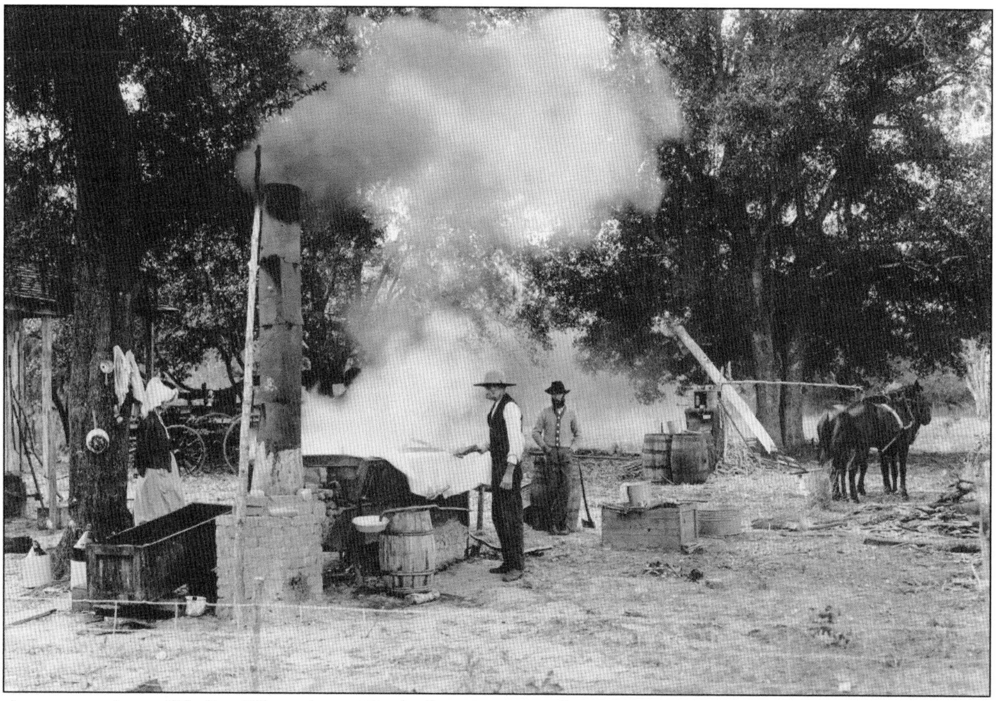

An insert about Wesley Chapel in a *Dade City Banner* of 1919 reported, "Most everybody of Wesley Chapel are grinding cane now. They intend to have something sweet, since we can't get sugar." Cane grinding and boiling were necessary to the economy of Wesley Chapel. This photograph portrays syrup making, with a boiling vat and mule in the background. Sugar syrup sold for $1 a gallon, and 50 gallons of syrup could be traded for a horse. (Photograph by Burgert Brothers Commercial Photography Studio, courtesy of Hillsborough Public Library.)

A car at the base of a cypress log in the 1930s illustrates the enormity of cypress trees in the Wesley Chapel area. Leonard McGuinty is in the center of the vehicle. Former property appraiser Ted Williams explained that large timber companies or trusts acquired vast tracts of land that were depleted of lumber. Many deserted claims after they were used up, and the properties were sold for tax deeds. (Courtesy of Florida Library & Archives, Florida Department of State.)

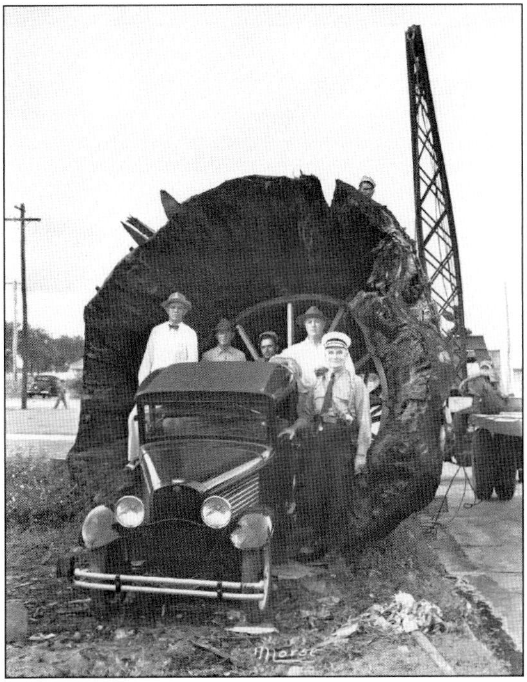

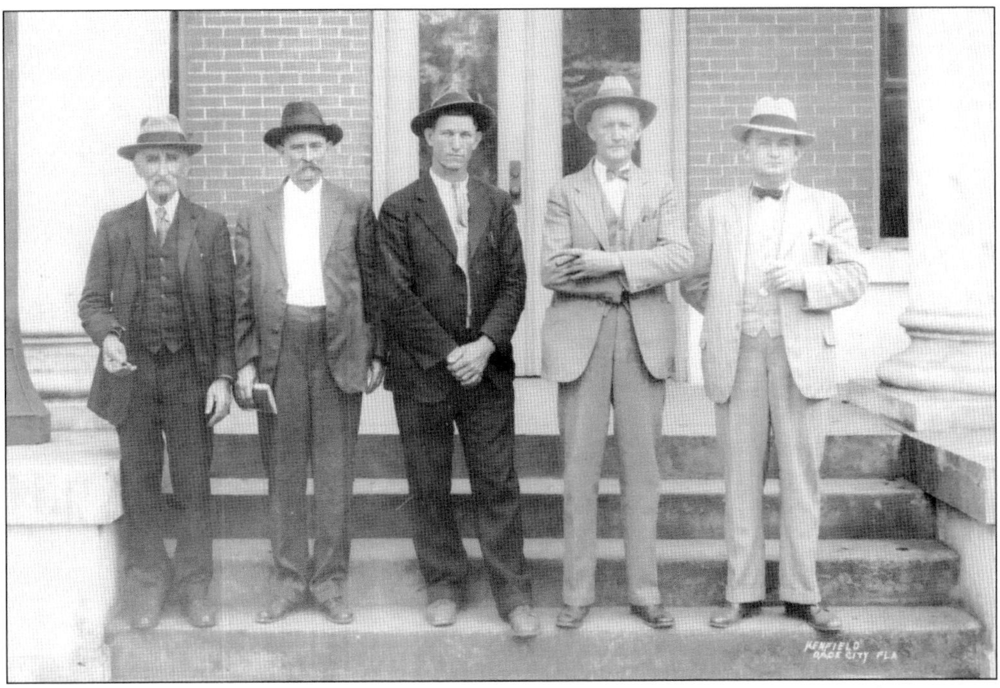

Fritz Boyette was appointed Pasco County commissioner in 1921 by the governor, replacing W.H. Mayo, who resigned. Fritz was a farmer and known for his corn, which was grown with "beggar weed," grass growing between the rows that supplied his livestock with hay. He also grew tomatoes, guavas, and a seedling grove in 1922. The county commissioners in this late-1920s photograph, from left to right, are D.H. McCarthy, Charles E. Dowling, Fritz Boyette, unidentified, and Dr. Bernard A. Thomas. (Courtesy of Helen Eck Sparkman Collection.)

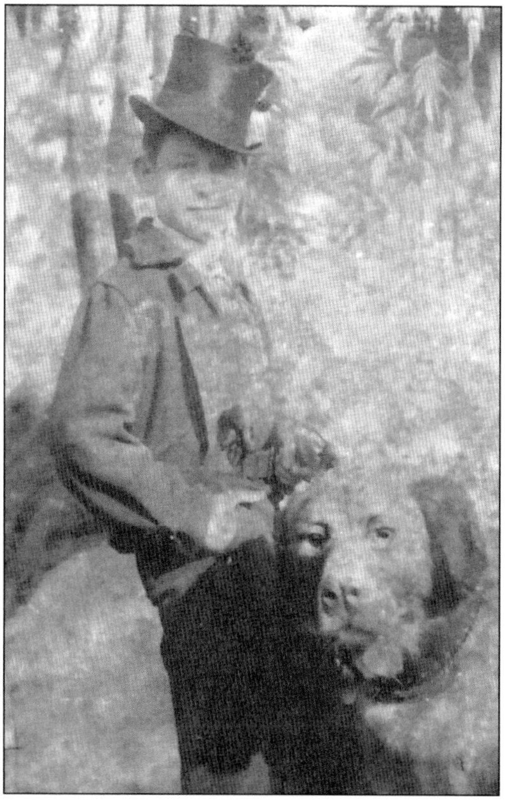

Robert G. "Bobby" Bryant from Wesley Chapel was the former tax collector and county commissioner for Pasco County. In the June 12, 1914, primary election, R.L Bryant was elected to District 1 County Commission. The other commissioners were Allen Bird, John H. Harper, D.H. McCarthy, J.M. Baillie, and E.M. Craig. The *Dade City Star* reported that "the count shows that something like eight hundred votes were cast, in fact nearly every one qualified to cast a vote, did so." Bryant poses here at the Florida State Fair around 1892. This image is an early tin photograph that has darkened with age but was stored meticulously in a family cedar chest so that it maintained visibility. (Courtesy of David L. Brown.)

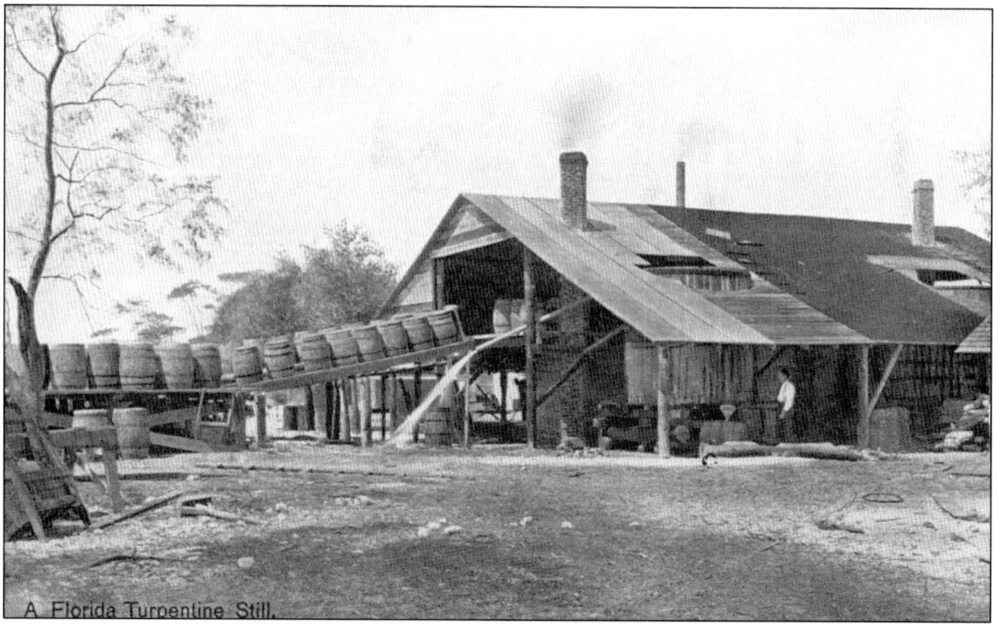

This 1908 photograph shows a turpentine operation. The gum from the trees was put into a boiler vat, where the turpentine could be collected. With the vat at boiling temperature, the turpentine was produced through steam passing through coiled pipes. (Courtesy of Florida State Road Department, Florida Library & Archives, Florida Department of State.)

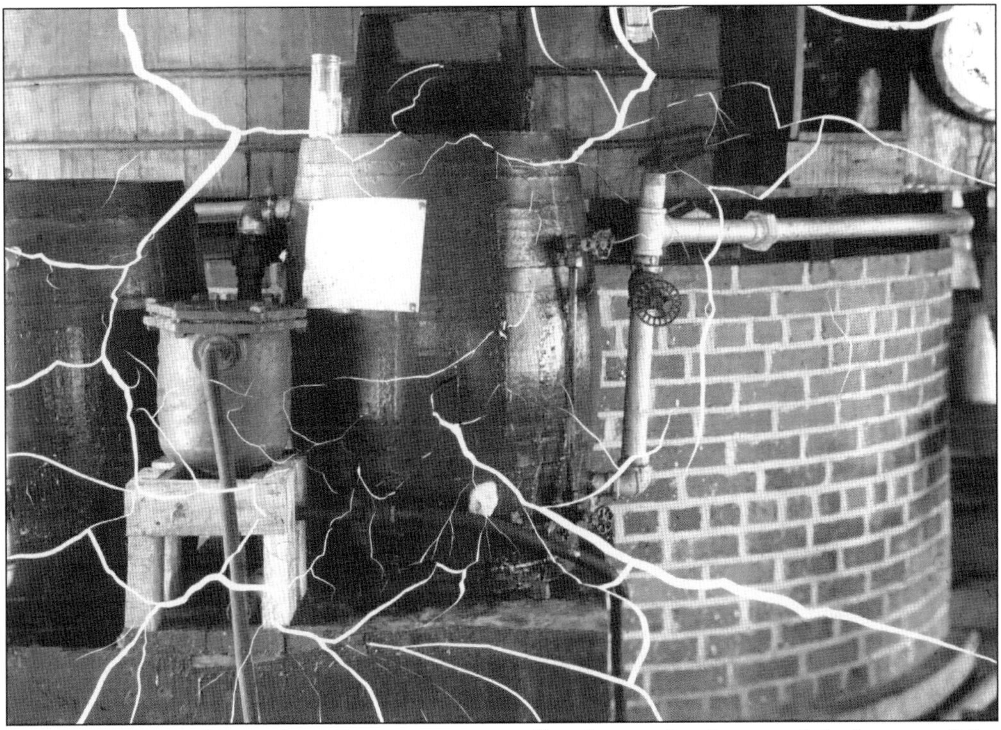

This photograph of an early-1900s turpentining still is from a glass-lantern slide. Lantern slides were used in photography in the 1860s. The Langenheim brothers of Philadelphia produced the photographic slides, which were used in "magic lantern" slide shows by speakers on lecture circuits. The slides were used until the 1930s, when they were replaced by 35-millimeter slides. (Courtesy of Alachua County School System, Florida Library & Archives, Florida Department of State.)

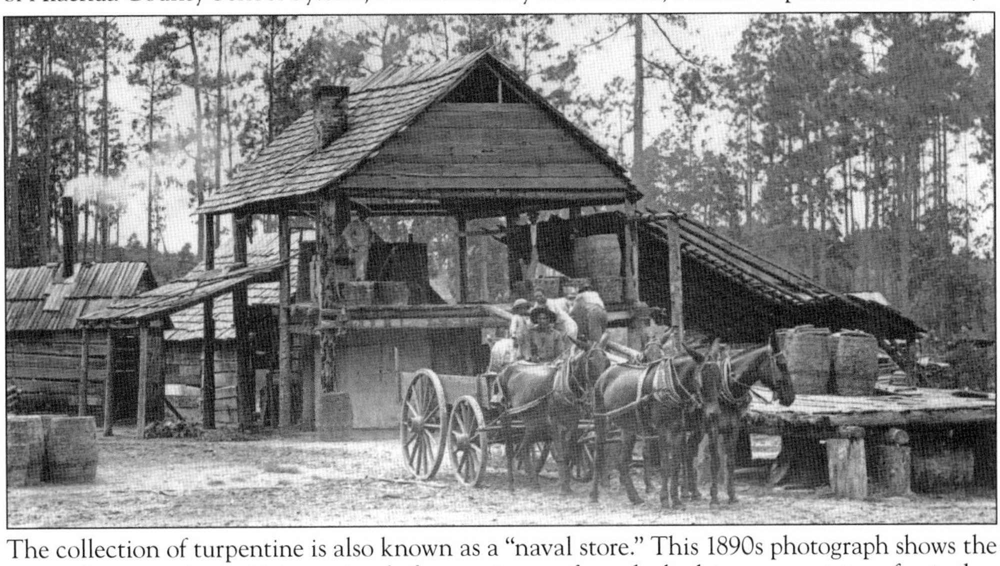

The collection of turpentine is also known as a "naval store." This 1890s photograph shows the turpentine operation, which consisted of extracting sap from the bark in narrow strips a few inches about the ground. Metal or earthenware cups were then placed at the bottom of the cuts so that the gum sap flowed into them. Thousands of trees were tapped in this manner to make the gum crop. (Courtesy of Florida Library & Archives, Florida Department of State.)

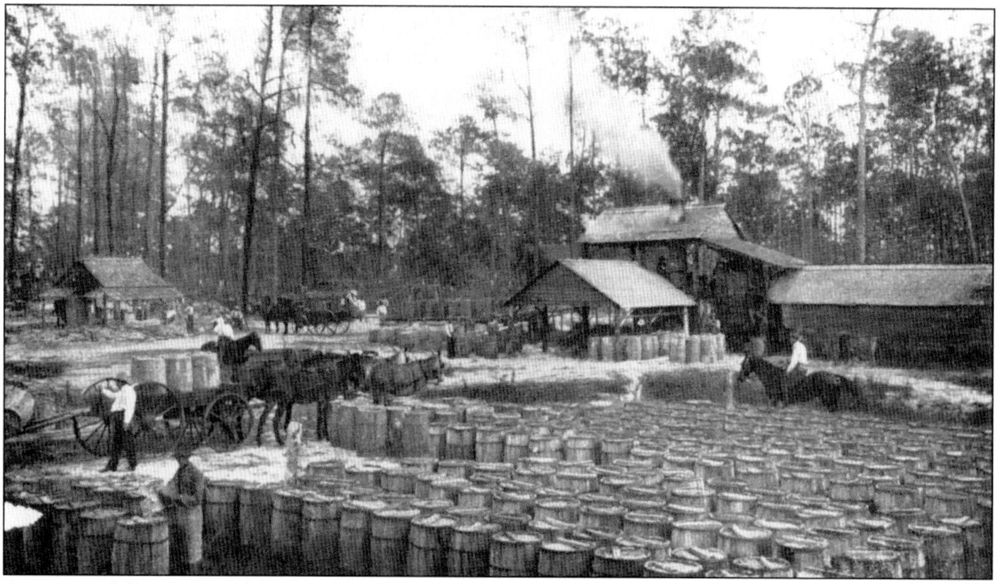

A postcard from 1911 depicts the Florida turpentine industry. Cups were emptied into barrels on wagons and taken to a copper shop at the still, where the barrels were utilized for storing raw gum. (Courtesy of S.H. Kress & Company, Florida Library & Archives, Florida Department of State.)

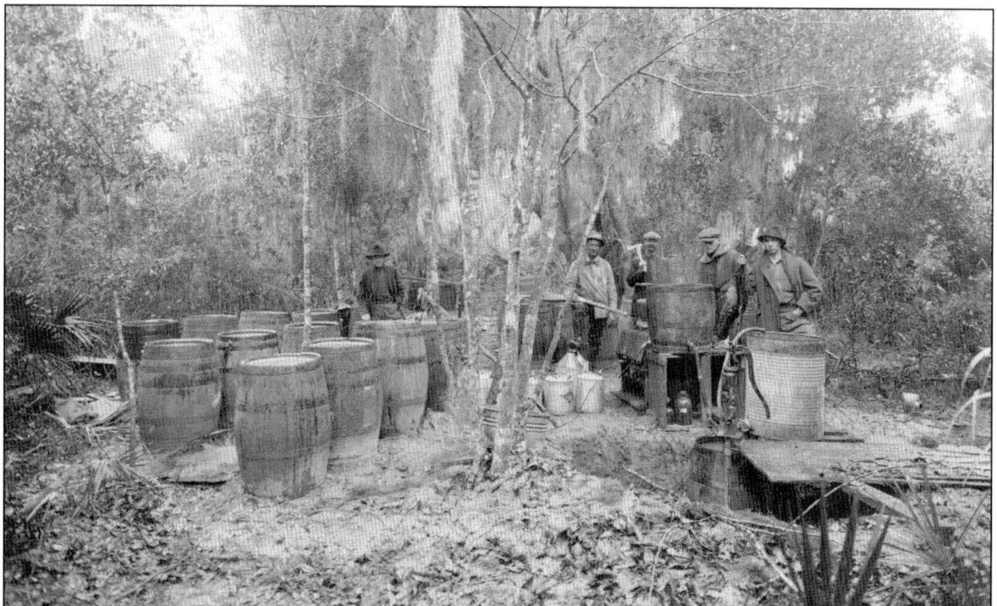

The May 4, 1926, *Dade City Banner* reports that "Deputy Sheriffs Bernard and Leon Hudson, O.H. Samuels and W.P. Burkett brought in a 250-gallon still found in the swamps of Wesley Chapel. They also found 80 gallons of liquor, a 1926 model Ford coupe, a 38-caliber six-inch Smith & Wesson special model revolver, and 43 barrels of mash. The officers watched the moonshiners operating the still but when they made their appearance on the scene the operators dived into the swamp and escaped." This photograph shows moonshine still after a raid. (Courtesy of Burgert Brothers Photographic Collection.)

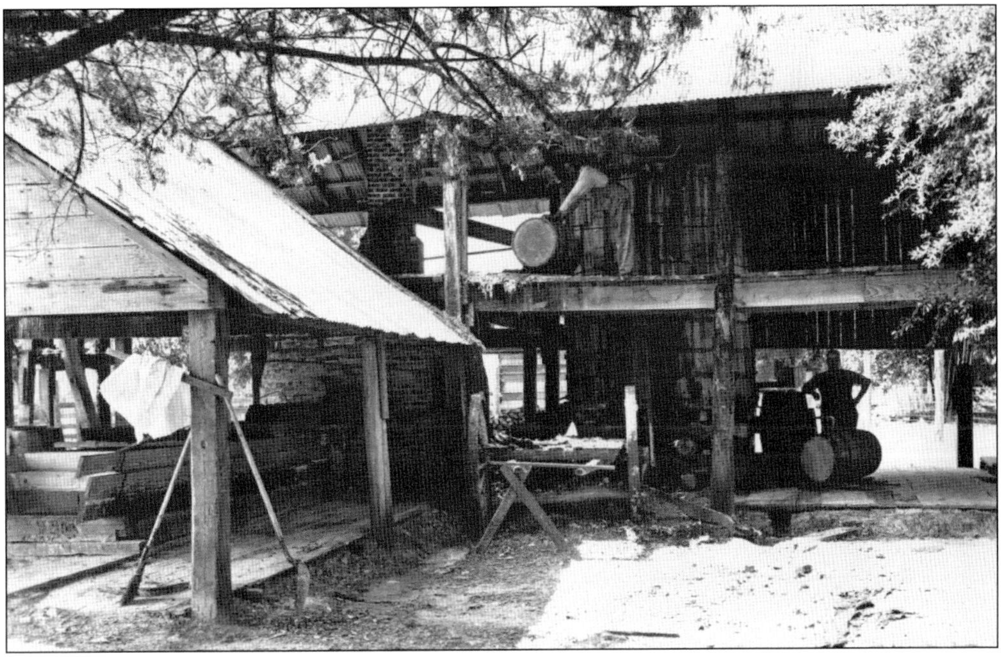

A turpentine community thrived on the area that is now the Brown Family Cemetery. Numerous workers were dependent on turpentine and lived in the area with their own commissary and homes. This photograph was taken around 1938–1939. (Courtesy of Florida Library & Archives, Florida Department of State.)

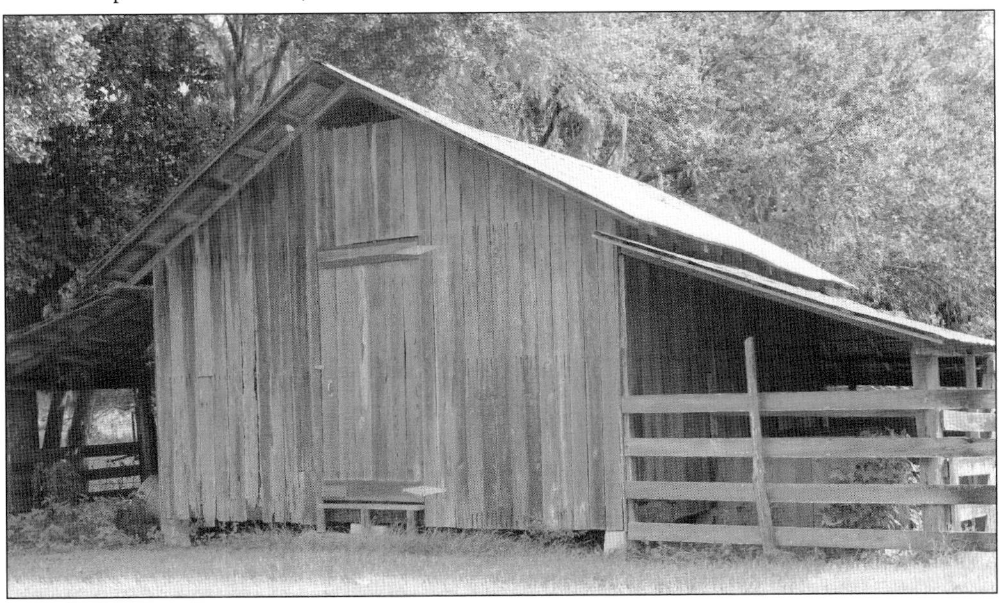

The original home of the turpentine foreman is still standing on the Brown property, which was part of the Ruben Barnes Ranch. According to David L. Brown, the building was constructed by a turpentine company in the mid-to-late-1800s. It was dismantled by Robert DePue in 1939 and moved to its current location about a mile from the original site. The original location of the turpentine community is evident due to the redbrick chimney base still adjacent to the family cemetery. The shared well is also visible. (Courtesy of Ernest Wise.)

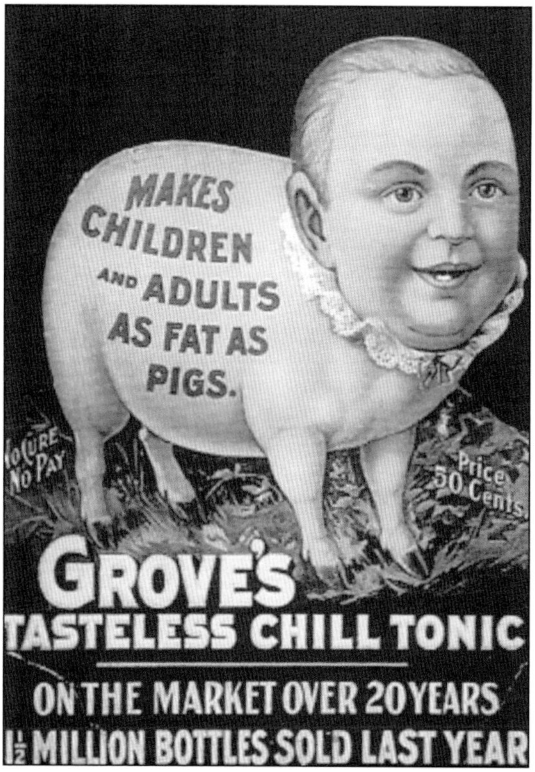

Edwin Wiley Grove, a well-known medicine man of St. Louis, purchased several thousand acres of farmland in 1921 in Wesley Chapel and intended to develop it. Grove was a self-made millionaire, most famous for his Grove's Tasteless Chill Tonic. It was a quinine mixture that he developed in 1878 that eliminated the bitter taste used to treat malaria. Some sources claim that by 1890, more bottles of Grove's Tasteless Chill Tonic were sold than bottles of Coca-Cola. (Author's collection.)

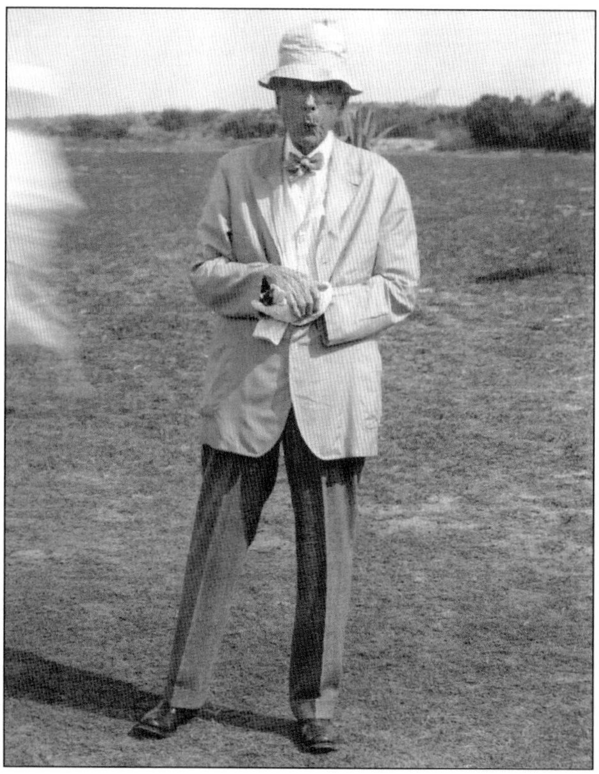

Pictured on one of his trips to Florida, John D. Rockefeller acquired timberland in the 1920s known as the Lumber Trust, which comprised thousands of acres encompassing Wesley Chapel. It was later acquired by James Barney Porter. (Courtesy of Florida State Road Department, Florida Library & Archives, Florida Department of State.)

Five

INSTITUTIONS

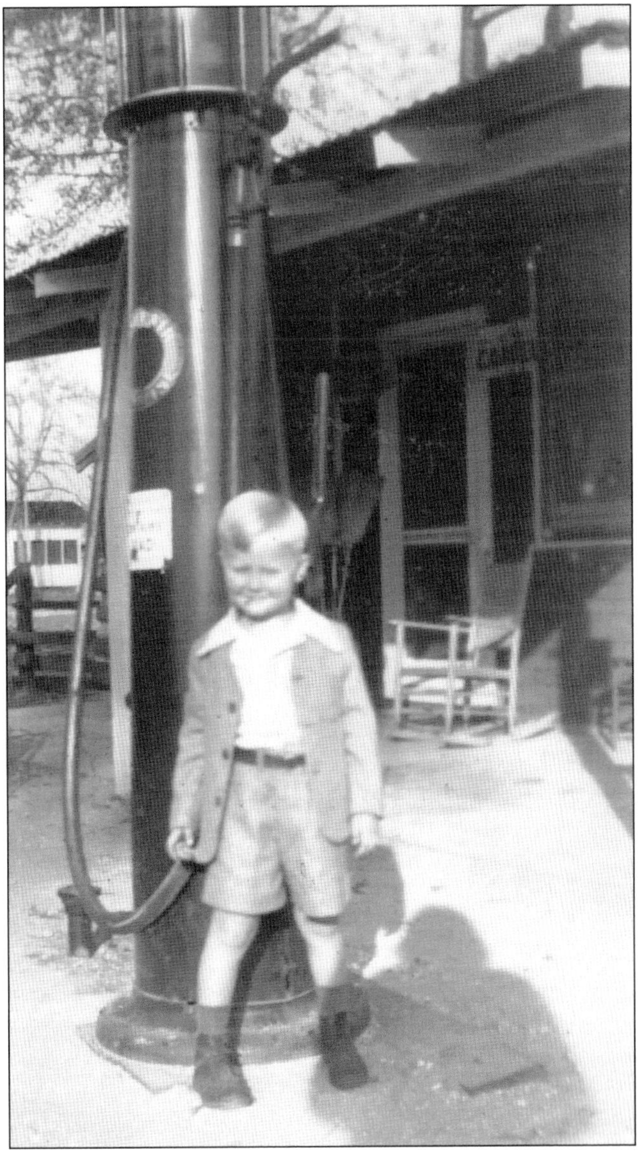

A 1946 photograph of the first Wells General Store at the corner of Boyette Road and Highway 54 shows Bobby Wells, son of Delbert and Ella Mae Wells, in front of the family store. Cullen Boyette said of the store, "It had a little bit of everything. He had a meat case and some dry goods and some cold drinks. He also had some staples . . . some nails, a few rolls of fencing, . . . a little bit of chain, things you needed every day. I reckon that's why they called it a general store." (Courtesy of Sue Boyette.)

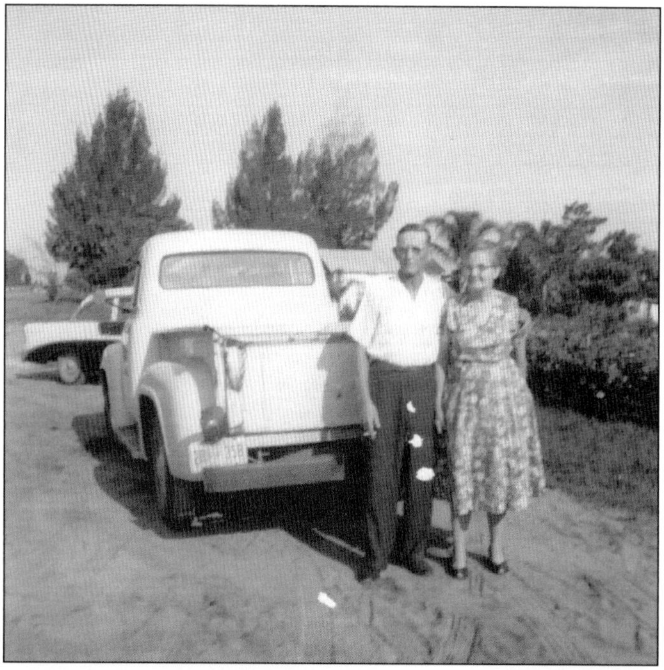

Ella Mae Wells and Delbert Lewis Wells pose by their pickup truck. Delbert owned the Wells General Store across from the church in Wesley Chapel. The general store was a small shop for congregating and buying goods, with a gas pump out front. (Courtesy of Sue Boyette.)

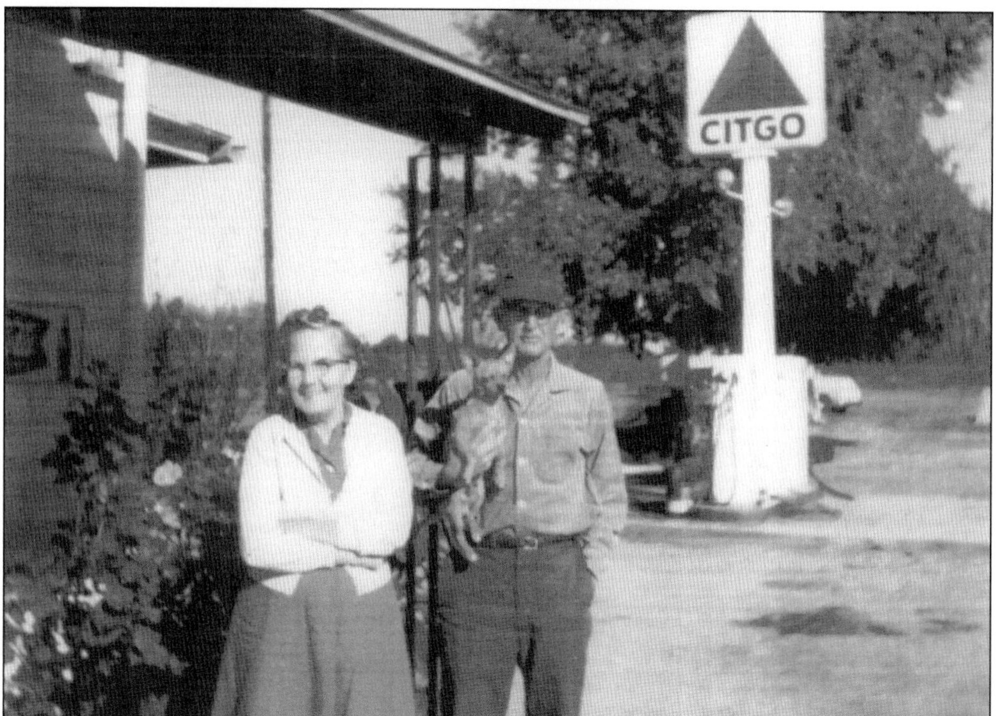

The Wells General Store (later simply Wells Store) had a dry-ice station and kerosene pump. Earlier, the community's general store was the Stanley General Store, operated by Jesse Stanley. David L. Brown said of the store, "It did not have a cash register, but simply a drawer in the counter that kept the money. There were no windows or doors in the store, only shutters. Cypress poles held up the structure, and chicken coop lights hung from the rafters." (Courtesy of Cletia Pierce.)

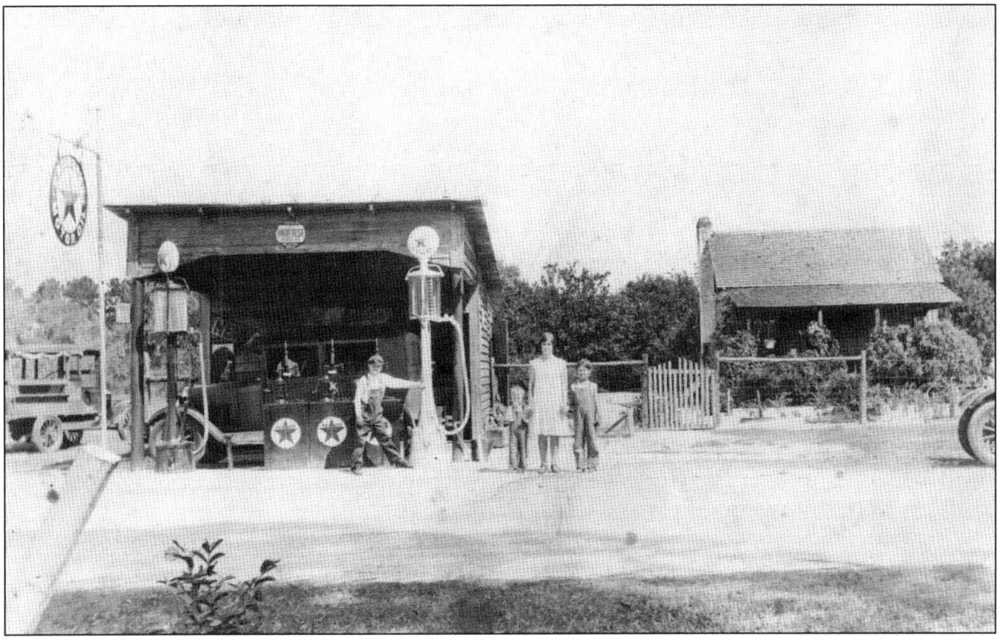

The original Hill Grocery & Gas was located at the northeast corner of Highway 54 and Eiland Boulevard, with the residence in the back. In this photograph taken around 1928 is the family of James Henry Hill—from left to right, Vernon T., James Monroe, Ida Geiger Hill, and Elsie Jeanette Hill. The store was operated by James Henry and his wife, Ida, and later operated by their son, James Monroe Hill, and his wife, Georgia Thompson Hill. The store served the community for over 60 years. Kruth Sombutmai purchased the store in 1990, when Hill retired, and referred to store management as "his American dream." The store was closed in 2007. (Photograph by 5th Avenue Photography, courtesy of Shirley Hill Sheppard.)

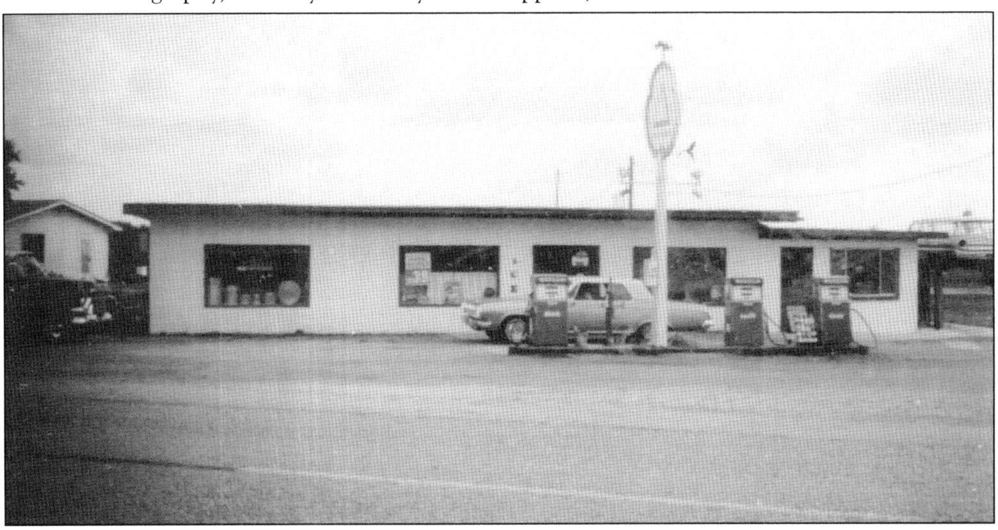

Hill Grocery & Gas was relocated across the street from the original store around 1937 at the southeast corner of Highway 54 and Morris Bridge Road. In this photograph are a car lift (to the right), gas pumps, and signs posted in the window for bargains on grocery items. Shirley Hill Sheppard and Eddie Lee Hill remember working at their parents' store as children. (Courtesy of Eddie Lee Hill.)

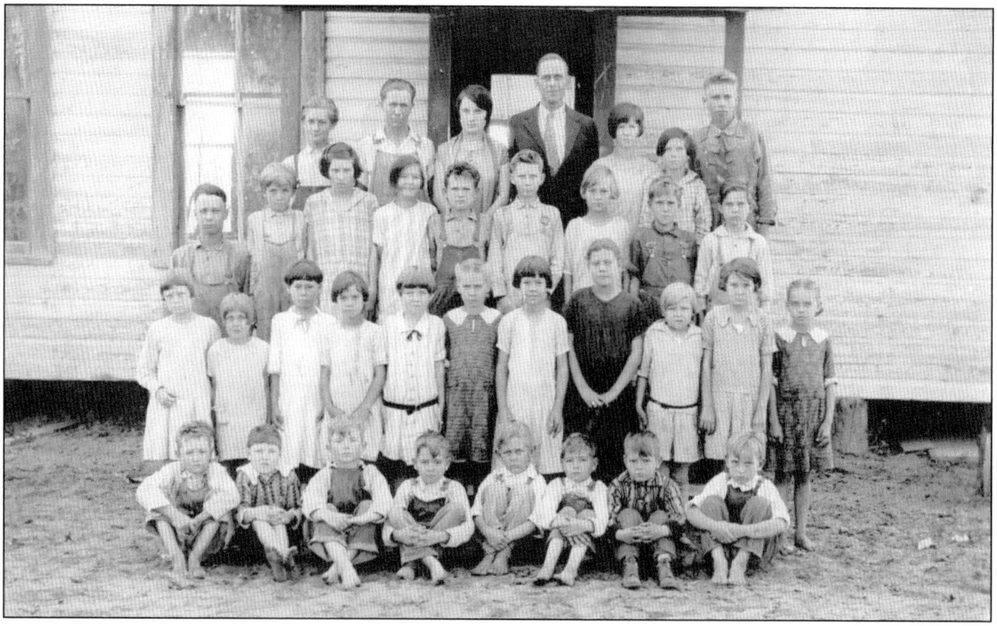

Two teachers and 33 students are in this photograph taken around 1922 or 1923 at Wesley Chapel School. From left to right are (first row) Archie Tucker, unidentified, Roscoe Stanley, Woodrow "Woody" Cooper, Clyde "Ted" Boyette, Pasco Cooper, Woodrow Strickland, and Albert Wells; (second row) unidentified, R.V. Cooper, unidentified, R.V. Thomas, Thelma Stanley, Estelle Godwin, Evelyn Thomas, Ronnie Thomas, Clemmie Cason, Juanita Wells, and Hazel Godwin; (third row) Baskum Thomas, Edward Thomas, Doris Boyette, Dona Cooper, Thomas "Tom" Boyette, Millard Wells, Hazel Boyette, Clyde Cooper, and Earl Boyette; (fourth row) William "Will" Tucker, Virgie Boyette, Georgia Wells (teacher), M.E. Lefler (teacher), Lena Mae Wells, Marie Boyette, and Austin Godwin. (Courtesy of Wayne Sweat.)

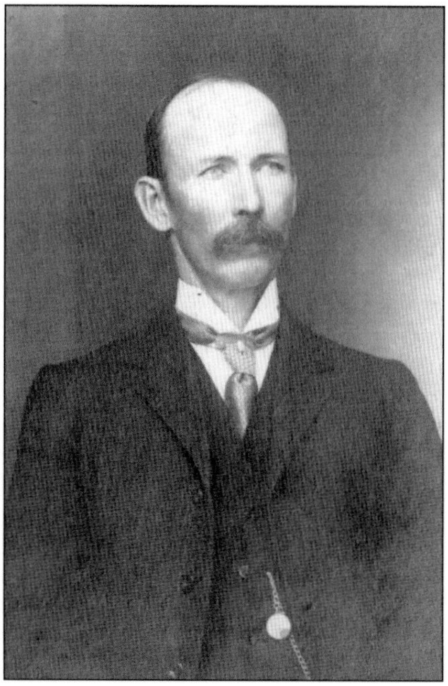

Another official from Wesley Chapel was John Barnes, originally a teacher in Tampa. He was the brother of Francis Asbury Barnes and uncle of Ruben Barnes. John was superintendent of public instruction for Pasco County in the early 1900s. He was born on June 30, 1864, to pioneer Methodist minister James F. Barnes and Sarah E. Barnes. John died in 1947. (Courtesy of David L. Brown.)

Isabel Barnes was the final teacher at the Wesley Chapel School's two-room building before it was closed due to consolidation. Other teachers fondly remembered were Georgia Wells, Annabelle Frierson, and Doc Cripe. Cletia Pierce described Barnes, her fourth grade teacher, as incredibly warm and compassionate. Mary Depue Nutt lovingly remembered riding with Barnes, her step-grandmother, each day to attend school. (Courtesy of Elisabeth Strickland.)

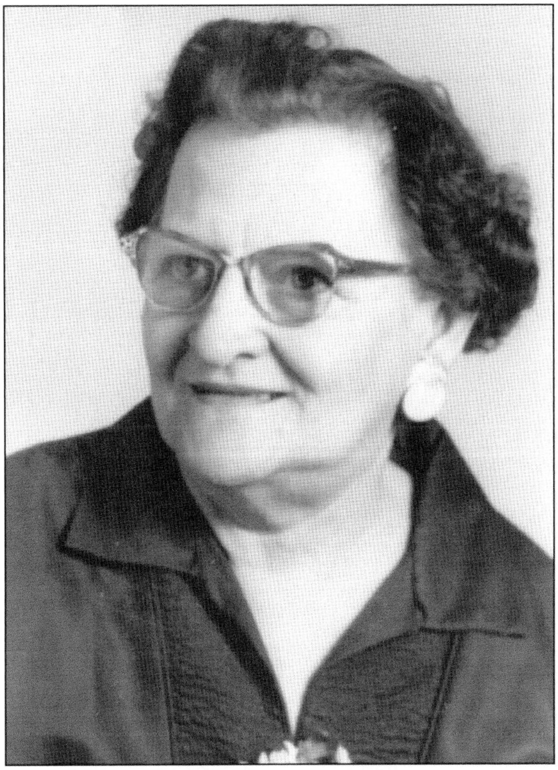

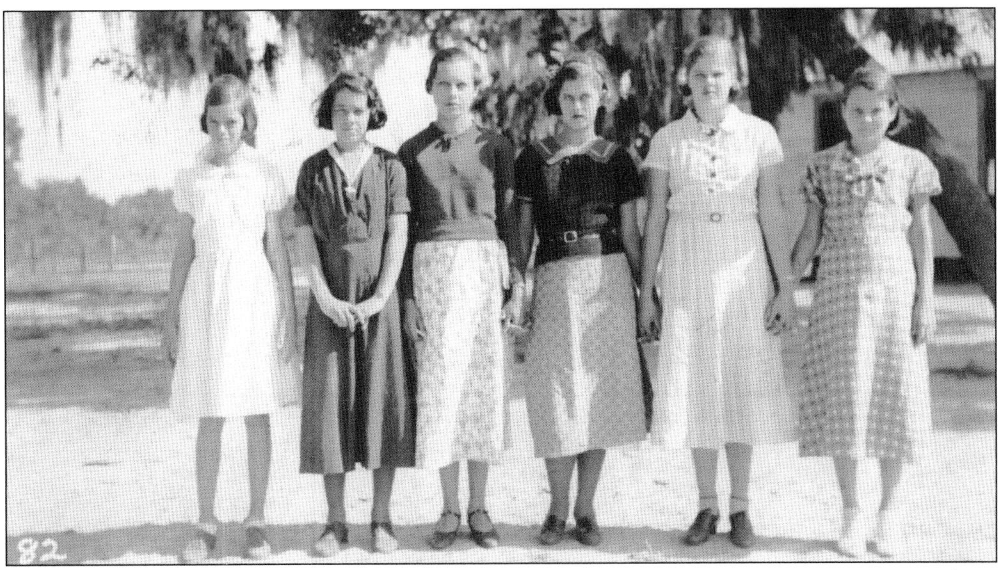

Wesley Chapel School seventh and eighth graders are pictured in the mid-1930s. They are, from left to right, Ruth Smith, Wyona McCloskey, Hazel Godwin, Ruby Tucker, Vida Barnes, and Marie Childers. The school was a two-room configuration with a lower and upper room for first through eighth grades. It was located to the east of the Double Branch Church. Luther Smith wrote, "The school was at the corner of my daddy's land. A little old box, one-room schoolhouse. That was in 1906, the year I was six years old. The teacher was Nancy Mobley from Dade City." (Courtesy of David L. Brown and Ruth Smith Adams.)

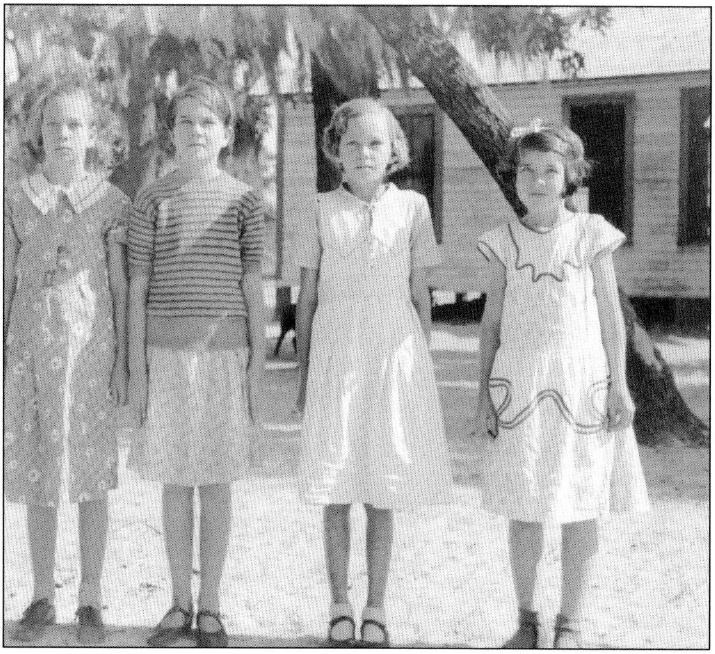

The log cabin one-room school was utilized by the early pioneers, while later generations attended the two-room school, with one room for primary classes and the other for intermediate classes. Pioneers wrote of the little persimmon switch that hung near the teacher's desk in the era of corporal punishment. Pictured are elementary classmates of Martha Barnes. (Courtesy of David L. Brown.)

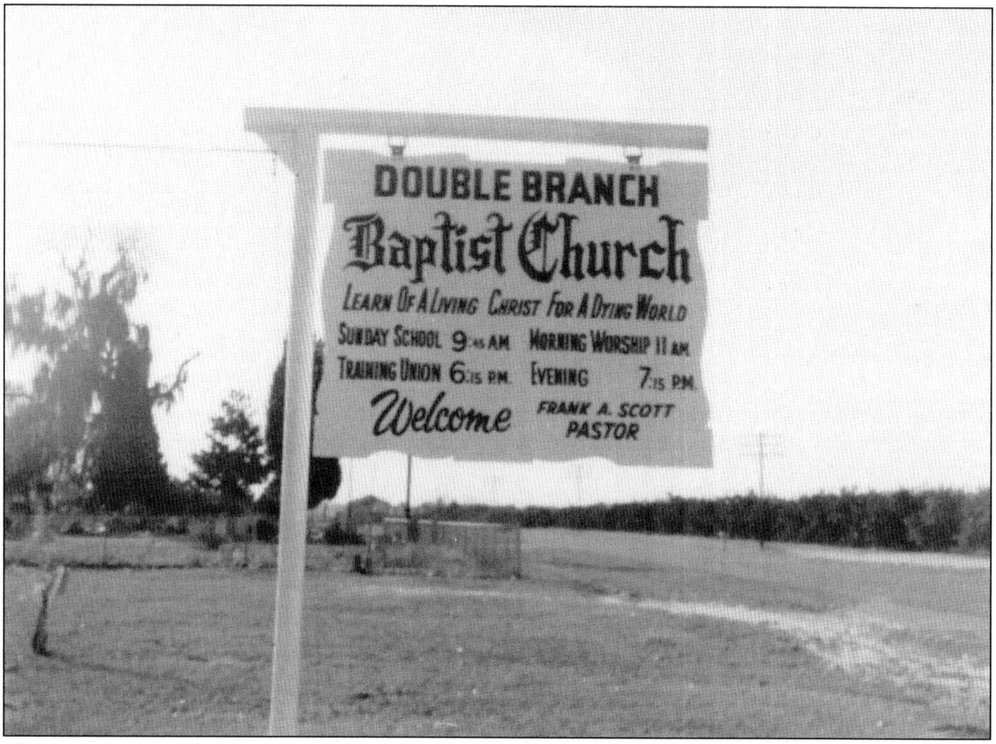

The sign for Double Branch Baptist Church is clearly displayed, prior to its renaming in 2000. The Double Branch Baptist Church was named for two landmark branches of water converging on the property by Boyette Road and dates to 1880. In the 1940s, the church hosted the Pasco County Singing Convention, which drew large crowds for the singing celebrations. The church continues in operation as First Baptist Church of Wesley Chapel. (Courtesy of Sue Boyette.)

Baptizing was a ritual at the Double Branch Baptist Church and was often done at King Lake, a popular fishing location, and Clearwater Pond on Wiregrass Ranch. Bill T. Brown and David W. Gaskin are being baptized at King Lake on March 23, 1952, by pastor C.R. Swartz Jr. (Courtesy of Sue Boyette.)

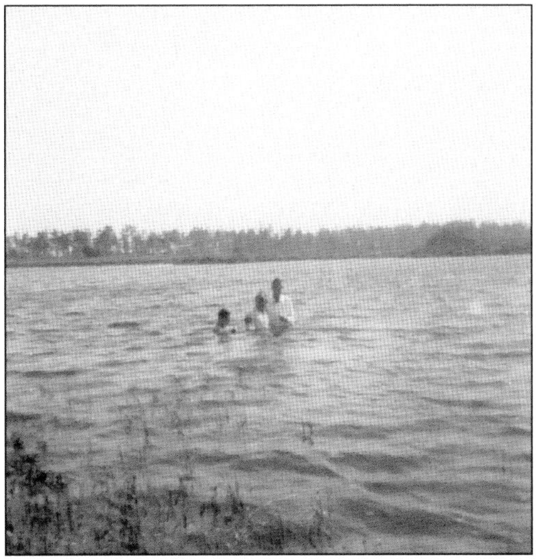

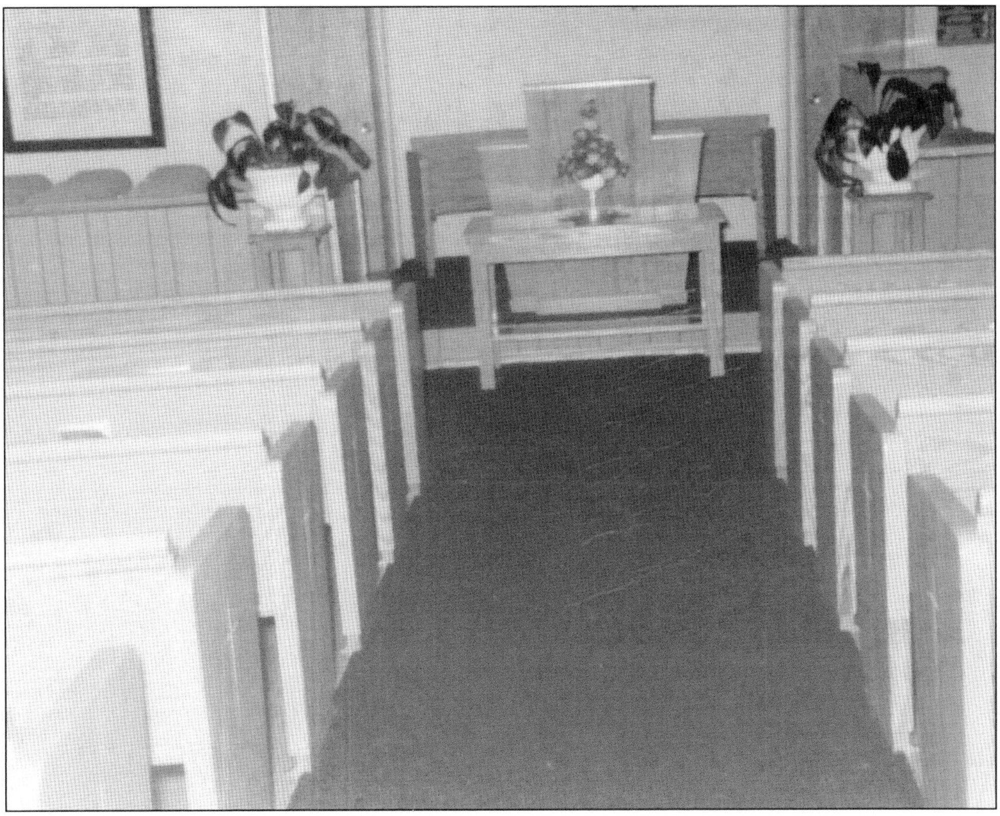

The Double Branch interior is depicted in this 1966 photograph. Before Pasco County was established, Wesley Chapel was part of Hernando County, and a covenant was issued in June 1878 by Hernando County. Although some of the document is illegible, portions of it state, "The church at Double Branch having been regular baptized . . . do agree and covenant together to try as best we can to keep the house for God by coming together in church capacity to watch over each other for good . . . to administer wholesome discipline for . . . disorderly members and that we will endeavor to sustain an Evangelical minister." (Courtesy of Sue Boyette.)

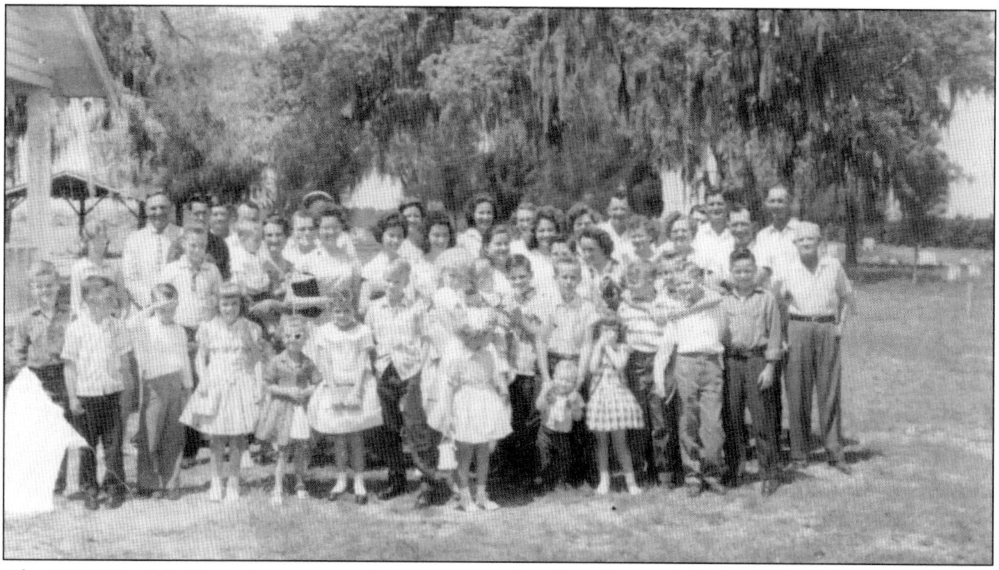

The 1960 Double Branch congregation poses on the church grounds. From left to right are (first row) unidentified, Randy Gillette, Doy Smith, Marlene Goodwin, Sandy Philmon, Sabra Cooper, Charlie Hill, Linda Ellerbe (holding unidentified), Sue Boyette, Billy Hill, Boone Goodwin, Tommy Philmon (little boy in front of Boone), Bertha Goodwin, James Tucker, Leonard Goodwin, Acie Ellerbe, and unidentified; (second row) Vonceil Smith, unidentified, Selma Gillette (with baby), Mamie McKendree, Joann Gillette, Linda Gillette, Elizabeth Gillette, Ruth Tucker, unidentified, Evelyn Goodwin, Genevieve Smith, Gwen Ellerbe, Earl Goodwin, and Hardy Cooper; (third row) two unidentified, Wilbur Tucker, Ed Goodwin, Joyce Boyette (with hat), unidentified, Violet Hill, Colene Philmon, Fern Goodwin Wells (in front of Colene), unidentified, Willie Smith, unidentified, Clarence Ellerbe, and Cleo Boyette. (Courtesy of Sue Boyette.)

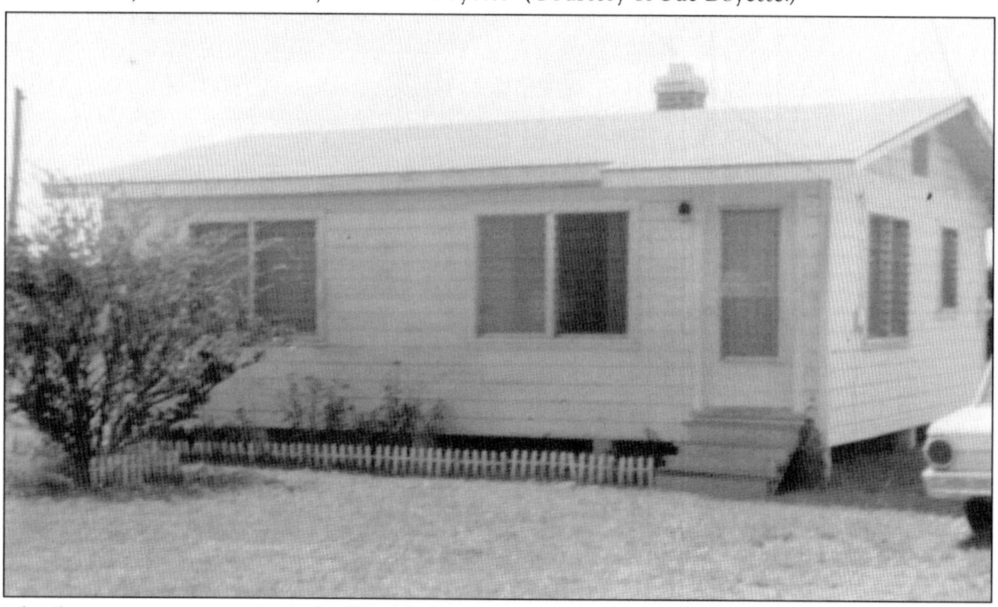

The first parsonage was built for Double Branch Baptist Church in 1960, and this photograph was taken in 1966. The parsonage was situated where the Wesley Chapel School was previously located. (Courtesy of Sue Boyette.)

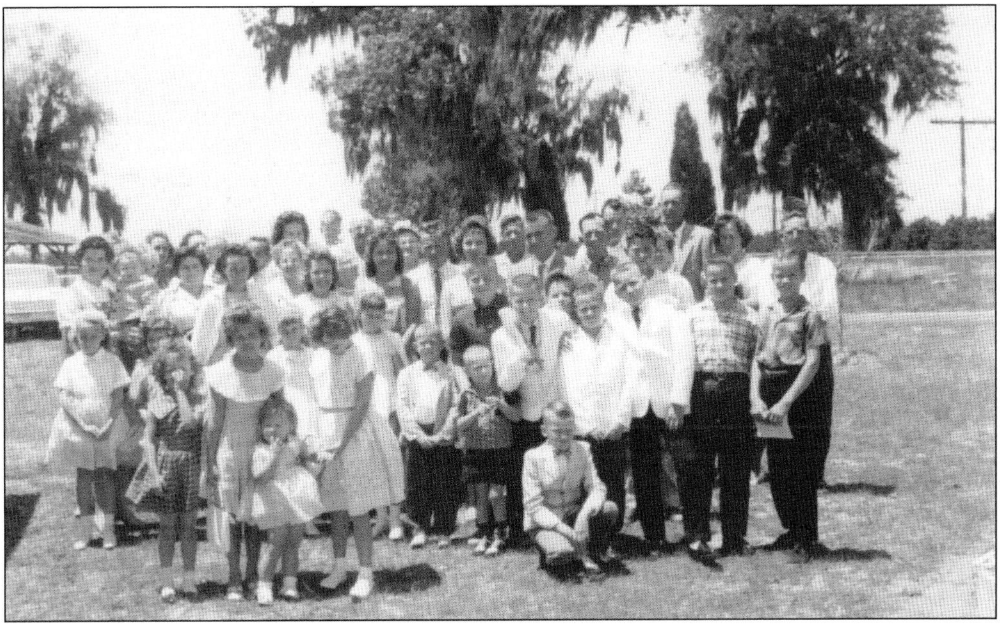

The Double Branch congregation is pictured in 1962. From left to right are (first row) Sandy Philmon, Sabra Cooper, Vicky Goodwin, Marlene Goodwin, and Doy Smith; (second row) Sue Boyette, Bertha Goodwin, Beverly Boyette, Barbara Boyette, Virgil Boyette (boy with bow tie), Harvey Boyette, Acie Ellerbe, Billy Hill, Cliff Cooper, Calvin Boyette, unidentified, and Charlie Hill; (third row) Evelyn Gaskin, unidentified, Ruth Tucker, Evelyn Gaskin, unidentified, Fern Wells, and James Tucker; (fourth row) Colene Philmon, two unidentified, Leonard Goodwin, Violet Hill (with Ella Mae Wells in front of her), Edward Hill, two unidentified, Robert Wells, Linda Goodwin, Wilbur Tucker, Ed Goodwin, Earl Goodwin, Willie Smith, unidentified, Genevieve Smith, Cleo Boyette, Esther Boyette, and Delbert Wells. Mary Jane Godwin deeded land in 1890 on the day she finished her homesteading qualifying period. (Courtesy of Sue Boyette.)

Pastor C.R. Swartz Jr. started his career at Double Branch Baptist Church in 1952. Church member Roy Burnside remembered that a few parishioners had a routine of opening one of the windows before the service so that they could spit out the window. Burnside also recalled that two young boys decided to play a trick on some churchgoers. The boys nailed the window shut so that when the parishioner tried to raise it, it would not budge. "He was not too happy about that," said Burnside. (Courtesy of Sue Boyette.)

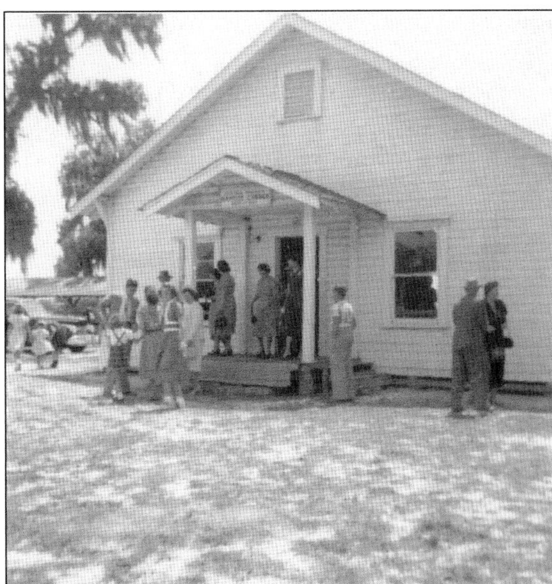

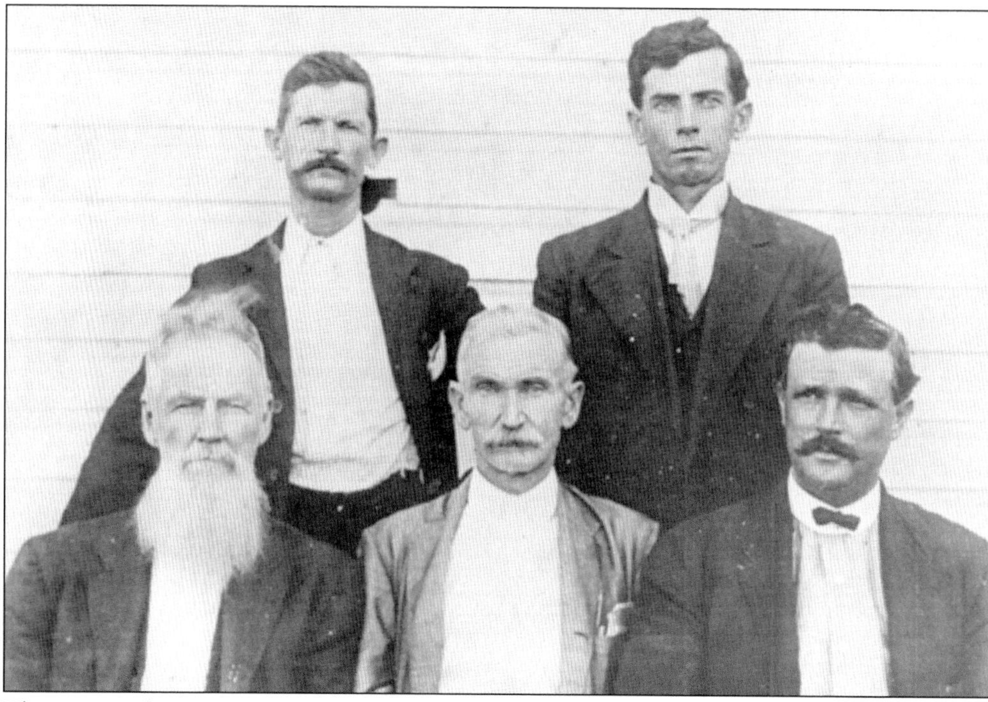

The circuit-riding minister at Double Branch, James Irvin Spivey was also a member of the Pasco County Commission from 1909 to 1920. He was known as Gen. John B. "Gordon's Bull" in the 26th Georgia Infantry during the Civil War. A $1,000 reward was posted for his capture because of his piercing vocals while bellowing commands such as "charge" to the troops. His legendary voice was said to be heard from up to a mile away. James was at Appomattox with Gen. Robert E. Lee at the surrender and later moved to Florida in 1875. From left to right are (first row) Spivey, John Thomas, and H.A. Brown; (second row) A.G. Schiselbauer and Elias W. Gillette. (Courtesy of Jeff Miller.)

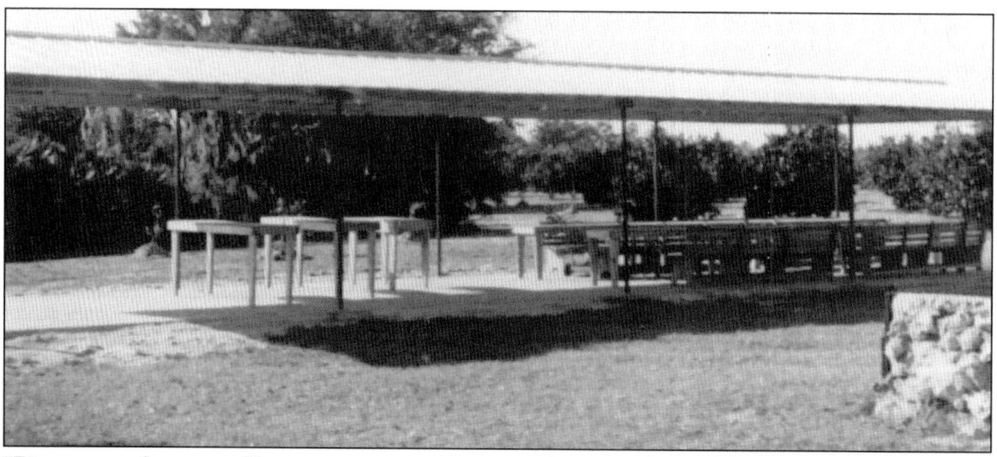

"Dinner on the ground" was a pioneer expression for spreading a blanket and feasting on a carry-in dinner (noon meal) with family and friends. It was a tradition after the Wesley Chapel singing convention. In contemporary Wesley Chapel, a covered picnic area with tables replaces the blankets. In 1919, the *Dade City Banner* reported, "Everybody seemed to enjoy the sing all day Sunday. Everyone spread dinner on the ground. There was plenty of dinner and plenty of nice singing." (Courtesy of Sue Boyette.)

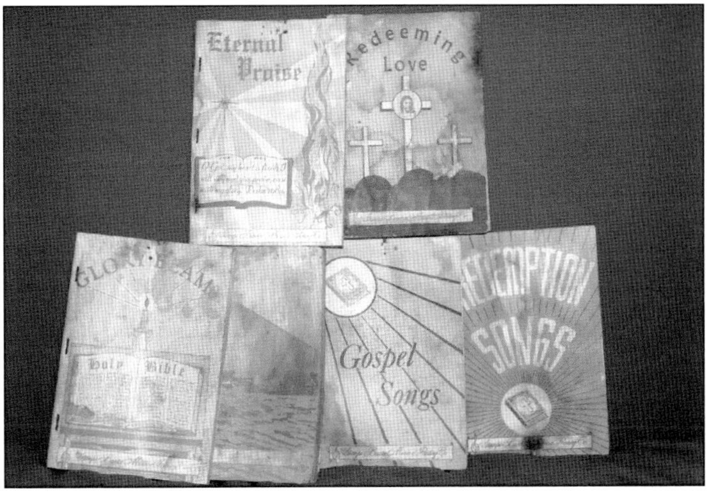

Shape note songbooks were printed by Stamps-Baxter Music & Printing Company, which originated in 1926. The singing convention was promoted by the publishers of these songbooks. According to Bill Smith, the singing convention was the Grand Ole Opry of Wesley Chapel. These books were owned by Luther Smith. (Courtesy of Bill Smith.)

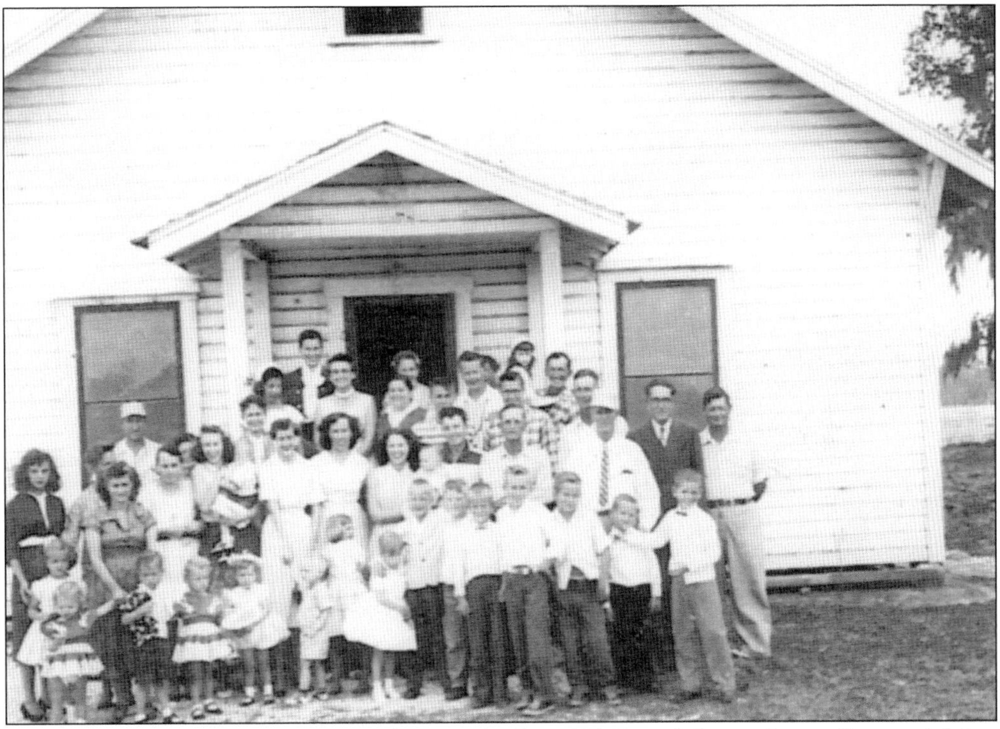

The Double Branch congregation is photographed in 1959. From left to right are (first row) Sabra Cooper, five unidentified, Sue Boyette, Calvin Boyette, James Tucker, Charlie Hill, Leonard Goodwin, Boone Goodwin, Cliff Cooper, and Billy Hill; (second row) Pamela Yates, Linda Cooper, unidentified, Evelyn Goodwin, Colene Philmon, Tommy Philmon, Joyce Boyette, Esther Boyette, unidentified, Anita Reid, Carletta Reid, Jimmy Reid, Delbert Wells, Fernie Cooper, Hank Smith, and Wilbur Tucker; (third row) Oliver Strickland, two unidentified, Fern Goodwin, Ed Goodwin, unidentified, and Cleo Boyette; (fourth row) unidentified, Orine Cooper, Ruth Tucker, unidentified, Robert Wells, and Earl Goodwin; (fifth row) Violet Hill, Ella Mae Wells, unidentified, and Bertha Goodwin. If someone did not show up for church, pioneers would check to make sure the family was well. (Courtesy of Sue Boyette.)

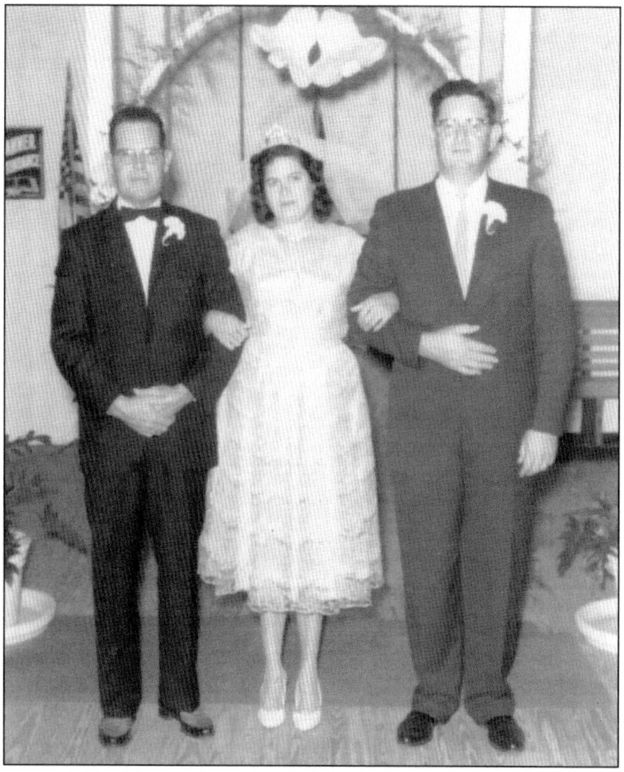

From left to right, clergyman Robert Weaver, Nannie Mae Weaver Wells Tucker, and Dick Tucker pose at West Side Baptist Church (now North Bridge Baptist Church) on the latter two's wedding day. Tucker, a war hero and prisoner of war, attended a celebration hosted for him in November 1953, upon his homecoming. The *Zephyrhills News* reported, "The young soldier, reared in Wesley Chapel, enlisted in the Army in January 1945 and reenlisted in 1949. After several overseas assignments, he was taken prisoner in Korea in 1950, and was a POW for nearly three years. The young soldier, smartly dressed in his Army uniform, proudly wore the Bronze Star and Purple Heart." (Courtesy of Anna Jo Bracknell.)

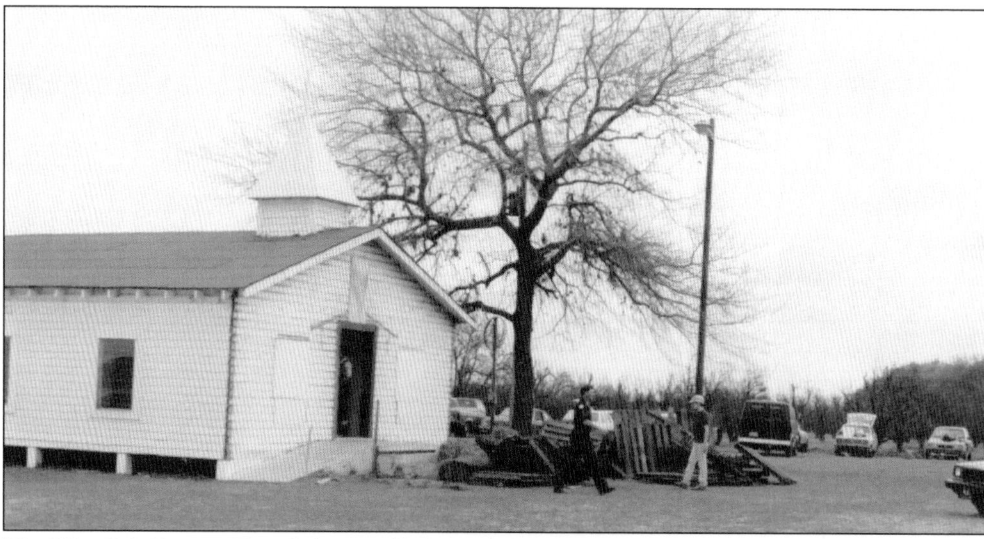

The West Side Baptist Church (originally Six Mile Pond Baptist Church) was built on land donated by Floyd Kersey's family. The Kerseys, Ellerbes, Wells, Smiths, Stanleys, Hales, Weavers, Chanceys, and Pringles were a few early families. The original building was wood-framed with outhouses. The Sunday school rooms were in the main auditorium, which was divided by curtains, and the offering plates were made from pine needles that Lenora Robinson Weaver braided together. There was no air-conditioning at the time—just open windows—and eventually, when a church could afford them, oscillating fans. For funerals, card-stock fans were distributed. (Courtesy of Steve Searles.)

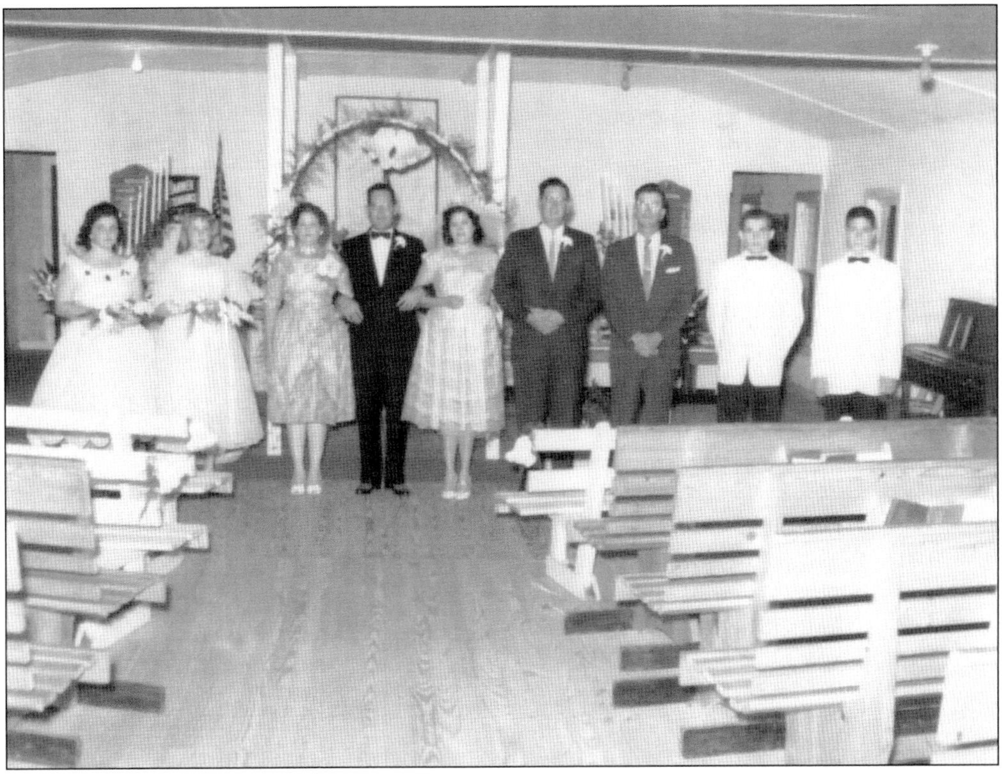

The wedding party at Westside Baptist Church in November 1960 includes, from left to right, Anna Jo Davis, Ruby Hale, Hazel Stanley, clergyman Robert Weaver, Nannie Mae Tucker, Dick Tucker, William Smith, Norman Weaver, and Junior Wells. (Courtesy of Anna Jo Bracknell.)

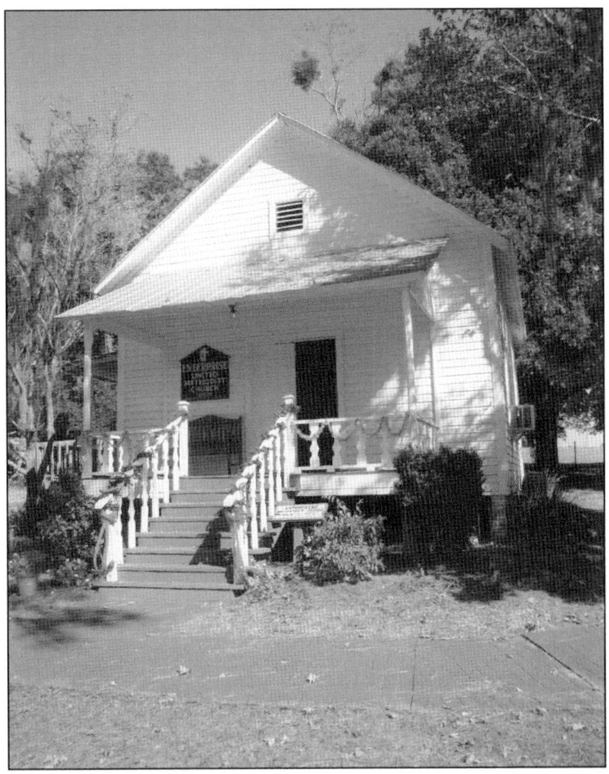

With a heritage of religious leadership, Francis Asbury Barnes helped build the Enterprise Church, which was later moved to the Florida Pioneer Museum and Village as an exhibit. Francis settled in Wesley Chapel with his family in 1879. His father, James Franklin Barnes, migrated to Florida in 1852 and was the founding minister of the Enterprise Methodist congregation. When the Civil War broke out, he left and started the congregation that became Mount Zion. (Courtesy of Jeff Miller.)

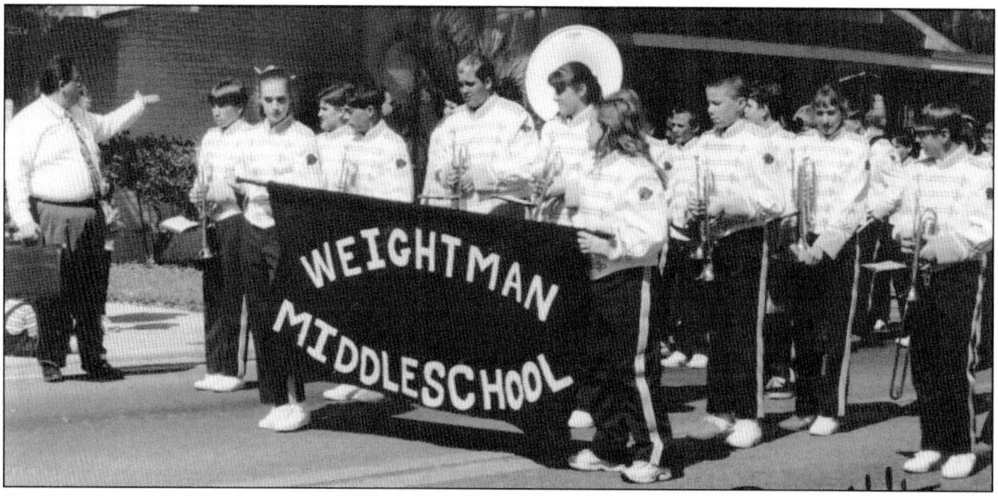

Opened in 1991, Weightman Middle School had the distinction of being the first professional development school in partnership with the University of South Florida. The school was named for Supt. Thomas E. Weightman. The Weightman Middle School marching band is pictured in the February 16, 1999, Pasco County Fair parade. (Photograph by Janelle Maffett, courtesy of Pasco County Fair Office.)

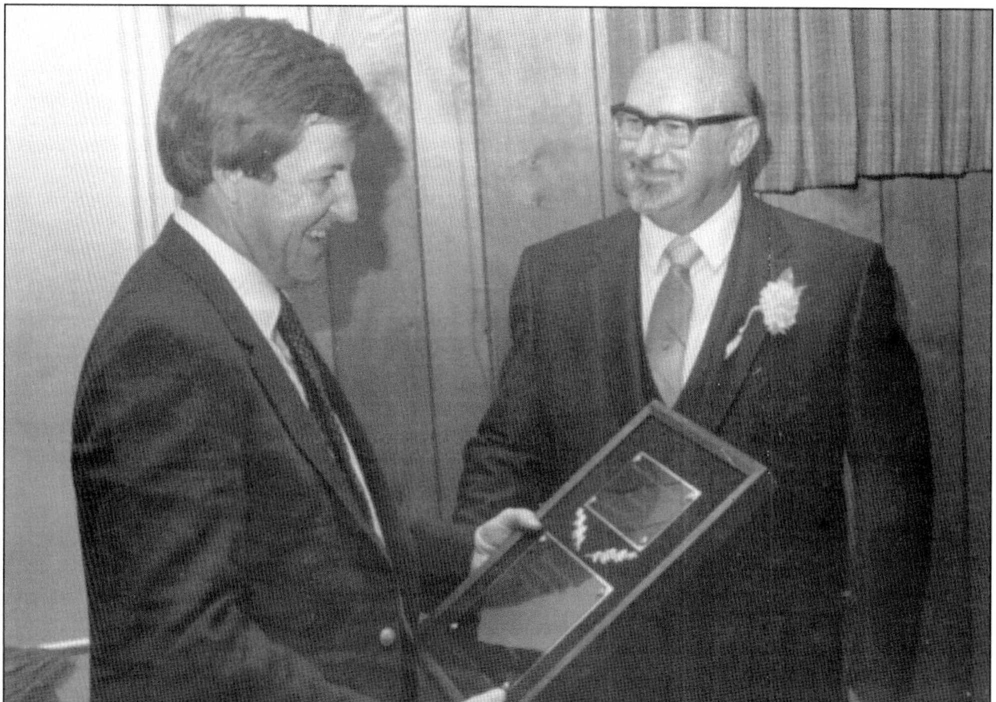

Thomas Weightman (left) is the namesake for Weightman Middle School in Wesley Chapel. He is pictured in 1985 with chamber of commerce director Earl Meyer. "Tom Weightman, serving Pasco students as a teacher, coach, dean, assistant principal, principal and assistant superintendent, was the Pasco County Schools superintendent from 1974 through 1996. In those 22 years, the Pasco County School District grew from a sleepy rural district to a suburban, progressive one that led the state of Florida," said Dr. Mary Giella. (Courtesy of *Sun Coast News*.)

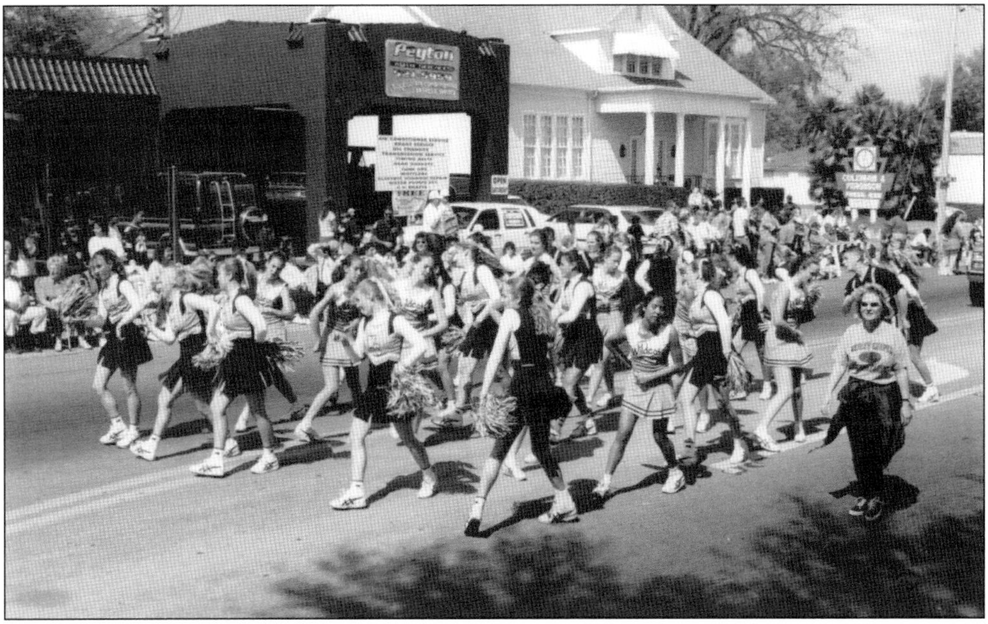

Wesley Chapel High School opened in 1999 as the first high school in the area. It featured the Center for the Arts at Wesley Chapel, which included a stage, sound booth, and state-of-the-art equipment that was readily used for recitals, plays, community celebrations, and public presentations. This photograph depicts the Wesley Chapel High School marching band participating in a Pasco County Fair parade. (Courtesy of Pasco County Fair Office.)

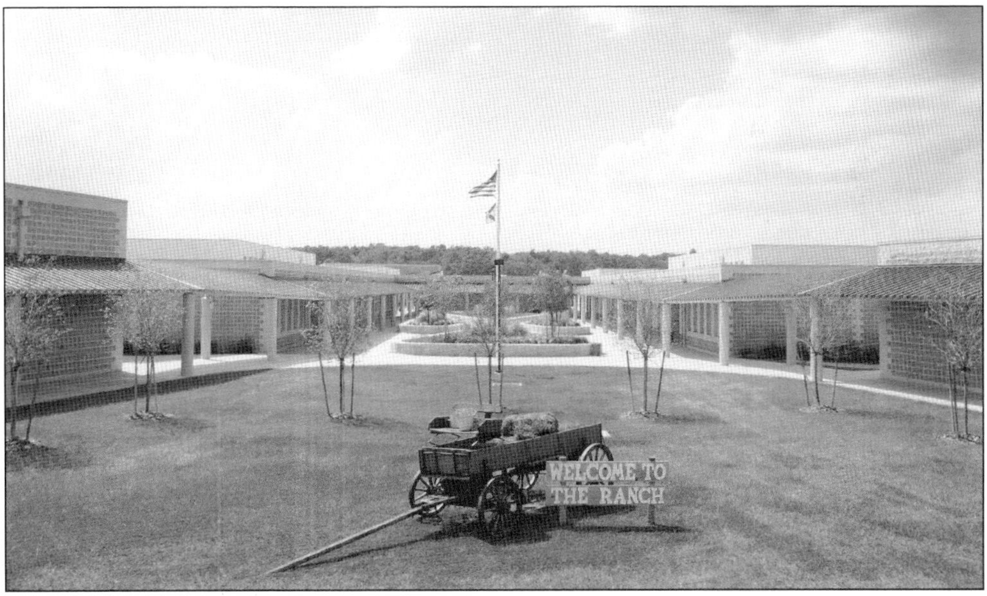

Wiregrass Ranch High School opened in the fall of 2006, with principal Ray Bonti. The high school's mascot selection was the Bulls, while John Long Middle School chose the Longhorns. Janet Watson wrote in the *Tampa Tribune*, "The original property known as Wiregrass Ranch consisted of 14,000 acres that was purchased from a Rockefeller Land Trust by James Barney Porter back in 1941. It was unfenced land that had been timbered during the Great Depression." (Courtesy of Pasco County School Board.)

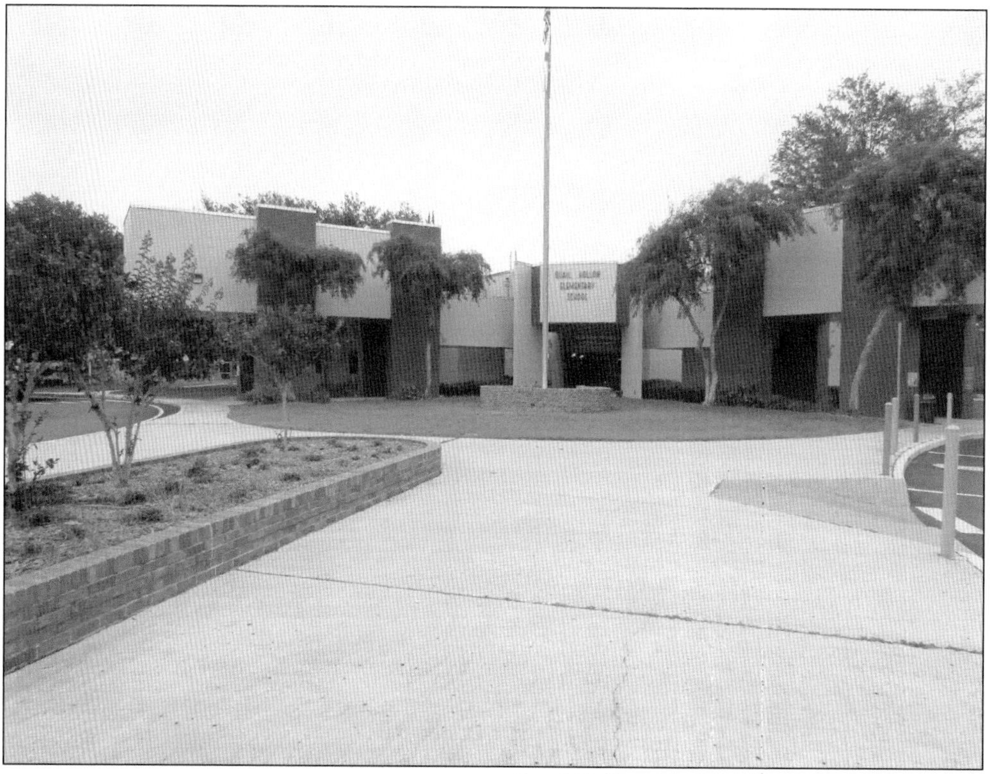

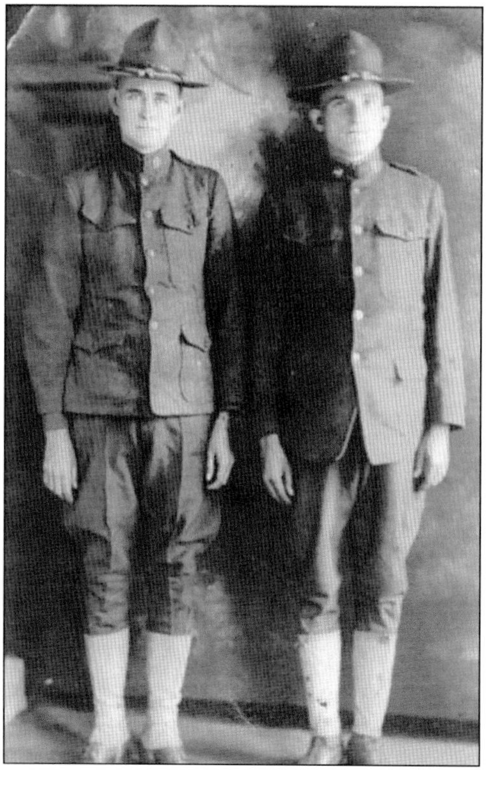

Quail Hollow Elementary opened in 1974 with 554 students. Student growth surged in 1970 and 1971 from 13,530 to 17,000. The building was an open concept school with moveable classroom walls designed by Eoghan Kelley. Quail Hollow in the Wesley Chapel area was one of nine circular school structures built by Pasco County in the early 1970s. (Courtesy of the *Laker-Lutz News*.)

Many Wesley Chapel natives have served in the military. Ruben Barnes (at left) and his unidentified friend display their World War I military uniforms in 1912. The doughboy uniform was made of either cotton or wool and included an olive drab "O.D." shirt and trousers, leggings, and hobnailed trench shoes, with a campaign hat to top it all off. Born in October 1887 in Wesley Chapel, Ruben died on May 2, 1971, in Zephyrhills. (Courtesy of David L. Brown.)

Cleo B. Boyette, son of Thomas Samuel Boyette and Ida Mae Bissett Boyette, poses in his military uniform with his mother in 1945. He enlisted in the US Army on November 7, 1942, at Camp Blanding in Starke and married Esther Lee Burnside in 1946. Cletia Pierce's memory of her Uncle Cleo was that whenever work was done, he sat on his back porch or under a tree and whittled with his knife and a piece of wood. He was also regularly seen with a pipe in his teeth. (Courtesy of Sue Boyette.)

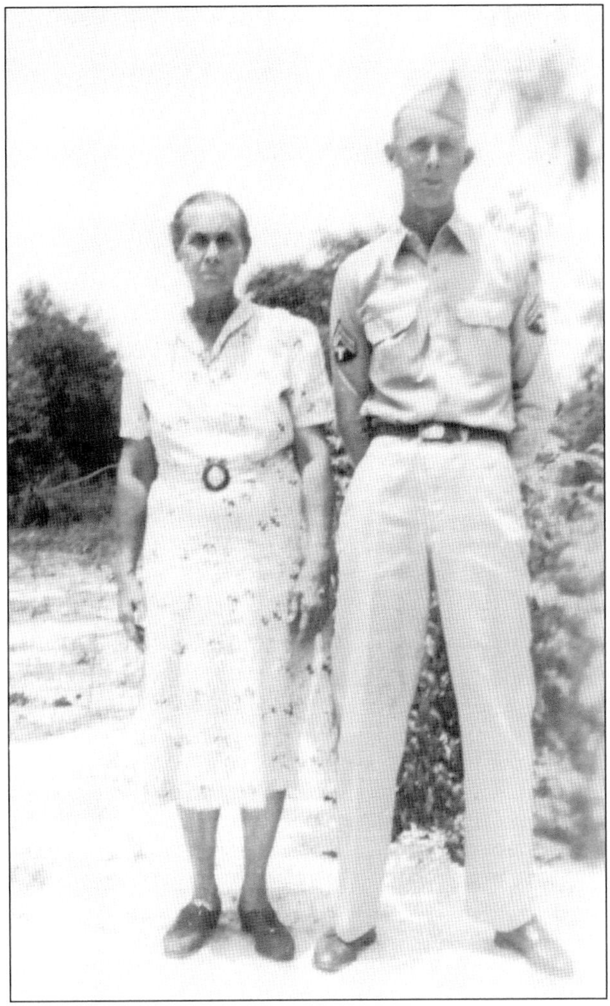

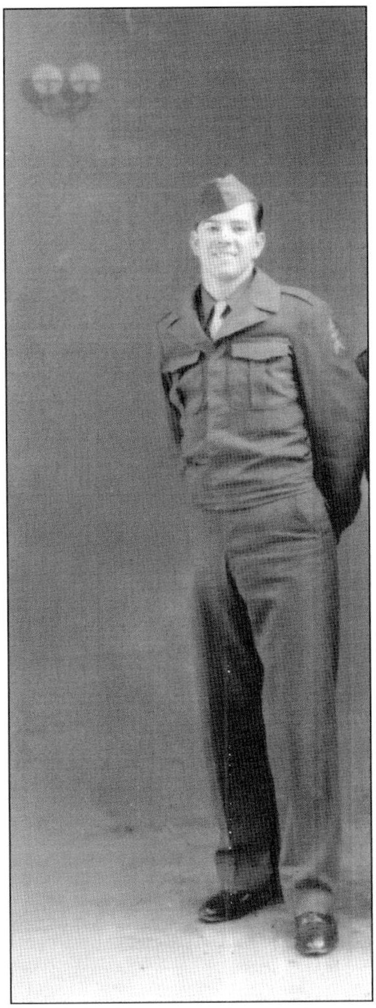

Bill Smith vividly recalled exiting the movie theater in December 1941 on the day Pearl Harbor was bombed to hear the daunting news that would bring the United States into World War II. He was stationed for a year in Japan, and his division was the first to enter Nagasaki, soon after the dropping of the atomic bomb. Three Army Air Corps training crashes occurred near what is now Wiregrass Ranch, all of which Bill witnessed before joining the military. (Courtesy of Ruth Smith Adams.)

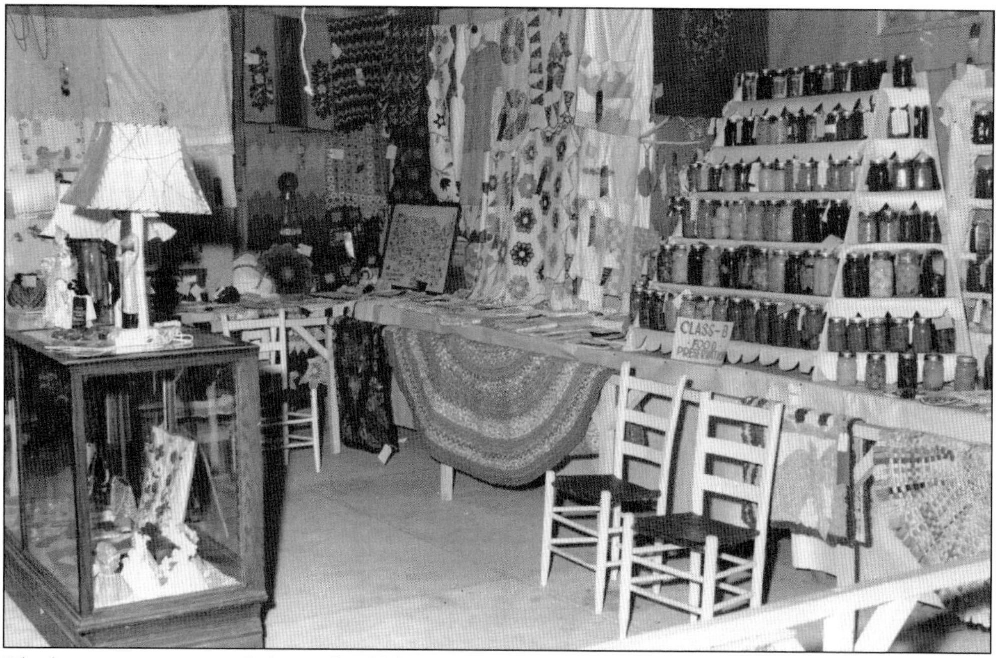

The home economics exhibit at the 1952 Pasco County Fair displays a variety of homemade wares. Wesley Chapel was a small town, and families had to work diligently to make ends meet, without modern conveniences. "We had no washing machine, so to wash clothes, we would take a big kettle and boil water, then wash our clothes in it, using a washboard. We'd then put the clothes on a log and beat them with a battling stick. We made our own lye soap and that's what we used to wash everything with. Many didn't have running water until the 1950s, and then things started getting better," said Lillie Stanley. (Courtesy of Pasco County Fair Office.)

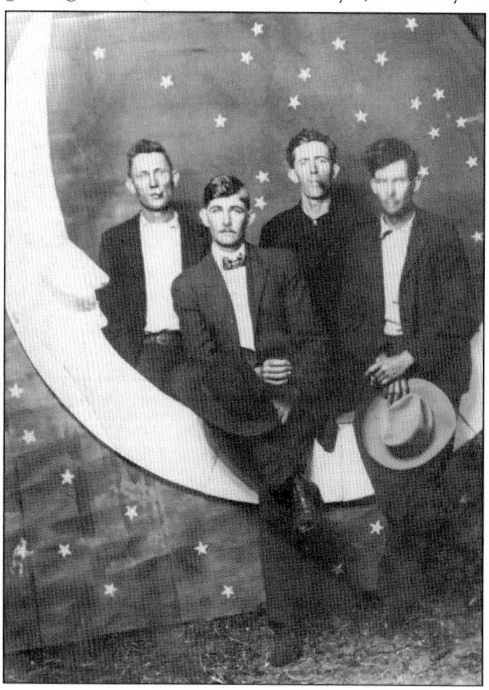

For an agricultural community in rural Florida, county and state fairs are major events and places to receive information as well as entertainment. Second from the left in this photograph is Ruben Barnes, who poses at the Florida State Fair in 1925 at the *Man in the Moon* exhibit. At far right is Raleigh Stanley. (Courtesy of David L. Brown.)

Six

Contemporary Wesley Chapel

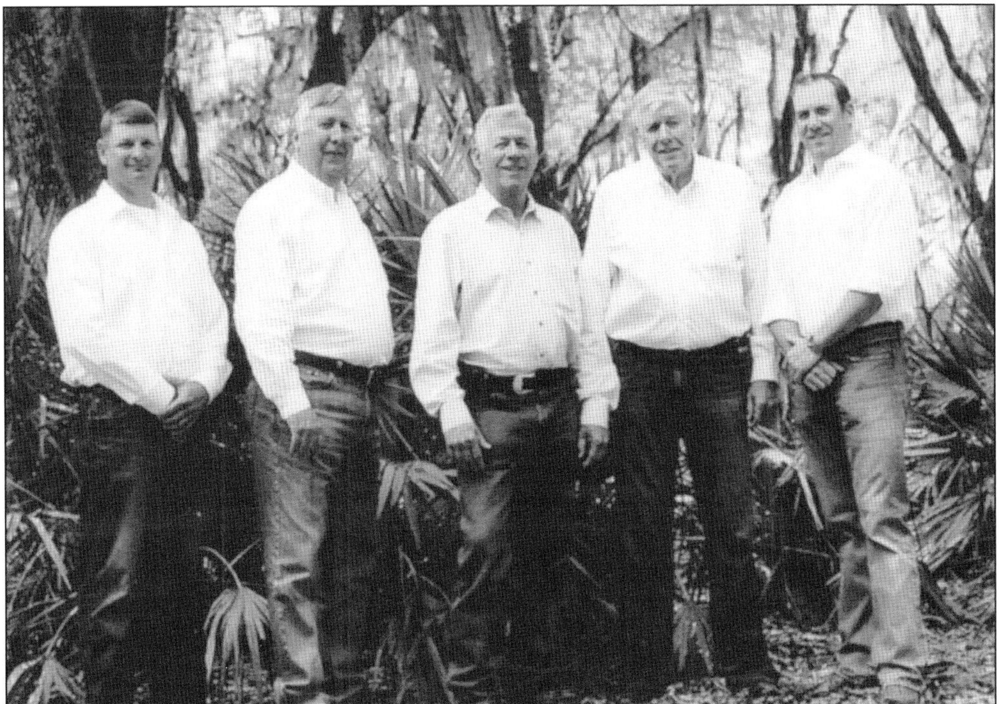

From left to right are Hatcher Porter, William "Bill" Porter, Tom McDonald Porter, James "Don" Porter, and James Don "J.D." Porter Jr. at the Wiregrass Ranch. James Hatcher "Wiregrass" Porter and Martha McDonald Porter were the parents of William, Tom, and Don. Bill Porter said his family was committed to stewardship, and as they saw Wesley Chapel transition away from an agricultural area, they contributed to educational and civic-minded growth. (Courtesy of Porter family.)

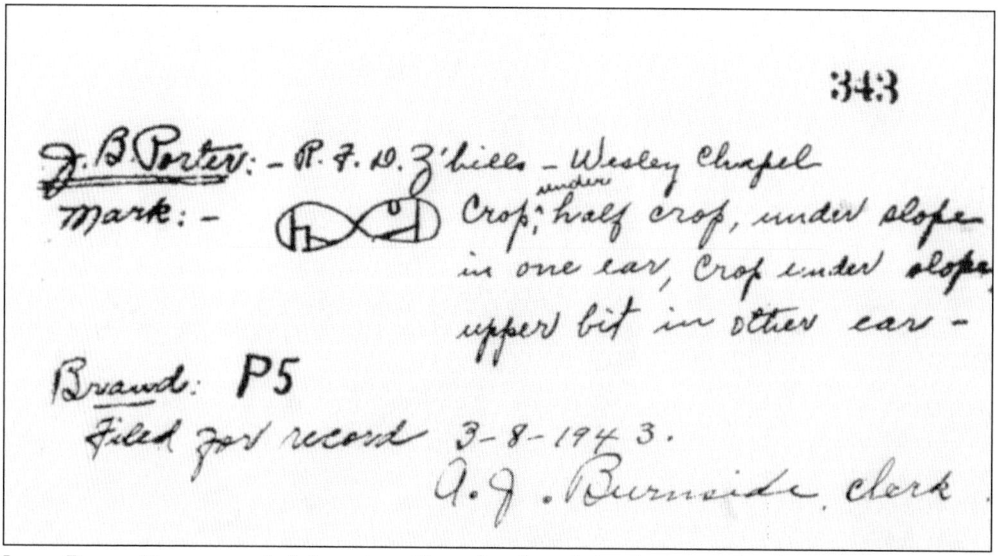

343

J.B Porter: - R.F.D. Z'hills - Wesley Chapel

Mark: - Crop; under half crop, under slope in one ear, Crop under slope upper bit in other ear -

Brand: P5

Filed for record 3-8-1943.

A.J. Burnside, clerk

James Barney Porter recorded the original brand and mark for the Porter family livestock on March 8, 1943. His son James "Wiregrass" Hatcher Porter was the first to actually live in Wesley Chapel. Ted Williams, a school board member during the 1968 teachers' strike, took it upon himself to recruit teachers to fill vacancies. He convinced Wiregrass, who he knew had a math degree, along with several other community members. Reluctantly, Wiregrass filled in for a few months at Sanders Elementary School. Grandson J.D. Porter recalled that his grandfather's former student sent thank-you letters to his memorial in 2003. (Courtesy of Pasco County Clerk's Office.)

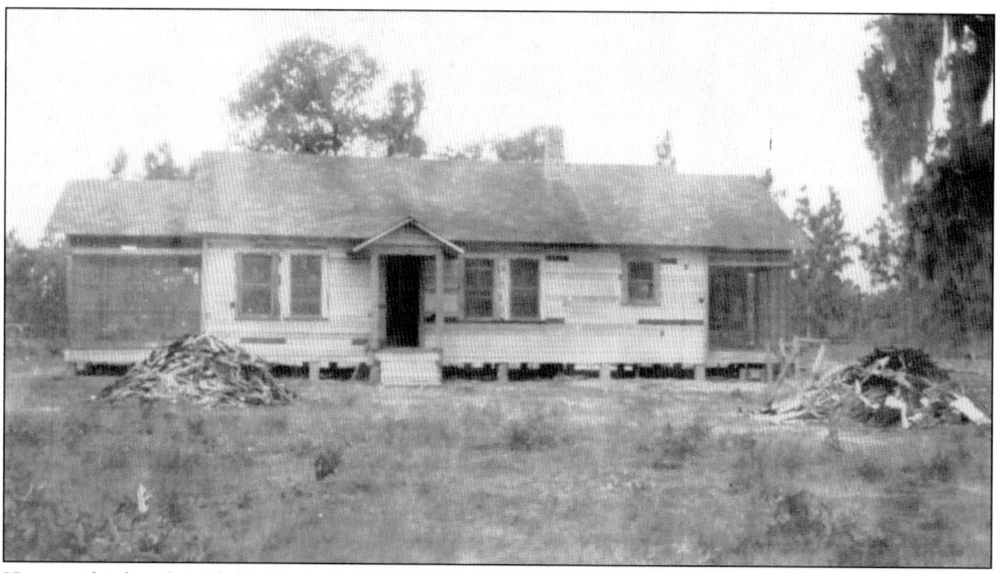

Known for his frugal fiscal management, James "Wiregrass" Porter lived with his family in a dilapidated frame house, which had been moved to their ranch property when they arrived in Wesley Chapel from Plant City. The structure was the former home of Jack Gillette, which had been later occupied by Angelo Sangiorgi. The house had no electricity, so meals were prepared on a Coleman stove. This photograph was taken in 1946, and in 1960, Wiregrass built a brick house on Highway 54 that became his home and headquarters until he died at age 86 in 2003. (Courtesy of Quinn Porter Miller.)

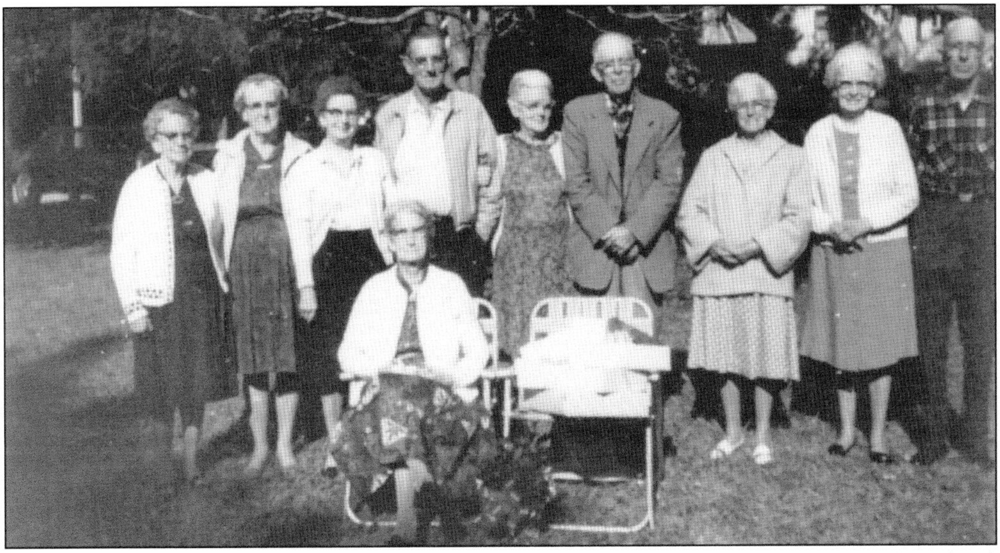

The last Stanley reunion in Wesley Chapel occurred around 1985. From left to right are (standing) Louneta Stanley Smith, Eleanor Stanley Hill, Edith Stanley Broecker, Roy Stanley, Mae Stanley Gaskin, Rollie Stanley, Dosha Stanley Fagan, Donnie Stanley Godwin, and Jesse Stanley. Sitting at center is Hattie Stanley Ryals. Everyone in this picture is now deceased. There were a total of 15 Stanley children: 11 girls and four boys, including two infant daughters and a 23-year-old daughter who passed away, as well as Dallas, who passed away in 1950. (Courtesy of Marco E. Stanley.)

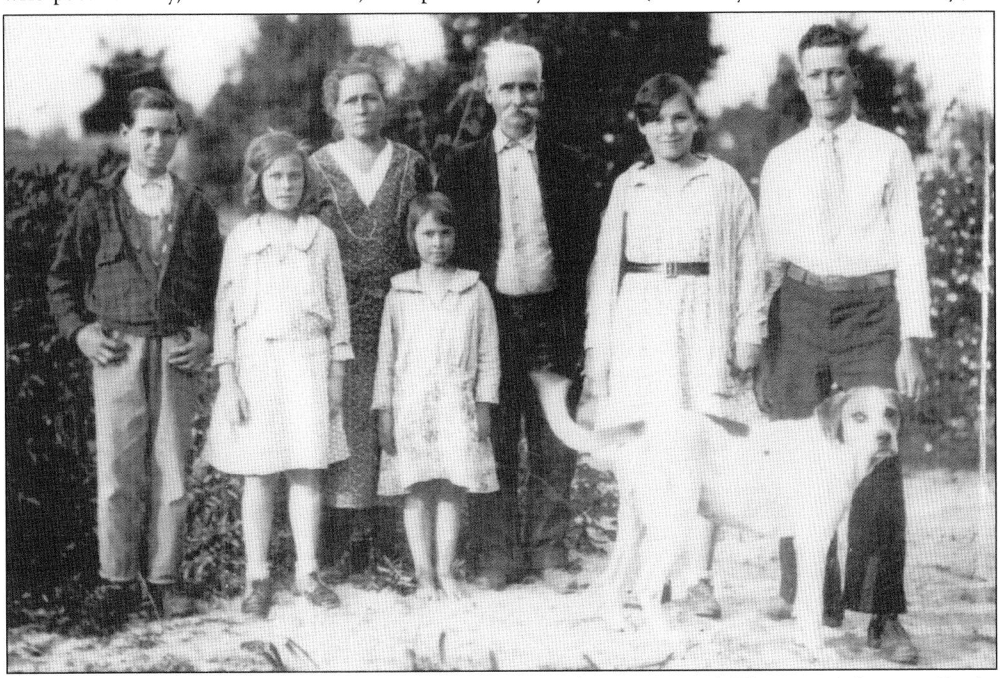

The Sherrod Ryals family is pictured. From left to right are Daniel, Florence, Margery, Ruth, Sherrod, Lena, and Stanley. Sherrod was the son of Civil War veteran Daniel C. Ryals and Mary Studstill Ryals. Both are listed in a past census of Wesley Chapel. Some of the Ryals land is still owned by family members and lies along Eiland Boulevard in the present-day Wesley Chapel boundaries. (Courtesy of Eunice Ryals McElveen.)

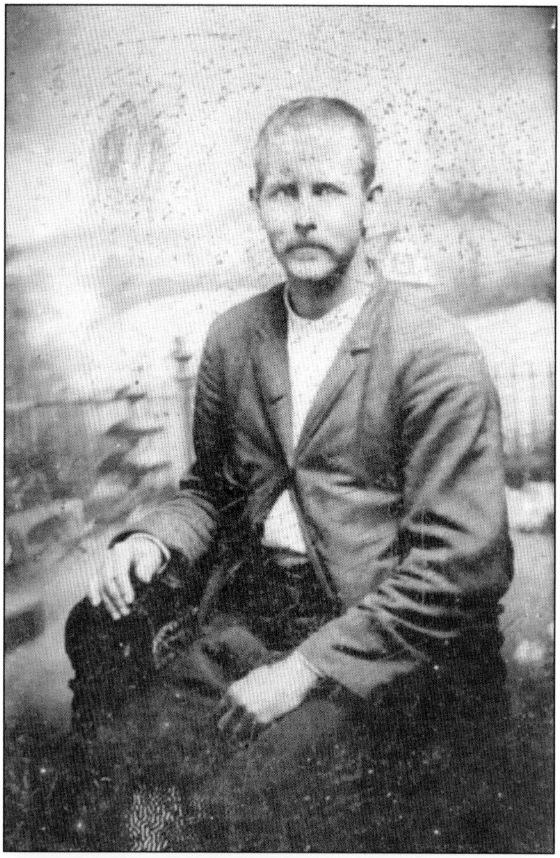

Sam Geiger, brother of Margie Geiger Barnes, poses for a Burgert photograph in Ybor City. Sam's pasture covered all of the present-day Lake Bernadette subdivision and some of the adjacent property, including part of what is now Geiger Cemetery. Lake Bernadette was built in 1983 and includes a golf course and development. (Courtesy of David L. Brown.)

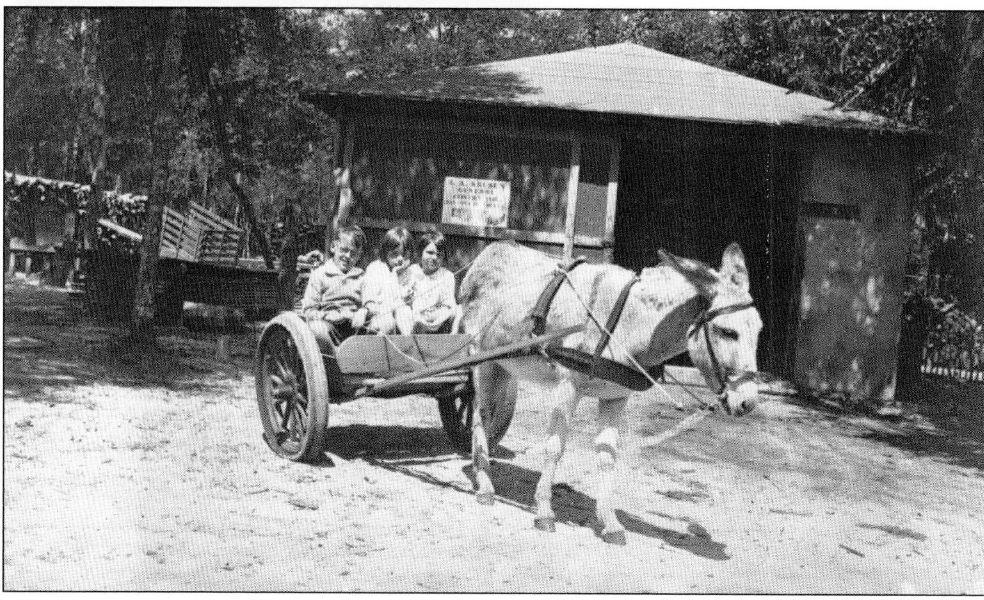

In 1933, the children of I. Andrew Krusen and Dorothy B. Barron ride with a friend in a donkey-driven cart on the ranch. From left to right are Charles "Buck" Krusen, unidentified, and Christine Krusen. (Courtesy of Florida Library & Archives, Florida Department of State.)

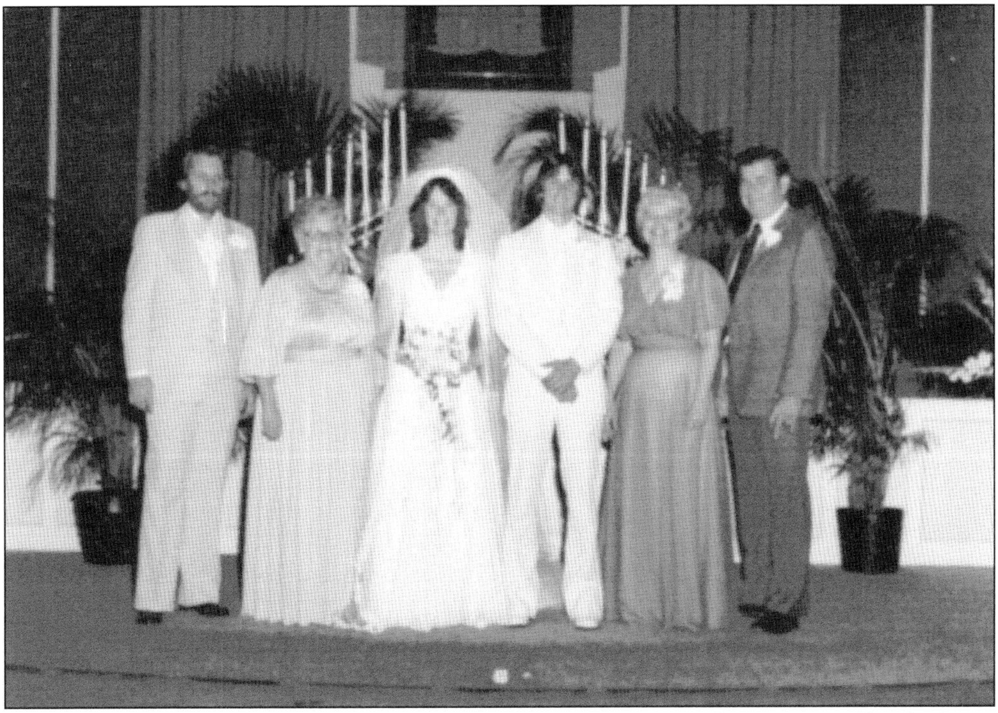

In this photograph taken on May 10, 1980, at the First Baptist Church in Bartow, Florida, Bruce B. Downs—the namesake of Bruce B. Downs Boulevard—is shown at his son's wedding. From left to right are Clarence Odell Robinson, Myrtle Lee Robinson, Sarah Robinson Downs, Bruce "Barkley" Downs Jr., Patsy Ruth Spencer Downs, and Bruce B. Downs. Daughter-in-law Sarah recalls that Bruce's grandson, Bruce B. Downs III, was seven weeks old when the boulevard was dedicated. Family attended the dedication, including Bruce's daughter Luanna Downs Sheridan and five-year-old grandson Justin Marshall Sheridan. (Courtesy of Sarah Robinson Downs Bruce.)

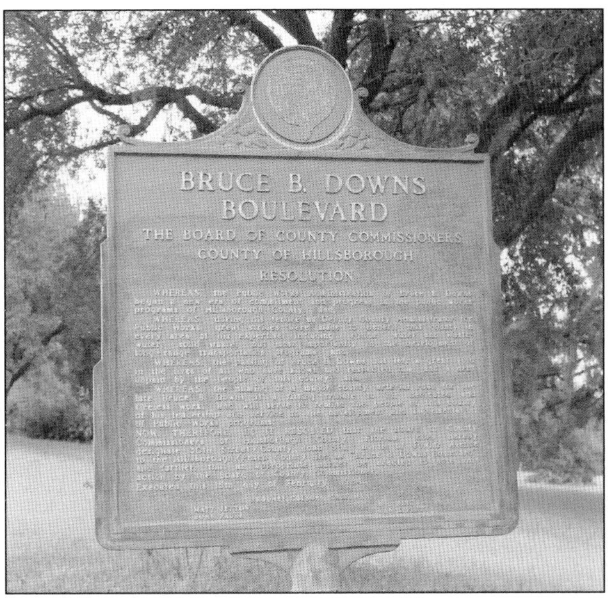

This marker is located on the east side of Bruce B. Downs Boulevard, approximately 100 yards north of the intersection with Fowler Avenue on University of South Florida property. The boulevard is the main thoroughfare across Wesley Chapel. Bruce Barkely Downs Jr., credited with improving infrastructure to finance the building and repair of roadways, was an engineer with the Florida Department of Transportation for 29 years and then director of public works for Hillsborough County. (Courtesy of Ernest Wise.)

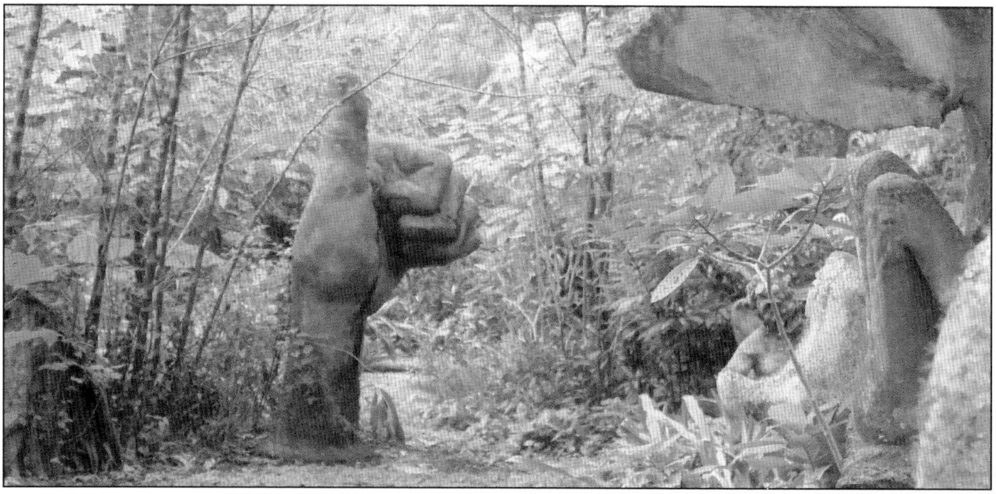

This sculpture entitled *Thumbs Up* is a focal point of the home studio of Lewis Van Dercar in Wesley Chapel. The sculpture honors the 11 athletes who were kidnapped and killed by terrorists during the 1972 Munich Olympic Games. Bobby Ebie Van Dercar explained that his grandfather Lewis wanted to symbolically memorialize the tragedy. The *Thumbs Up* statue is surrounded by numerous works by Lewis, who died in 1988. Lewis was a merchant marine during World War II and then began a career in art. (Courtesy of Ernest Wise.)

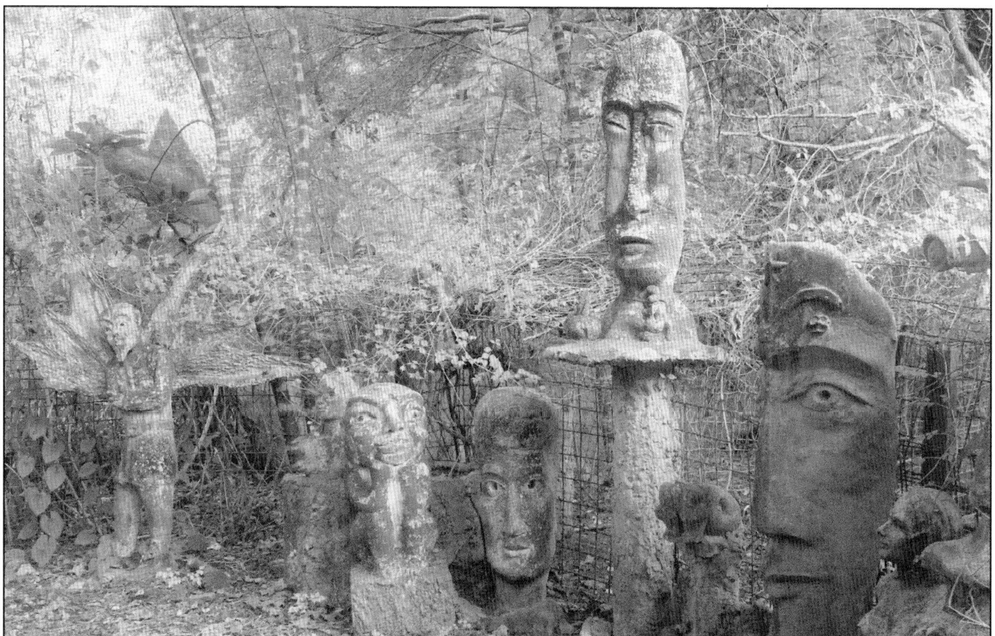

Whimsical sculptures adorn 25950 Queen Sago Place. Lewis Van Dercar built a unique geodesic dome house covered in ivy on his 14-acre estate in Wesley Chapel. The home remains today and is surrounded by approximately 200 of Lewis's concrete sculptures. Often compared to Andy Warhol and Salvador Dali, Lewis worked in a variety of mediums in Miami for 30 years before moving to Wesley Chapel. He created oil and multidimensional paintings and his own technique of sculpture, which was utilized in many public locations, such as parks and zoos. His work has been valued and collected—both during his lifetime and posthumously. (Courtesy of Ernest Wise.)

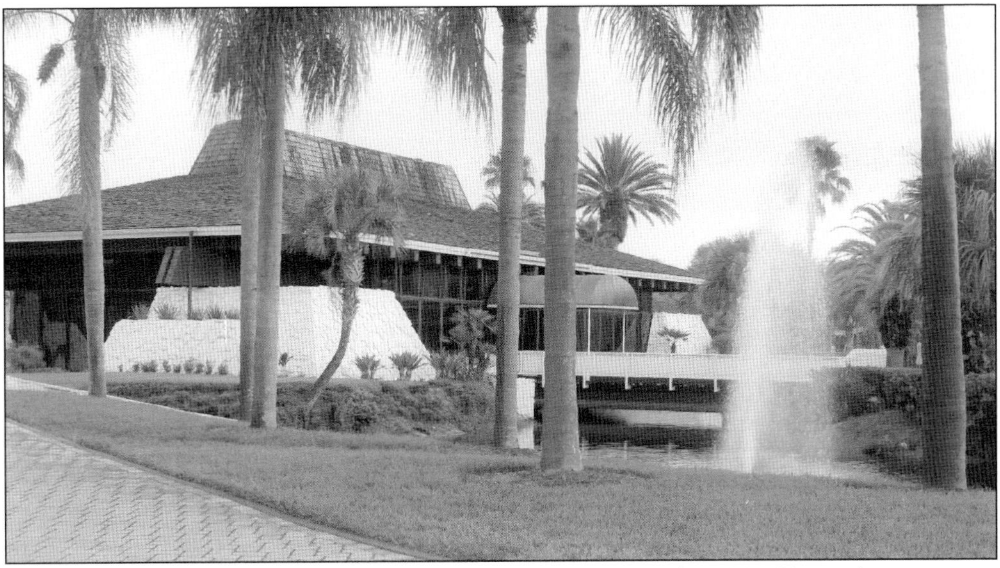

Saddlebrook, located one mile east of I-75 on Highway 54, opened in 1981. Planned as a resort, it hosts meetings and conferences. Two golf courses were designed by Arnold Palmer, and a tennis facility opened in 1986, which has 45 courts of clay, grass, and hard surface. International tennis stars Jim Courier and Jennifer Capriati of Pasco County trained at Saddlebrook. The preparatory school was founded there in 1992 and is now an accredited college preparatory program. Athletes from third through twelfth grades work on their tennis and golf skills while completing their education. (Courtesy of Ernest Wise.)

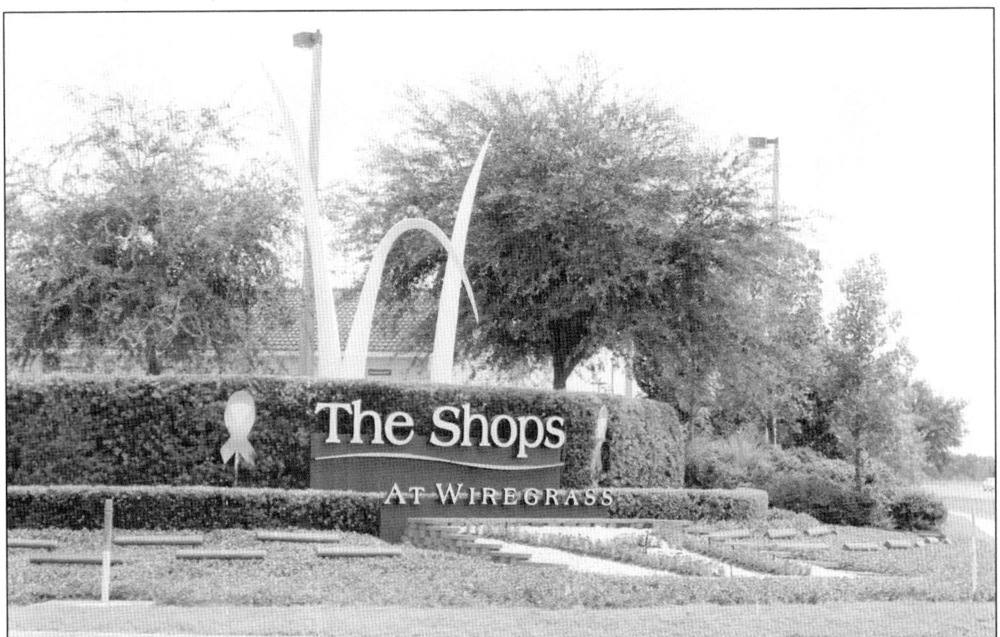

The Shops at Wiregrass opened in 2008 on 67 acres. The space has become a town square meeting place and hosts holiday events and an open market. The Grove is also a shopping area off Highway 54 that features a large movie theater and many big-box stores. Wesley Chapel was named by *CNNMoney* magazine as one of the top places to live in Florida. (Courtesy of Ernest Wise.)

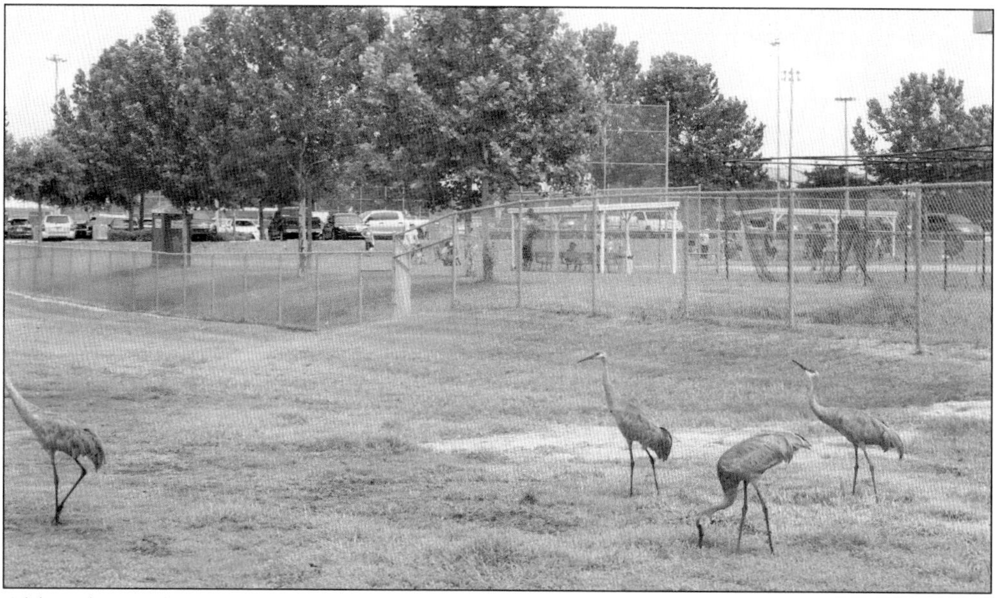

Although a modern park is available in Wesley Chapel, the classic sandhill cranes are reminiscent of the surrounding woodland wildlife. The Wesley Chapel District Park is located at 7727 Boyette Road and has four baseball fields, eight soccer fields, a fitness trail, and more. The Wesley Chapel Athletic Association cosponsors a variety of leagues that practice and compete there. The park encompasses more than 140 acres and, according to Rick Buckman of the Pasco Parks and Recreation Department, has approximately 50,000 visitors per month. (Courtesy of Ernest Wise.)

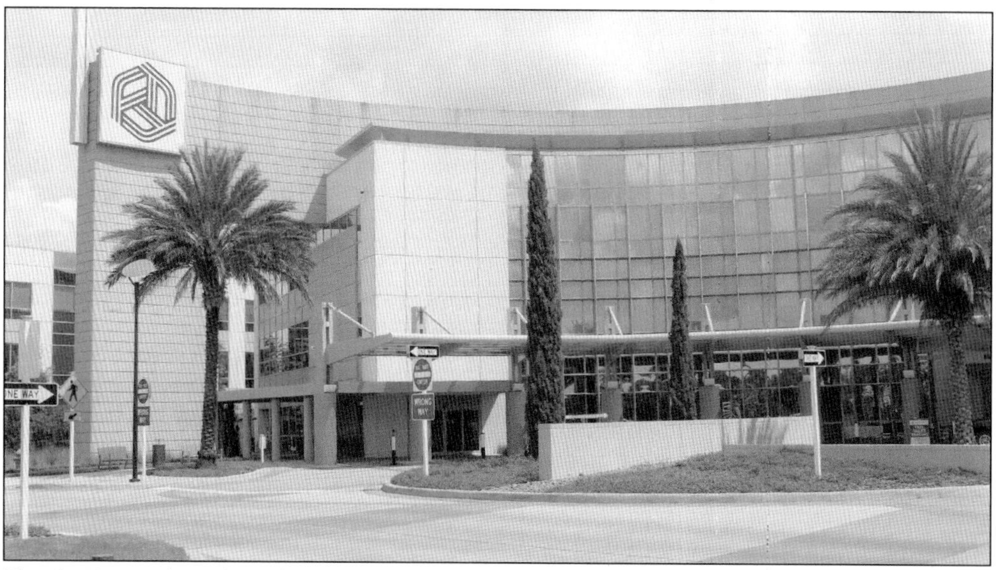

Florida Hospital Wesley Chapel opened in 2012 and added over 450 jobs to the area. Built at a cost of approximately $121 million, the facility offered extensive medical services. Medical clinics, physician's offices, and related services were also constructed in the surrounding area. The Wiregrass Porter Ranch family donated that land and are particularly proud of the hospital services, which remind them of the nurturing compassion of Martha McDonald Porter, a registered nurse who greatly respected the contributions of nurses to the health of a community. (Courtesy of Ernest Wise.)

Seven

HISTORIANS AT WORK

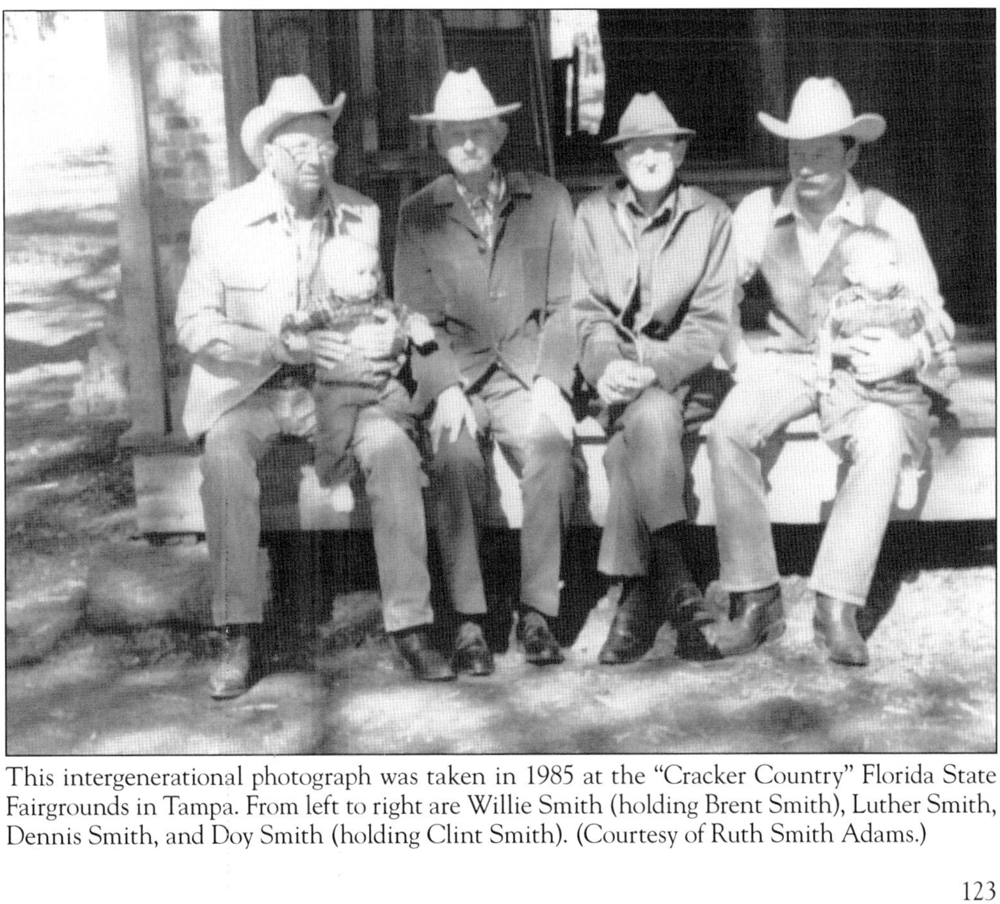

This intergenerational photograph was taken in 1985 at the "Cracker Country" Florida State Fairgrounds in Tampa. From left to right are Willie Smith (holding Brent Smith), Luther Smith, Dennis Smith, and Doy Smith (holding Clint Smith). (Courtesy of Ruth Smith Adams.)

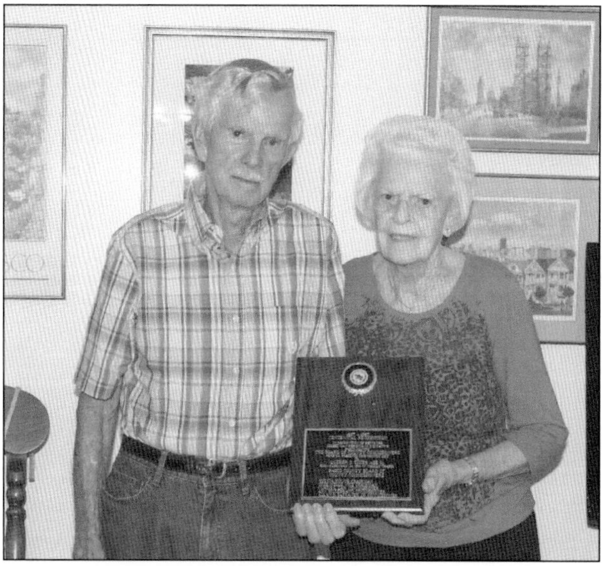

Bill Smith and Ruth Smith Adams display their "Pioneer Founding Families of Pasco County" plaque. Bill and Ruth are descendants of the founding family of William R. Smith and Annie E. Sims Smith. The Homestead Act of 1862 gave pioneer families 160 acres if they resided on the land for five years and improved it. Land could also be acquired after six months of living on it for $1.25 an acre. Daniel Henry Smith was a close friend of fellow settler Francis Asbury Barnes, and they worked to divide up some of the land between them. (Courtesy of Ernest Wise.)

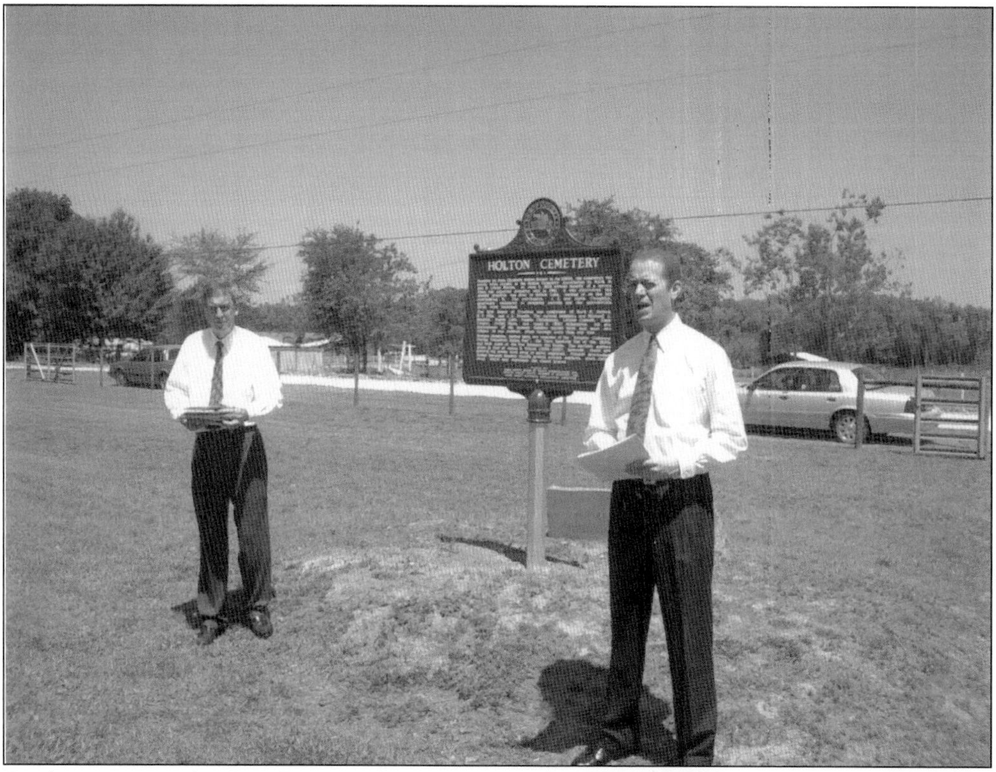

Cochairman Michael C. Boyette (left) and chairman Scott Black of the Pasco Historical Preservation Committee speak at the dedication of the Holton Cemetery historical marker. The original acreage used for the cemetery was donated by Julia Elizabeth Holton Benner in 1882, and other acreage was given by Mark H. and S. Louise Holton. The first board of trustees included Mark H. Holton, E.F. Ellis, and J.E. Branch. Numerous pioneer families are buried at Holton Cemetery, including veterans from both sides of the Civil War. The oldest marked grave is of James B. Wilson (1834–1883). (Courtesy of David Boyette.)

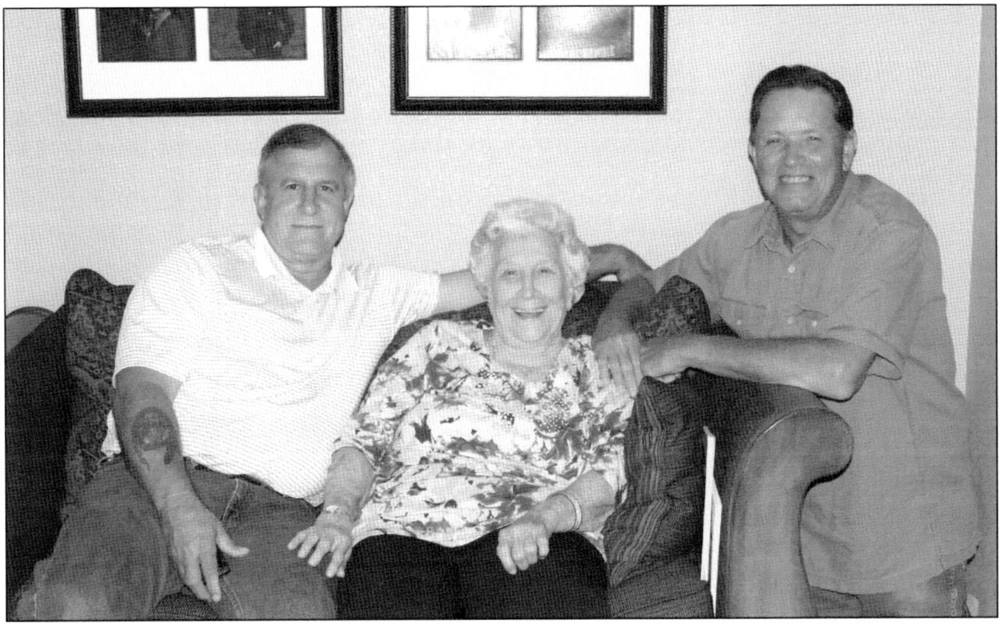

Three natives of Wesley Chapel—Marco E. Stanley, Lillie Eva Sapp Stanley, and Roscoe "Rocky" Stanley—provided firsthand information about Wesley Chapel and generously shared family photographic collections. Lillie said the most significant legacy of Wesley Chapel was the caring community that looked out for each other. At age 95, she credits her longevity to "good genes." (Courtesy of Ernest Wise.)

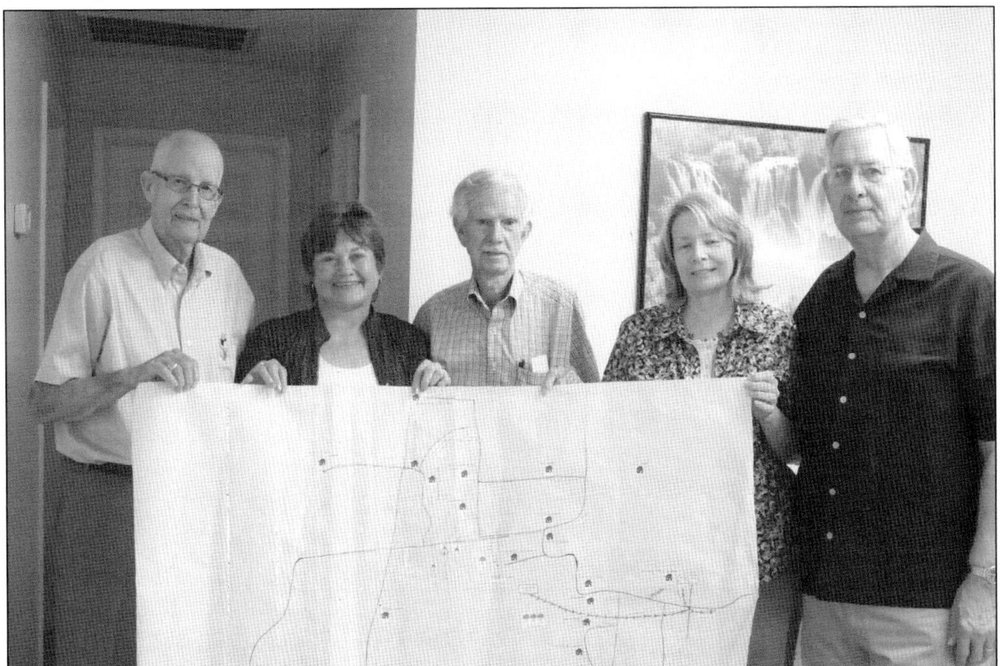

In this photograph, a chart of the early Wesley Chapel settlements is shown. From left to right, Roy Burnette, the author, Bill Smith, Sue Boyette, and Frank A. Scott Sr. display a map of key frontier sites of Wesley Chapel. (Courtesy of Ernest Wise.)

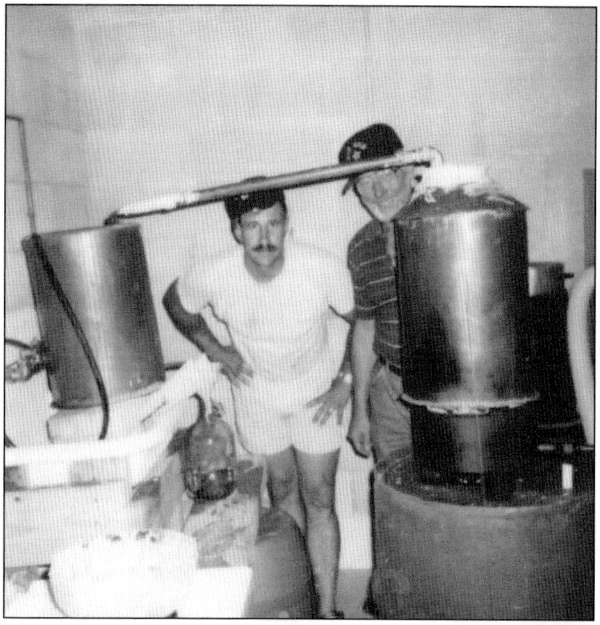

Marco E. Stanley (left) and Keith Lane Stanley are descendants of Wesley Chapel frontier settlers. They both revere early stories and carefully preserve photographs, passing the legacy along to their children. This 1989 photograph shows Marco and Keith with a modern moonshine-making apparatus. Keith is the nephew of Clarence Lane, who was particularly renowned for moonshining during the Great Depression. (Courtesy of Keith Lane Stanley.)

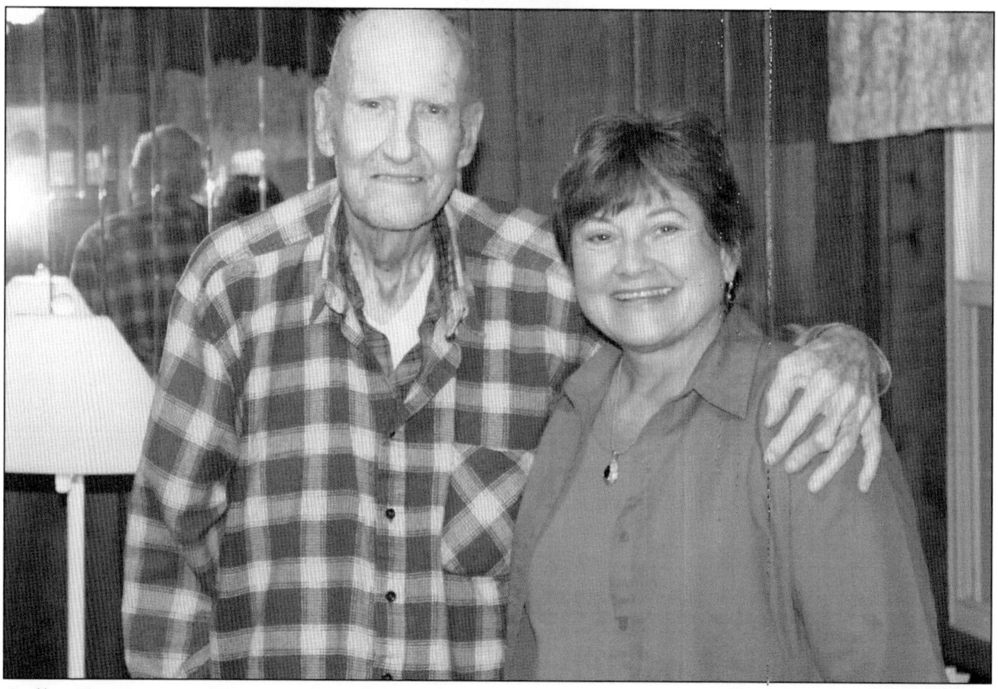

Cullen Boyette, age 81, remembered doing his homework by kerosene lantern at the dining room table in the evening. At the time of his attendance, Wesley Chapel School was for first through sixth grades and had previously been for first through eighth grades. Cullen later attended Dade City Junior-Senior High School. "A bus driver from Fivay, Florida, was responsible for picking up the kids from Land O'Lakes and Wesley Chapel and transporting them to Dade City. Cullen and pal Ronald Strickland, son of Morris Strickland, were school buddies. There were eight students, and they tutored other students. Sadly, Cullen passed away in September 2015, just a few months after he was interviewed for this book. The author is at right. (Courtesy of Ernest Wise.)

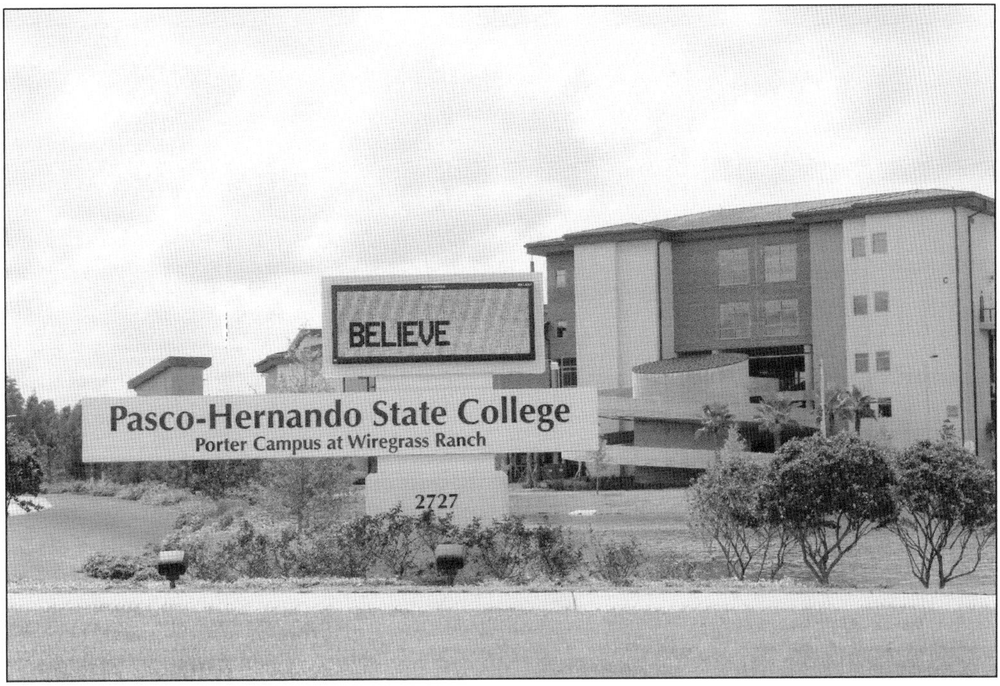

Pasco-Hernando State College stands in striking contrast to the original Wesley Chapel School log cabin for pioneer children. The college, on Mansfield Boulevard, is situated on 60 acres donated by the Wiregrass Porter Ranch family. It opened with 1,600 students in 2014 and has a nursing unit in honor of Martha McDonald Porter. According to J.D. Porter, the site was chosen in part because remnants of a homestead that his family knew as the Mandy School (presumably from Amanda Cooper Godwin) were nearby. (Courtesy of Ernest Wise.)

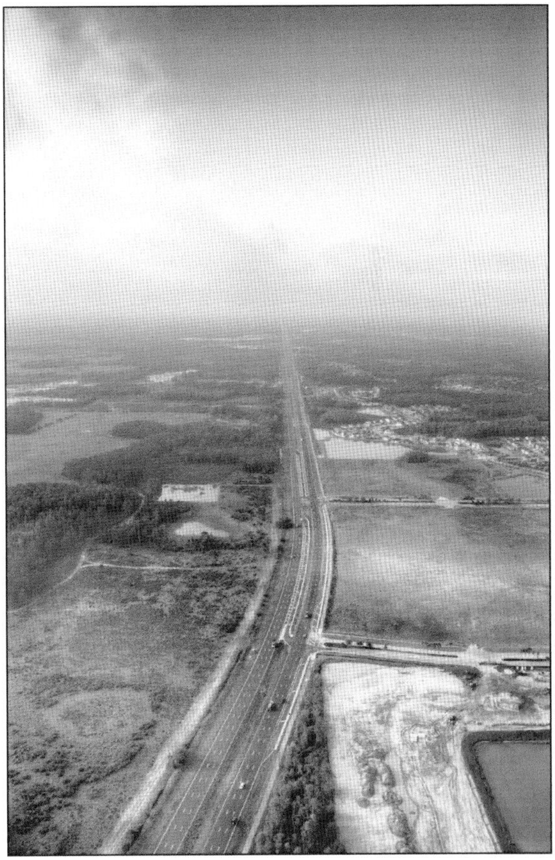

Richard and Kathy Riley enjoyed a hot-air balloon flight in Wesley Chapel. This photograph was taken from the balloon in 2014, though inclement weather caused the flight to be rescheduled several times. The picturesque ride, which originated from the Tampa North Flight Center in Wesley Chapel, reveals a contrast to early pioneer maps that documented only a handful of settlers. (Courtesy of Richard Riley.)

Discover Thousands of Local History Books Featuring Millions of Vintage Images

Arcadia Publishing, the leading local history publisher in the United States, is committed to making history accessible and meaningful through publishing books that celebrate and preserve the heritage of America's people and places.

Find more books like this at
www.arcadiapublishing.com

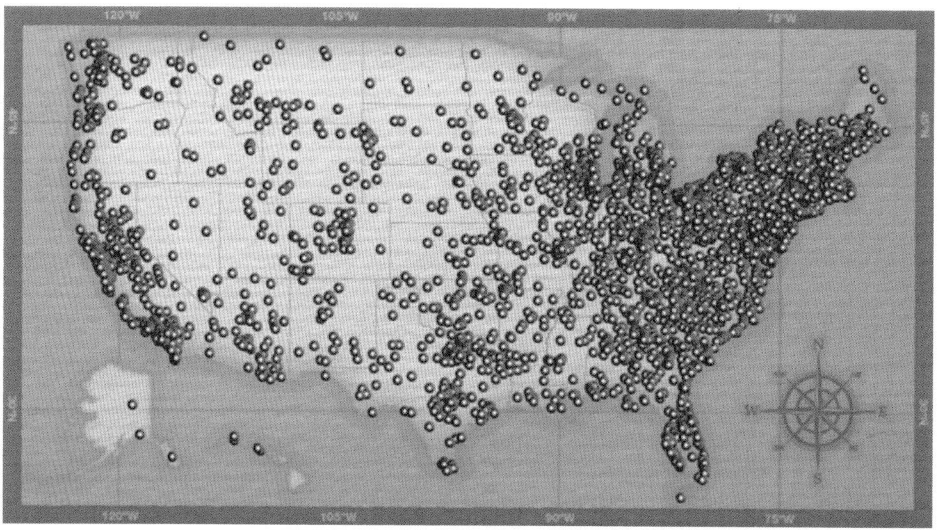

Search for your hometown history, your old stomping grounds, and even your favorite sports team.

Consistent with our mission to preserve history on a local level, this book was printed in South Carolina on American-made paper and manufactured entirely in the United States. Products carrying the accredited Forest Stewardship Council (FSC) label are printed on 100 percent FSC-certified paper.

MADE IN THE USA